A Life of Faith

A Life of Faith

◆

My Journey

Elsie Moses Huck Detweiler as told to Douglas V. Jewson, M.D.

iUniverse, Inc.
New York Lincoln Shanghai

A Life of Faith
My Journey

Copyright © 2005 by Douglas V. Jewson, M.D.

All rights reserved. No part of this book may be used or reproduced by any means, graphic, electronic, or mechanical, including photocopying, recording, taping or by any information storage retrieval system without the written permission of the publisher except in the case of brief quotations embodied in critical articles and reviews.

iUniverse books may be ordered through booksellers or by contacting:

iUniverse
2021 Pine Lake Road, Suite 100
Lincoln, NE 68512
www.iuniverse.com
1-800-Authors (1-800-288-4677)

ISBN-13: 978-0-595-37582-0 (pbk)
ISBN-13: 978-0-595-67533-3 (cloth)
ISBN-13: 978-0-595-81976-8 (ebk)
ISBN-10: 0-595-37582-0 (pbk)
ISBN-10: 0-595-67533-6 (cloth)
ISBN-10: 0-595-81976-1 (ebk)

Printed in the United States of America

Contents

Foreword vii
Introduction ix
The Beginning 1
From Here to 13 18
Looking Both Ways from 13 34
Embarking on the Adventurous Christian Life 45
Stauffer Henry Moses 56
Albany 83
Dothan Alabama 111
Picking up the Pieces 135
Return to Dothan 139
Sowega Youth Home 146
Faith Cottage 150
William Huck 154
The Women's Mission 158
The Women at The Mission 161
Surgery and Cancer Scare 169
Marriage to Bill Huck—and The Mission 171
Life after Bill 179

A Voice Crying in the Wilderness 206
Personal Life Following Retirement 211
Village Atlanta and God's Math 215
Winding It Up 226
Linwood Detweiler 236

Foreword

I was first introduced to Elsie Moses Huck at the original Women's Mission on Ponce de Leon in the fall of 1980 when I sought to do volunteer work there. Her courage, compassion, and vision impressed me at once. Fascinated, I listened to virtually her entire life story from pioneering with her husband in the home mission field of rehabilitation for alcoholics to her present work with homeless women. Others would benefit from her experience and needed to hear what she had to say.

While volunteering at the Women's Mission, I also donated time to the Men's Mission. A striking contrast was readily apparent. At the Women's Mission there was no drinking and no "check-out" time. The atmosphere was that the women were in a recovery-oriented mode, that they had a home, however temporary, and that they were safe and loved.

With the passage of time, I was honored to watch them move to a "new" and expanded Mission in an abandoned and then renovated school in the industrial section of Atlanta. Upon her retirement, I observed first-hand the remarkable process by which her dream of a rehabilitation facility for homeless women with children was realized. Elsie demonstrated the extraordinary ability to surround herself with people who made her dream come true. My wife and I were privileged to be on the board of Village Atlanta and saw the entire project from its inception to its completion.

The cover story of the September 9, 1996 *U.S. News and World Report* was entitled *The Faith Factor: Can churches cure America's social ills?* Her narrative addresses this issue from her perspective. Although not a "how-to" manual, it provides a sense of direction that others with a similar burden can follow.

Listening to her heart-felt verbal history of her life of faith moved me deeply. In changing the format to the written word, and in the editing process, I hope I have not interfered too much with the emotional impact her story may have on you. Hers is a powerful autobiography at a time when too few stories like this are available.

Douglas V. Jewson, M.D.

Introduction

Today is August 18, 1994. Diane and Doug have requested that I sit down in front of their tape recorder and record memories of my life of faith and work in the home mission field. Friends and acquaintances have also suggested that I document my memoirs because of the remarkable ministries that I have been blessed to be a part of over the past half century. To these ministries, however, I really brought nothing but a vision of what could be. Then, I was surrounded by people who helped make these dreams come true. I have never before been inclined to do any writing, but I'm going to at least attempt it now. I hope the result will bring glory to God as much as the ministries have. In spite of obstacles, living my life by faith has been an exciting adventure. The primary intended audience for my story is my own family, my children and grandchildren, so they will know something of the background of their predecessors. I pray they will come to salvation by personal faith and this by the grace of God. We are not saved by our works, but we are created by God to do good works. From there, my further prayer is that all others will recognize them by their fruit and that they will do the will of their heavenly Father.

> Ephesians 2:8-10 (NIV) For it is by grace you have been saved, through faith-and this not from yourselves, it is the gift of God—not by works, so that no one can boast. For we are God's workmanship, created in Christ Jesus to do good works, which God prepared in advance for us to do.

> Matthew 7:16-22 (NIV) 16 By their fruit you will recognize them. Do people pick grapes from thorn bushes, or figs from thistles? 17 Likewise every good tree bears good fruit, but a bad tree bears bad fruit. 18 A good tree cannot bear bad fruit, and a bad tree cannot bear good fruit. 19 Every tree that does not bear good fruit is cut down and thrown into the fire. 20 Thus, by their fruit you will recognize them. 21 Not everyone who says to me, 'Lord, Lord,' will enter the kingdom of heaven, but only he who does the will of my Father who is in heaven.

The Beginning

I am going to begin at my beginning, with my origins and my birth and childhood. I was born in 1920, on June 24, the fifth of seven children, in Allentown, Pennsylvania. My parents were Ard Stein Barr and Elsie Mabel Schlicher. They married in 1907. My father was a silk ribbon weaver in East Greenville, Pennsylvania, when he met my mother. It was a small town and they were both Pennsylvania Dutch, which means they were of German ancestry. "Dutch" is derived from the German word "Deutsche," meaning German. They spoke Pennsylvania Dutch to each another exclusively though they and their parents knew the English language as well. Pennsylvania Dutch was a dialect handed down from generation to generation since the original migration from Germany.

Mildred, their first daughter, was born in 1908. Linwood, their second child, was born in 1910. Iva was the third child, born in 1912. mother and dad taught the first three children to speak Pennsylvania Dutch. These three children didn't know any English until they went to school.

During the early years of my parents' marriage, they lived among their brothers and sisters and their own parents. Dad was employed in the ribbon mill and became quite skilled as a weaver. Mother's dad (Clement Weiser Schlicher) was the Chief of Police and played in the town's German band. My dad's father (Pierce Baer) owned the town's tombstone business. They all attended church religiously. The first service was in German and the later service in English. They attended the English service.

For generations, the families married and settled in town or in nearby villages. It was a major event when my parents decided to leave East Greenville and move to the big city of Allentown, about thirty miles north. Allentown was the textile center in the Northeast for silk fabric and ribbons. It is located in the Lehigh Valley. The Lehigh River separates Allentown from Bethlehem, the steel-manufacturing city. The move to Allentown took courage. Dad was now working as a weaver at the largest ribbon mill in the country. This was a highly skilled position that paid well and allowed him to provide quite nicely for his growing family. Since they were now living among families with backgrounds other than German, they made the decision to speak only English to their children.

My next sister, Nina, was born in 1918, five years after the birth of Iva. This was a scary time since that was the year of the great flu and pneumonia epidemic that swept the country. There were also many deaths from diphtheria and typhoid fever during that time. Nina contracted pneumonia when she was only nine months old. She was so sick that the doctor made daily house calls until she started to recover.

Mother told of a neighboring family who attended a funeral to bury a child who had died of diphtheria. Upon returning home from the funeral, they found another child had died. Those were hard days during 1918. mother had no family nearby to help her. 1918 was also the end of the First World War.

In our home on Elm Street, Dr. Beck brought me into the world on June 24, 1920. I was their fourth daughter! My ten year-old brother insists he proudly announced the birth of his new baby sister to his class at school the next day. School had been out for several days but the students returned on the morning of the 25th for their final report cards and their promotion slips. In Pennsylvania, school always started after Labor Day and continued till the latter part of June.

I looked different from my siblings because I was the only red-head in the family. My dad named me Elsie Schlicher (Schlicher was my mother's maiden name) after my mother because he thought I looked like her. Actually, Grandpa Schlicher was the redhead. My mother was named Elsie after Elsie Dinsmore, a book character in the mid-1800's who was a Christian girl. By "coincidence," there is "A Life of Faith" website now (2005) with further information about her. That site is www.alifeoffaith.com.

When I was almost three, another baby was added to our happy family. This time, Linwood finally had a brother. Mother returned the favor to dad by naming him Ard S. Barr, Jr. Except this time, the S. stood for Schlicher instead of Stein, so technically Ard was not a "Jr." Ard had big brown eyes like dad's and was a lot of fun and brought much joy to our family. Linwood now had a buddy. This became Ard's nickname. "Buddy." He has been Bud ever since.

Our home was a three-story duplex. Mother and father lived comfortably there with the five children. Because we were so close to town, it had a very small yard, just a stoop out front down to the street. If my memory serves me right, the yard was no bigger than the width of the house. The yard was square, so it was no deeper than the width of the house either. It was surrounded by a high fence.

There were now six of us children, but we divided naturally into two groups. The older three were fifteen, thirteen, and eleven; the younger three were six, four, and one. My recollection is that mother never let the younger group go out of the yard to play with any children in the neighborhood. She always opened the gate graciously and invited any children in who wanted to play with us. Mother loved children. She especially wanted to know where her own were at all times. She assured the other mothers that she would carefully watch over their children when they were in our yard.

My earliest memory was when I was three years of age. My big brother Linwood wasn't in the house where he was supposed to be doing his homework. Dad went out front to see if Linwood was with his friends. Right before dad's eyes, Linwood came speeding down the hill on his wagon and was hit by a car rounding the corner. My memory is of mother putting Bud, the baby, in Mildred's hands and rushing to the door. Immediately on seeing Linwood, she went into a dead faint and had to be carried back in by a neighbor. I can still see her on the old Victorian couch. At that age, I didn't know what to make of it.

My next memory is of the happy days that followed. Linwood couldn't go to school because his broken leg was in a big cast. Mother saw to it that he practiced a long time each day on the piano. He had time as well to give me a lot of attention.

My memory is also clear on some of the furnishings we had in that house. We had a beautiful glass-shaded lamp sitting on a claw-leg table in the middle of the room. The decor was similar to that in many parlors of the time. There was a table in the middle of the room with a lamp. The lamp cord went to the ceiling above it. The big family Bible sat on the same lamp table. The setting was quite beautiful. I also have pieces of a traumatic memory of Nina pushing me on my little kiddy-car right into the lamp table. The lamp fell and broke.

My next memory is when my father decided to give up ribbon weaving and go into the restaurant business. He liked cooking, enjoyed helping my mother cook, and had some knowledge of cooking. He decided to go into partnership in Lansdale, Pennsylvania, with my mother's sister's (Helen's) husband, Isaac Hartzell. Isaac was an accountant, and his job was keeping the books and doing the business administration while my father did all the other work and supervised the cooking. (That is where I started school, in the first grade, in Lansdale, Pennsylvania.) Ours was a railroad restaurant. Big steam engines pulling trains with many passenger cars came through Lansdale every day on their way to Philadelphia. They came right across the main street and stopped directly in front of the restaurant. I stood at the restaurant window and watched the people filing out of the big trains. It was a very busy restaurant. The patrons were mostly railroad and businessmen during the week. On the weekends, it became a family restaurant. I remember going there every Saturday evening. I always wanted a hot roast beef sandwich. My dad made the best vegetable soup and hot roast beef sandwiches. However, the big demand was for home-baked pies. My mother was an expert baker, being a Pennsylvania Dutch cook. Because she wanted to be at home, and saw the need to be there with her children, she turned our large kitchen into a bakery. My memory is that these were happy days for me. My mother was always home with us and she had a jolly neighbor woman helping her. Brown sugar, raisins, and other goodies were stored in big containers. Nina, Bud, and I loved to invade them when she wasn't looking.

Our home in Lansdale was a large, single house with old maple shade trees in a big yard surrounded by a picket fence. We children had plenty of room to run and play. The aroma of pies hung in the air all day long. I don't remember her baking cakes, but she made apple tarts, cherry pies, shoo-fly pies, and things like that. She baked thirty-five pies every day of the week. On Saturdays, she baked seventy-five pies to take care of the weekend business.

Every Sunday morning, my mother took us downtown in her model "T" Ford to the Reformed Church. These were the only occasions I remember my mother driving. Linwood hand-cranked the car to get it started. During the winter, the side flaps were on. These were curtains with celluloid windows. During the summer, we had strict orders to keep our seats and not stick our heads out the sides. We were probably going fifteen miles per hour!

I was happy playing under the big maple trees in our yard with my siblings and the neighborhood children that came over. However, this period was short-lived. We only lived there about two years. My uncle didn't manage the business affairs or his own family affairs very well. His office was in Philadelphia and his family lived in Lansdale, a distance of about 35 miles. He finally decided he'd have to end the partnership for "financial reasons." He had been using the income from the restaurant to finance a "questionable lifestyle." (He had been having an affair and possibly was also being blackmailed by this woman to keep it quiet) This was very disappointing to my parents because their restaurant business was growing and they were successful in their piece of the partnership.

Because of these extenuating circumstances, my parents decided to move back to Allentown. This was at the end of my second grade. We moved into a rental house back in Allentown. My dad operated a little neighborhood grocery store with the help of my older brother and sisters. However, this was the beginning of the big chains like A&P and American Food Stores. The little corner grocery stores were beginning to fade away. People passed us by and went to the bigger stores. I remember dad saying that his cost for the groceries he sold in the little grocery store was the same as what people could buy things for in the newer chain stores.

Consequently, dad decided to go back to the silk mill. At that time, we moved to a very large house at 2011 West Allen Street. It was on the other side of Allentown, a side of town that was still in the suburbs. It was a comfortable house and was actually the only house on that block with fields on both sides and in the back. Across the street was a row of newly built houses so I had plenty of playmates. Mother and dad felt that their moving days were over and decided to buy the house. Dad had received a small inheritance and he could handle the monthly mortgage with his salary.

The year was 1927. I started the third grade at Jefferson School, about two miles away from home. That next year, a new school, the Muhlenberg School, was built near our home. I started the fourth grade in that new school.

The first eight years of my life were happy ones. Frequent moves and financial ups and downs didn't affect the closeness of our family. My parent's love and commitment to each other and their children created a nurturing environment for all of us. In November 1928, Ida Jean, my baby sister, was born. Her birth brought me much happiness as well as joy to the rest of the family but resulted in added financial responsibility for my dad. At the time of her birth, dad only had part-time work. Rumors that the silk mills would close down became a reality. Linwood graduated from High School and was the first to leave home. He moved to a boarding house in another town and became an apprentice in tool and die making. Mildred had taken a job as a clerk in a large department store and now Iva quit High School at sixteen to work in the same department store.

The events of 1929 changed the course of our lives. After the big Wall Street crash, there was no hope that the silk mills would start up again soon. Pure silk was imported from China. Owning pure silk dresses and ribbons became a luxury. The silk mills were the primary industry of Allentown, which became one of the first cities in the East to suffer mass lay-offs. My dad was laid off work completely when the mills shut down. The newspapers were full of "sheriff sales" of people all around us who were losing their homes.

Our family's only steady source of income now was the small salaries my two older sisters brought into the home. We no longer owned an automobile and the girls walked into the city every day. Some evenings, they brought two Irish Catholic girls home for supper and to spend the night. They were Doreen and Eleanor Dougherty. Their mother had died recently and their father was an alcoholic. Their family unit was breaking up.

My parents said, "We have room for them. No one is sleeping in the attic. If we hang quilts up there, the upstairs can be made cozy."

So in spite of the changing times, hard work, and struggles, evenings were a time of singing around the piano and four hard-working girls dancing around the room, one of them usually waltzing with my baby sister in her arms. Mildred was the pianist. My sister Iva was the comedian of the family. She and Doreen created much to laugh about when times were bad. With four girls paying board and room at seven dollars a week each, we always had food on the table. Mother and dad thought they would be able to save the house.

I watched my dad paste rubber soles on his shoes because he walked all day long to look for work. Mother saved the cards from the Shredded Wheat cereal boxes that separated the biscuits. If she saw a hole in our shoes that might tear our socks, she placed one of the cards inside that shoe. To this day, the smell of ether brings back a vision of dad sitting at the newspaper-covered kitchen table pasting soles on our shoes. The glue that he used contained ether.

Dad did whatever work came along. He washed dishes if a restaurant was short on dishwashers. He came home one day having had a day's work planting celery. He picked peaches and apples in season. Dad was a quiet, responsible man. When things looked really bad, he started whistling a tune and told mother that the next day would be better.

We were blessed that mother was a good homemaker, seamstress, baker, and cook. She darned our stockings, mended our clothes, and was totally consumed and busy with her family. There was never any question whether she would try to work outside of the home. Our family was so large there was no way that she could have earned enough to provide what she saved by staying at home.

At the age of eight, I was very sensitive and inclined to be a worrier. My mother called me a "worry-wart." Even as a young child, I had many fears and worries. When I heard my parents talking, I listened to their conversation to learn the latest news. As I look back on those times, there was a lot to worry about with all the changes in the economy.

Once we moved to the bigger city, Allentown, my parents became aware that people with a Pennsylvania Dutch accent were subjected to a lot of teasing. They wanted the best for us and determined that they were going to stop talking Dutch to their children. From the time we moved to Allentown, they never again spoke Dutch to their older children. We younger children never learned to speak it. We were discouraged from even trying. It was explained to me very early that it would make me speak English in a way that wasn't "acceptable" to well-spoken people. Speaking Dutch was a "no-no." That didn't keep me from being really curious because it was interesting. Although mother and dad never again spoke Dutch to us, they continued to speak it to each other. Nor did my older siblings speak it to each other or to us. When mother and dad had a conversation at the table, it was always in Dutch. We children responded in English if they spoke to us in Dutch. Yet, they mostly spoke to us in English. It was just such a natural thing. It was something I grew up with. Mother would pass the potatoes to dad, and say, in Dutch, "Do you want potatoes?" He would pass them on and address the next person in English. It was just something that was accepted in our family.

I understood Dutch perfectly. I was always really curious and I worried constantly. I knew the only way I could worry properly was to know what was going on financially with the family. I listened to all of my parents' conversations and I knew when they were having a struggle paying on the mortgage or the electric bill or any kind of utility bill.

With four working girls and three school children, mother had to pack seven lunches every day. Every morning, I awoke to see mother with loaves of bread and all kinds of sandwich fillings. Every evening, she cooked a nutritious meal for all these people. It was difficult. Though we had a large yard, and though we grew tomatoes and other garden produce, we still had to purchase a lot of food. Our main after-school snack was apples because we had an apple tree in the yard. Also, mother used to dry bread crusts in the warming oven of the large (coal-burning) cooking range to make her own breadcrumbs. When we said we were hungry between meals, we were offered either a toasty, dry, crisp piece of bread from the warming oven, which we dearly loved, or an apple. I don't think we suffered any lack of nutritious food because of the Depression.

The three older children were now young adults. Nina, Bud, and I became the three that required the most attention. My parents were a lot more lenient in allowing us to go beyond our own yard. We didn't have a fenced-in yard but traffic was slow and sporadic and we weren't in the downtown area of Allentown. We were in what then was a little bit more "suburban." There were row houses across the street, but we were in a house with open fields on both sides. I recently saw the house and it had been restored. It is still a very lovely home. In fact, I think it is the most attractive home in that block since it was restored. While we still lived there, houses were built on the one side of us all the way to the corner. Nowadays, Allentown has grown way beyond that old house and it is no longer in the suburbs.

Nina was a carefree leader. She loved to bounce balls from the time she was very young. Now, she gathered the neighborhood children to play baseball in the field beside the house. She organized sidewalk races and roller-skating with the kids across the street.

It was good for me that Nina had a carefree personality. Because of her happy nature, she was a bright spot in my life. She was always full of fun. She was a good reader. I remember her reading the funny papers to me every Sunday afternoon when we were just seven and five years old respectively. As she grew older, she delighted in correcting everyone's English.

Of course, we had our fights. She was quick to hit. Because she was bigger and stronger, I never won.

When it came to washing dishes, Nina and I were always stuck with that work detail. It never even dawned on us that the four older girls should help. Mother always felt that the only work Nina and I did was walk two miles to school each way. She did all the cooking, helped clear the dishes from the table, and put the food away afterwards. There were many dishes to wash and a lot of cleaning up to do after the evening meal. Nina and I did those chores while the "older" girls went on their way. They were either dating or doing what older teenagers did in those days. If we had any help at all, it was from mother. We had to do the dishes for ten every evening. There were mother and dad, the four "older" girls, the three of us school kids, and my little sister. Over the weekends there were usually more. Either grandma and grandpa came to visit, or Linwood was home from Boyertown.

Sometimes there were other visitors. In those days, few people had telephones. The Pennsylvania Dutch tradition was to visit relatives unannounced. It was common for relatives to show up and stay for the evening meal. At those times, on weekends, usually everybody pitched in and helped with the dishes.

My parents taught us to work. From the time I could stand on a stool, I was expected to dry the spoons or the unbreakable things. By the time Nina and I did all the dishes, we learned about division of labor. She enjoyed washing more than drying, and I enjoyed drying more than washing.

We younger children learned to respect our older siblings. When we had chicken for Sunday dinner, the older ones decided what they liked first. By the time Nina, Bud, and I came along, I guess we just thought we liked the gizzard, the neck, and the wing better than the breast and the drumstick! I think the older ones convinced us of that, and I think Nina convinced me that I liked drying dishes better than washing them. We were never finished in the kitchen until all the dishes were washed, dried, and put away, and until the kitchen floor was mopped. Mother thought the dry mop gathered the crumbs better than the broom.

I remember once I was mopping under the kitchen cabinet. Nina stepped on the mop handle and it broke. The break was jagged, so we were able to stick it back together. She and I were frightened and put the mop away in the closet as though it wasn't broken, hoping my mother would think she broke it when she took the mop out of the closet. However, she didn't buy that she had broken it just by picking up the mop by the handle. I don't know whose idea that was. It could have been mine. I don't want to make myself look like a saint. I wasn't. I was just a worrier and I'll get to more of that later.

My earliest recollection was being Nina's bedmate. I don't remember ever sleeping in a crib. Usually my dad came to the bedroom to hear our prayers. We then drew an imaginary line down the middle of the bed. If I got my foot on the other side of that line, I got a whack from her. I am sure I hit her, too, if she got her foot over the line. We talked ourselves to sleep most of the time. She was a good sister and friend.

Nina and I were compatible simply because we were so very different. Ida Jean says she remembers me cutting up just to hear Nina laugh. Nina was just that kind of person. She found a lot of pleasure in funny things and in happy things. When somebody described me, they said I had a good sense of humor and that I was a lot of fun. I didn't see myself that way. I guess if that part of me was developed at all, it was because Nina thought I was funny. I cut up just to hear her laugh and to please her. Maybe that carried me through the years that I worried and I felt like I was taking the burden of the family on my shoulders. Worrying didn't do a bit of good. I don't think I ever helped anything by worrying. Nevertheless, it was my nature to worry.

I'd like to address the subject of discipline in a large family like ours. My mother strongly believed that to spare the rod would be to spoil the child. She was very strict. I don't remember being physically punished very often, but she did have a yardstick and she did use it on occasion. Once, when I was about seven or eight, she came after me and Bud with her yardstick. I don't remember what we did but I'm sure I deserved the punishment. Mother came to the bottom of the stairway while I ran to the top. She ordered me to stay there. I knew it wasn't because she wanted to measure me. Bud got his spanking first. The vision of her spanking Bud and then coming up those steps was greater agony than the actual paddling. When she spanked me, the yardstick broke. My brother always declared that she weakened it on him and that is why it broke on me. I was extremely humiliated. After she was through spanking us, she sent us to our rooms. She said, "When you are through crying, you can come out."

I remember coming out of my room, going up to her, and just hugging her and kissing her. It wasn't at her insistence that I did that. I just needed to know that I still had her love. I never held the discipline against my mother.

To the best of my memory, my dad never spanked me. Mother was the disciplinarian. Dad was very firm. When he spoke, I obeyed.

Some more about my family life is coming to my mind. I mentioned the discipline, and that for deliberate disobedience there was a warning and then a paddling. I don't remember getting too many of them. If the three of us, Nina, Bud, and I, were fighting and we tried to blame one another when she came on the scene, she said "I don't want to hear who started it, you were all into it." She would just go from one to the other and give us all a paddling. We all cried together and pretty soon we were all playing together peacefully. I think that is why there was such harmony. I don't remember her ever shaming or blaming. We knew what we would not get away with, including tattling. Punishment was given out to all of us equally. There was really no individual who ever got it; unless, of course, one was being disobedient independently of the others. For that, there was individual punishment.

Nina and I had to do all the dishes after the evening meal. One night, I got into a fight with Nina. I don't remember if I hit her or not. Dad heard us. He came out to the kitchen and said, "Now girls, I want you to stop your fighting and start singing." It was really hard to start singing after we had been in a good verbal battle, but he just requested that we sing. Dad was such a sweetheart. We just wanted to please him and we wanted his blessing. So Nina and I put our arguing aside and sang.

My mother had blue eyes, was fair, and had very long brown hair. She had a big knot on the back of her head and she used giant hairpins. As a little girl, I used to think that it must hurt for those hairpins to go into her head to hold her hair up!

My father had black hair and big brown eyes. Of the seven of us, three had blue eyes. There were three with brown hair and brown eyes, three with brown hair and blue eyes, and me with red hair and blue eyes. Of the twenty-seven cousins, only two of us had red hair. My cousin, Russell Hartzell, was the only other.

Anyway, back to brown eyes. I was afraid of brown eyes. I loved my father dearly, but when he looked at me firmly, I thought he was cross. I guess when my mother looked at me, I never realized when she was cross or upset with me because her blue eyes weren't as intimidating. I didn't want my father's brown eyes to look at me with disapproval. Nina also had brown eyes. Mother told me that shortly after I was first able to talk understandably, I came crying to her once and said, "Nina is looking funny at me again." Nina was very cross with me and I didn't like the way she was looking at me. So, obviously, even Nina's brown eyes were intimidating. I always wanted them to twinkle at me rather than look angry with me. Maybe that is why, in later years, I picked a husband with blue eyes.

Well, back to the brown eyes again. As you remember, I said that I was very curious about what was going on in the family. I was nosy and I wanted to hear the family gossip. I don't remember my mother ever saying anything negative about any of the relatives on either side, so I guess I never thought there was any negative thing about any of them.

When the aunts and uncles and their families visited, they spoke Dutch to each other. Mother was one of seven children and my father was one of five. Of course, all their siblings had children. When families visited, the cousins went to another room or out in the yard to play. If I happened to come in for a glass of water, and if I happened to overhear an animated conversation in the living room, I'd stand at the door to hear what the adults were saying. If the subject was something that I was curious about, I'd stand and listen while my cousins continued to play. I remember my father looking with his brown eyes, first at me and then at the door. That meant, "You go back out the door that you came in." I would obey immediately. I obeyed as my father guided me with his eyes. On occasions in the evenings when there were a few relatives around without children, he and mother spoke Dutch in the living room. As I hung around to listen to their conversation, he got my eye and looked at the open stairway. I knew that meant for me to go to bed.

Years later, I found in Psalms 32:8..."I will guide thee with mine eye." (KJV) The New American Standard (NAS) says "I will instruct you and teach you in the way which you should go; I will counsel you with my eye upon you." I like the King James Version best. When I saw that in later years, as an older Christian, my heart rejoiced. I realized that my father couldn't have guided me to go back out into the yard or to go up to bed if he hadn't caught my eye, which he wouldn't have been able to do if I avoided his glance or if I looked the other way and didn't really want his guidance. I realized also that God couldn't guide me if I didn't keep my eye on Him, if I didn't glance at Him, if I didn't look into His word, if I wouldn't let His eyes gaze upon me and guide me.

Because of the financial crisis, I became increasingly sensitive to my parents' feelings. I wanted to make everything right for my mother and dad. I was hypersensitive to my mother's sadness. Often, I found her crying after the mail arrived. There was a Mr. King who came to collect the mortgage payment. He always came when dad wasn't home but was out looking for work. Mother was in tears every time Mr. King left. I just dreaded when he came to the house. During one conversation, I overheard him say, "Well, Mrs. Barr, even if you lose the house, you have to remember that there was a crash on Wall Street and some people lost far more than you."

Mother said, "They couldn't lose any more than we did."

He asked, "How's that?"

She replied, "Because this is all we have. Even if they lost hundreds of thousands of dollars, we all lost the same amount if we all lost everything."

That summer, when things were the worst, my mother's aunt asked me to spend some time with her in East Greenville. She had no children. She had snow-white hair as did all my mothers' aunts and uncles. I also had some first cousins in the same town. I went to visit her and I remember how homesick I got. My thought was that if I weren't at home they could save some money because I wasn't eating there. There was nothing my mother ever said that made me feel that way, but I still felt that one less person might be a help to them financially.

I don't remember my parents ever having an argument. I mentioned that to mother once and she said "Well, we had disagreements, but we never aired them in front of you children." All I can remember during those hard years of the Great Depression was a great deal of understanding and sympathy between them. I remember their long, quiet conversations and their tenderness toward one another. It seems that financial difficulties frequently result in divorce in our present days. Looking back, it seemed that mother and dad really reached out to one another for support during the hard times. My parents were strong people and were very close to each other.

So that was the family I grew up in. I don't remember ever having a particularly close relationship with my mother or with my dad. I always felt secure in the middle of this big family. If I had any concerns…I guess if I talked or expressed my concerns to anybody about anything, it was probably with Nina. However, there was a lot that I kept to myself. Nina was such a carefree person that I didn't want to burden her. She laughed things off. I worried. When I look back, I see that we were so different in nature that I felt a lot of loneliness. I don't remember sharing my fears or thoughts with anybody. If there was anything I missed in my childhood, it was a close personal relationship with a parent that I could just say anything to or share my deepest feelings with. I didn't know how to do that.

The Depression hit my family very hard. It wasn't quite as bad for my mother's family. Her parents, my grandma and grandpa Schlicher, now lived in West Philadelphia on Chestnut Street. Grandpa Schlicher had been in the plumbing business in East Greenville. During my childhood, he took a job in

Philadelphia at the Boyertown Casket Factory display store on Arch and Ninth Street. The building was nine or ten stories high. There was an elevator which my youngest unmarried aunt operated.

Grandpa drove a LaSalle, which he parked in a garage during the week while he took the subway to work. On weekends, he and grandma visited their children in East Greenville and Allentown. They arrived on a Saturday noon and left Sunday afternoon to go back to Philadelphia.

Every summer, I spent a week in Philadelphia with them. Each day, grandma took me to market to purchase meat and fresh vegetables, which she carried home in her basket. One day of that very special week, I rode the subway with my aunt and watched her operate the elevator all day long in "my grandpa's building."

I also had an aunt, my mother's sister, Irma, whose husband had a small creamery in East Greenville. Occasionally, they visited us and brought groceries. I remember my grandmother asking my mother in Dutch, "Why is Ard so quiet? It doesn't seem like he appreciates the groceries we bring."

My mother said, "You don't know what it is like for a man who has always provided for his family to see his in-laws, at their age, bring groceries to feed his family. It is just hard for him to express his gratitude."

In recalling the visit to my great-aunt (Irma) and uncle (Arthur Kranzley) in East Greenville, I remember playing with my cousins in the neighborhood. I got extremely homesick, but only cried at night after going to bed. I had nightmares about home. One of my biggest fears was that my father would go to jail if he couldn't pay his bills. When I left to go home after being there for six weeks, Aunt Sarah gave me $4.50 for being a big help to her. I thought it might pay one of my parent's bills, and put it in the kitchen cabinet believing my mother wouldn't know who left it there.

I am so thankful for my family and the courage and the work ethic they taught me. Despite them, however, I was becoming increasingly depressed.

Another traumatic event occurred in my life that started my spiritual search at the age of eight.

Before the Muhlenberg School was built, I had to walk two miles to school each day. Phyllis Whitner, a little girl in my class, often joined us halfway to school and walked the rest of the way with us. She became one of my closest girlfriends that year. I really admired her. I remember having permission to rollerskate with her.

Before the end of the year, Phyllis became ill and died. I don't know the cause of her death but it was a short illness. I had just really admired her. She was a very beautiful girl. When I heard in school that she had died, it was such a shock to me. I had lost my paternal grandfather earlier, but Phyllis was a child like me, my dearest friend. I roller-skated with her and sat in class with her and all of a sudden she was dead. I probably didn't even know she had been sick. It was all the more traumatic because we also went to the same church and were in the same Sunday School class.

The really traumatic part of this was that our schoolteacher took the whole class to her house the day after she died. We walked from the school and filed through the front door, down the long hall, into her bedroom. She was lying on a bed with her hair combed back over the pillow. We were allowed to view our dead friend in her own bed! She looked like she was asleep. I don't remember anyone's emotion. I just know what I felt, which was numbness and fear.

The day of her funeral, our Sunday School class, which was a small group of girls, stood around her open grave and watched the casket go down. While the minister droned the last words of his "ashes to ashes, dust to dust" committal, each of us stepped forward and threw a flower, perhaps a rose bud, into her open grave. Not remembering any outward emotion that I displayed, I must have…I must have wept. I must have shown some emotion, because I remember my mother saying to me, "Don't cry over Phyllis, she is better off than you are. She is an angel in Heaven. If you are a very good girl, some day you are going to see her again."

With that, I felt the issue was closed as far as my mother was concerned. However, for me, her death set in my mind a great fear. Phyllis was dead. I knew in my own childish mind that I was next. I was going to be the next one to die. It was something I just felt was a certainty. My mother said I would see her again if I was a very good girl.

A long time later, I had a dream that showed the depth of my grief and what was going on with me emotionally. I don't know how long after her death I had this dream. The dream played a big role in my life for the next seven years. In the dream I saw Phyllis. She was beautiful and was bathed in light. I remember the brightness and how happy she looked. She said, "Come and play with me."

All I could see when I tried to go to her was this darkness between us and I couldn't move and I said, "I can't. You come and play with me."

She said, "No. No, I don't want to. You come to me."

There are several things about that dream that I realize now, many years later. I believe that God gave me that dream. First, she wasn't an angel. Scripture teaches that human beings will never be angels in Heaven. Second, she was very happy. It brought me some comfort to know that she really didn't want to come back. That helped me with my grief. I also didn't want to go where she was without my family. It perhaps increased my fear of the blackness between us and my inability to reach her. However, something my mother said, "If I would be very good…." Another time…and I think it was unrelated, but it was probably a by-product of all the questions and fears that this traumatic death experience caused in my own young emotions…I asked my mother if she was a Christian. She said, "Well, yes, everybody is a Christian. This is a Christian country and a Christian nation."

I asked, "Are you going to Heaven?"

She said, "We don't really know that until we die. We have to treat everybody the way we want to be treated and we have to be very good and then when we die God will judge if we were good enough, so we have to be very good."

That was her answer. Since she was my mother, I believed she had all the answers. In my own mind I was going to be the next one to die; I was going to die young. I definitely wanted to go to Heaven. Being very good was the prerequisite. Thus, I had no choice but to be good.

The double burden I bore made me want to stay close to my mother to feel safe and to obey her every wish. She told me I was the family "worry-wart," but she never seemed to have a clue about my growing fear of death. I worried over my family's financial troubles and now I had to deal with the fear of death and not being good enough to get into heaven. There was no one to share my worries with. It was a grief that I just couldn't share with anybody. It was a grief that I just didn't know how to talk to anybody about.

Nina was very carefree and happy and didn't always do her chores as she should. Mother sometimes had to reprimand her. I did my chores as I should and she didn't have to reprimand me. I often helped Nina with her chores so I thought that was being *really* good! I was being obedient and good and certainly that was going to help me get to Heaven. However, it created a situation with my nature that, had I not been in a happy family, probably would have given me many real emotional problems. My brothers and sisters helped me to maintain some balance and diverted me just enough from my personal problems.

Once, my mother said in Dutch to one of her sisters, "Elsie is the most helpful and obedient child." She didn't know I really wanted to be as naughty and as carefree and full of fun as Nina and Bud seemed to be.

Around this time, my mother was involved in her own personal search for God. I heard her say in some of her discussions with other adults, "Well, who does know the truth? Who knows the truth about which religion is right?" She asked her pastor that question once. He said there was some good in every religion.

A middle-aged couple lived nearby and they were very strong Christian Scientists. The woman became a close friend of my mother. She asked my mother if they could take Nina, Bud, and me to their Sunday School. Mother and dad weren't going to church very often in those days, although they were good people. They tried to get to the Reformed Church of America (RCA), where they were members, twice a year for communion (I think RCA is now the United Church of Christ). They sent us younger children to Sunday School, but we were allowed to come home afterwards without attending the Church service. The older children didn't go. We were all very moral, but I don't remember going to church very faithfully with my parents after we moved to Allentown and they had no car. Every Sunday morning, we walked to Sunday School. My dad walked us there and then came and met us and walked us home. I suppose it was no big thing for my mother to let us go in the neighbor's car to their Sunday School. Her pastor had said all religions were good.

This church was such a new experience for me. Everyone was so different, so full of outwardly showing love to everyone and also talking so spiritually about God's love. The neighbors stayed for church after Sunday School and I listened to the Christian Science lecturer. Two people stood up front and alternately read from the Bible and from *Science and Health With Key to the Scriptures*. For Sunday School, there was a general lesson that was to be done by everybody every week. You had to read the Bible and you had to read *Science and Health With Key to the Scriptures*. I don't remember how much reading there was, but I remember as a very young girl, by this time perhaps nine, they supplied me with my own copy of *Science and Health With Key to the Scriptures* by Mary Baker Eddy.

I sat with the Bible that I got for Christmas and with the *Science and Health With Key to the Scriptures* and read them together. When I came to a word in the *Science and Health* that I didn't understand, I looked it up in a dictionary. I read the lesson every week, and started feeling that if I did that faithfully every week before I went back to the Sunday School, I wouldn't die that week. I continued to read like that religiously in order to stay alive for another week!

There was so much said in the Christian Science lectures about *Science and Health with Key to the Scriptures* that I thought it must be second to the Bible. We were also taught that the Scientific Statement of Being was something that every good Christian Scientist should memorize. It was supposed to be the key to health and the key to good thinking. I quickly memorized it: "There is no life, truth, intelligence, nor substance in matter. All is infinite mind in its infinite manifestation. For God is All in All. Spirit is immortal truth. Matter is mortal error. Therefore man is not material, he is spiritual." I said that paragraph several times a day in my own mind, thinking that if I did that, I was safe. It was almost like carrying a rabbit's foot for good luck.

From Here to 13

During this time, there was an impending crisis in my family because of the imminent foreclosure on our home. Finally, we lost our house to the Great Depression and we moved to the country for a year.

My parents heard about a business opportunity halfway between Allentown and Boyertown. The opportunity was in a country setting and was with the owner of an empty farmhouse on land that was no longer being farmed. The owner, at any rate, thought that it would be a good business enterprise. He planned to put a service station on the main highway and turn the barn into a recreation place for the local people. The big farmhouse was made of brick and was on the other side of the barn facing a hard top road. Originally it had been a dirt road that wound its way down to a one-room school. The house had fourteen rooms, but no indoor bathrooms. Fortunately, there was an outhouse. Actually, it was a fancy brick out-house that matched the style of the brick house. It was a three-holer! Sometimes my big sisters took the lantern and went out there at night and sat on top of the seats and just talked. I loved to go with them. It gave me a sense of being one of them. There was a small galvanized tub in the house only large enough for the younger kids to get into for a bath. The water-pump was on the porch outside the kitchen. Dad had to hand-pump the water, carry it to the coal stove where it was heated, and then carry it to the tub. I don't know how the larger kids and the adults bathed.

In this country setting, my parents thought they could make a new start. They were optimistic, with all the land, and the opportunity to try to start something new, and my dad's willingness to do anything to care for his large family. So, we moved into this fourteen-room house. This was a very happy year. As I look back, I think what a wonderful thing it was for God to provide that year for us after we lost our home and before we moved to Boyertown.

During the time we lived in the country, I went to a one-room school and sat in the same classroom with Nina and Bud. She was in the seventh grade while I was in the fifth and Bud was in the second grade. I had finished fourth grade in Allentown and was promoted to fifth grade. When I started this school, we found that the fifth grade studies were the same as the fourth grade studies I had just completed. The teacher advanced me to the sixth grade. As a result, I graduated from High School a year earlier than I normally would have.

After a year, the economy remained depressed. The owner's plans didn't materialize for my family because he thought the business wouldn't be a profitable undertaking for him. We had to look elsewhere.

After that marvelous year of living in the country, we moved on to Boyertown. My dad got a labor job in the casket factory. My brother moved out of the boarding house and back in with us. He was able to pay room and board to my parents. Finally, my dad had steady employment, although at minimum wage. Franklin D. Roosevelt had assumed the office of President. The minimum wage was set at forty-four cents an hour by the National Recovery Act (NRA).

There was no Christian Science Church in Boyertown. I felt that as long as I kept doing the Christian Science lessons, I wouldn't die that week. Increasingly, I read the Bible. I read whole chapters at a time as I came to feel if I read a whole chapter, I wouldn't die that week. I spent less time with the Christian Science lessons. I thought I could substitute for the lessons by reading more from the Bible. I read the Bible out of fear. I concocted in my own mind what I had to do to please God in order to stay alive. I also agonized over what I had to do to be good so that, some day, whenever that was, I would get to Heaven.

Our new home was within walking distance of the Reformed Church. Ida Jean was now three years old and joined the three of us in going to Sunday School. She was my little girl. I became a slave to her every wish and tried to prevent her from receiving any discipline from mother. Ida Jean remembers me as the person who helped raise her.

As I read the Bible more, the Christian Science principles regarding God's love stayed with me. However, in my self-made beliefs, I had nothing on which to base the purpose of Christ. My mother taught me that Jesus was God's son. I believed that mentally, but I didn't understand God's love for me. I didn't understand the Gospel message, of course, since my mother didn't. I knew that God was love, and I thought a loving God would surely take me to Heaven if I died. I still said the Scientific Statement of Being, but I also read the Psalms so much that I memorized some of them.

I especially found comfort in reading the 91st Psalm. I read it every day and soon knew the whole chapter by heart. I did the same with Psalms 1 and Psalms 100. I picked small chapters to memorize at first. Through the next few years, I increasingly added to my religious menu more and more chapters of the Bible. The number of chapters that I read seemed more important than the particular books of the Bible I read. I felt like it was all God's word, so if I just read a bunch of short Psalms…and frankly, I picked some really short ones, like Psalm 117. By the time I was fifteen, I was reading up to ten chapters a day. That sounds like a lot. I figured when I read a lot of Psalms, it soon added up. If I were to describe this to a child psychologist today, he would say I was obsessive-compulsive. This was very compulsive behavior and it all stemmed from that original fear that I still had, the fear of death.

At eleven years of age, I started school in Boyertown Junior High as a seventh grader. I was the youngest and smallest in my class. They offered me the opportunity to repeat the sixth grade since I'd had sixth grade in the country and found school here more difficult. With my serious nature and by doing lots of reading, I persevered and was in the upper level of my class.

Boyertown was a small town and the main industry was the manufacture of Boyertown Caskets where Linwood and dad were employed. Iva was married when we still lived in the country. The two "adopted" sisters remained in Allentown. Mildred couldn't find employment in Boyertown so she took a job in East Greenville helping my Aunt Irma with her growing family. She came home weekends. Life certainly was changing and I missed my big sisters at our evening meals.

Our home was a large three-story duplex with five bedrooms and one bath. The rent was $25 a month. Dad earned forty-four cents an hour and was allowed to work forty-four hours a week (making a maximum income of $19.36/week) under the National Recovery Act. Linwood left his boarding house and returned home, adding ten dollars a week to the family income.

Dad tried to sell Stewart Products on the side for added income, but with little success. The products consisted of home remedies, cooking condiments, and toothpaste. Because I wanted to do my part, when I was twelve I asked dad if I could sell toothpaste. After having a couple doors slammed in my face, I went home in tears. That was the beginning and the end of my sales career! The incident shows the responsibility I felt for the family finances.

Mother and dad were good managers, but as hard as they tried, the combined income was not enough to provide the barest necessities. There was little money for clothes. During the next three years, they moved twice more. The first move was to a house on Franklin Street that cost eighteen dollars a month to rent. The second move was to a place in another neighborhood that rented for only fifteen dollars a month. The last move occurred after Linwood and Mildred were married and dad became the sole wage earner in the house.

The houses in this clean, well-kept Pennsylvania Dutch community were basically three-story homes. Some were single, some were duplexes, and some were long rows of houses. All had front porches with colorful awnings to keep the sun off while folks sat on their rocking chairs during the long summer evenings.

Mother and dad didn't attend church in Boyertown. They typically sent us off to Sunday School on our own. Mother prepared a big Sunday dinner because she never knew who would show up. Grandma and grandpa Schlicher still made trips to visit us. While mother prepared dinner, dad tidied up and dusted the downstairs. Dusting was something that had to be done everyday! We took long walks on Sunday afternoons if we didn't have company. It was always a fun day.

In reminiscing about my life to this point, I must conclude that I grew up in a very close-knit, very Pennsylvania Dutch family that survived the pre- and post-Great Depression years together. These were my formative years.

Mother and dad were very much in love. They were also loving and affectionate with their children. Mother was a strict disciplinarian but was always fair. On occasion, she insisted that dad step in when she felt Bud needed his firm hand. No one ever talked back. Never. That would have been cause for discipline. As a result, I don't recall much in the way of confusion. The rules were very simple and clear, and discipline was sure and swift.

Moving so many times for economic reasons was part of molding us as individuals and as a family.

Nina was always my bed-partner and we always had the same furniture in our room. As a little girl, I watched dad put up our bed, place the furniture, and tell me which side of the bed was mine. He wanted us to feel that nothing in our home changed just because we changed houses.

While I pursued my spiritual journey, my mother pursued hers. She really wanted to know the Truth.

Mother said later, "I could never understand Christian Science. I know the children went to their Sunday School, and Elsie really liked Christian Science, but it just never made sense to me."

That was something she didn't share with me at the time. I am sure that if she had the assurance of salvation herself, she would have been sensitive to my behavior. If she had been at peace in her own mind and had the assurance of her own salvation, she would have shared her discovery with her family.

In our second house after we moved to Boyertown, we had a neighbor, Mrs. Peters, who lived two doors away. She was a member of the Church of God. Within walking distance, on a hillside on our end of town, was a Church of God camp meeting grounds. Camp meeting was held there every summer for two weeks. Our neighbor considered herself to be a missionary and told mother she was praying for our family. I don't know if she had been an actual missionary when she was younger. At any rate, she started inviting our family to the services.

During the winter months, the neighbor woman invited mother to prayer meetings in her home. Mother said that Mrs. Peters was a lovely lady who was perhaps a little fanatical. My mother was a friendly woman who liked older people. Mrs. Peters said she *knew* she was going to Heaven. When mother went to her house, they got down on their knees to pray. They did this once a week. Mother always enjoyed visiting with her, but she kept saying, "I don't know how people can say they *know* they are going to Heaven. That is fanaticism."

As a result, I thought, too, that was fanaticism. My mother said it was, so it was. In the summertime, she invited us to go to camp meeting and I saw how fanatical it was because they clapped their hands, they raised their hands, and they went to the altar. Although my mother said it was fanaticism, she still kept going to their prayer meetings. I told mother I preferred the Christian Science religion and I didn't like it when the Church of God people preached about Hell. The truth really was that I was starting to see myself as a sinner in need of salvation when I just wanted to be a "good girl."

Our third home in Boyertown was a large, comfortable, older house right on the main street. Many of those houses had been made into business places. This house had been made into a millinery store where they made and sold women's hats. The woman who owned it bought some hats to sell, but she made a lot of them herself. It was proper in those days for everyone to wear a hat to church, to club meetings, to go shopping, or for luncheons.

The offer was for us to live there for fifteen dollars a month in exchange for keeping the place up for the owner of the hat store and keeping it heated.

As I look back, every house that we lived in always had a minimum of five bedrooms and one bathroom. On at least one occasion, the bathroom was outside. Of course, living in Pennsylvania, there was always a large basement with a coal-fired stove.

So, we moved to the main street in back and on top of the hat store. My parents' bedroom was actually over the store and had three large windows. Their room was so large that besides their bedroom furniture, they used the area in front of the three large windows as a sitting area. A wicker sofa and chairs were placed there. When parades passed, we had friends in to watch from the three large windows. At other times, we watched the shoppers go up and down the street. We had no front porch to sit on, but we now spent many of our evenings watching the activities on the main street. The adjustment to our new home was quick.

Though we suffered financial hardship, as did many families, our family remained intact. The problems in our lives drew us closer together instead of breaking us up or bringing us a lot of unhappiness. There were enough brothers and sisters that we didn't lack for playmates. We just had a few basic toys to play with like balls, hats, dolls, and roller-skates. We played a lot of hop-scotch and hide-and-go-seek with everybody else because we weren't the only ones that were suffering through the Great Depression.

Because of the happy environment in which I grew up, it was only in my quiet moments and my alone moments that I was given to being this despondent person that I remember myself being. But we did have a lot of fun growing up.

My own children are always amused when I tell them of the customs of our family and the things that we just accepted. The climate in Pennsylvania got quite cold so we had seasonal clothes. When I was very young and up until I was through sixth grade, as soon as autumn came, we got the long underwear out. We put clean underwear on every Sunday morning. Saturday nights were bath time. Barring accidents, we had to wear the same underwear all week and, of course, long stockings. After wearing it the first day, we put it on again the next morning, the same long underwear. We had to fold the underwear around our ankles to pull our stockings up over it. Clean outer bloomers and stockings were put on daily. My bloomers always matched my dress until I was eight years old. We wore the same dresses to school for a week at a time but changed into play dresses as soon as we got home.

Water for baths was always rationed because we had to keep expenses to a minimum. My father really rationed the water. We were only allowed to put about four inches of water in the tub on a Saturday night. The water was nice and warm. When we were all very small, Saturday night bath time was done on a production line starting with the youngest. Because I was in the middle of the younger pack, I never got the cleanest water, but I never got the dirtiest either. Mother sat on a stool by the bathroom basin and washed our faces and thoroughly scrubbed our necks and ears. We were then passed over to my dad who soaped us up and rinsed us off in the tub, wrapped a towel around us to dry us, and sent us off for our pajamas and on to bed. When we started bathing ourselves, we were told just how much water we could use, just about two inches at the bottom of the tub, and that was only on a Saturday night.

Every night, after our homework was done, we were sent to the bathroom one at a time. We had to fill the basin just half full with water and take a sponge bath from head to toe. We started with our neck and ears and worked our way down to our feet every night. Half of a little basin of water was much less than if we had used the tub. That one tub bath a week felt really good and we enjoyed not having to sponge bathe on Saturday nights.

Also, being Pennsylvania Dutch, mother was very rigid about her housekeeping chores. Her weekly schedule began with laundry on a Monday, washing clothes in the ringer washer, and then hanging them on the line. Every Monday after school, my job was to iron the dishtowels. Everything had to be ironed, including the dishtowels and the sheets. The pillowcases were always starched and sprinkled. If the wash was dry when we came home on a Monday afternoon, we ironed the things that could be ironed dry. On Monday night, mother sprinkled two basket loads of wash. One basket was starched and the other was things that did not need to be starched, but needed to be ironed.

Tuesday, for mother, was ironing all day long. When we got home from school Tuesday, she had some things kept back that she allowed us to iron. She reserved the men's' shirts for herself and my older sisters.

Wednesday was mending day. Mother opened up her Singer treadle sewing machine, and she mended clothes all day. She also got her button box out if a button had been lost and she reattached buttons. On a Wednesday night, she darned stockings. The men wore cotton socks and we children wore cotton stockings and there were always a lot of holes to be repaired. I never put a stocking on that had a hole in it. It might have had a hole when I took it off, but by the time it was back in my drawer, my stocking was neatly darned. I don't mean the hole was just pulled together. I mean, she taught us at a very young age how to weave in and out and make the hole look like a woven patch so that it would not pucker and end up on the heel or the toe of the wearer and thus be uncomfortable. As I grew older, I started wearing silk stockings. Along with that privilege, I had to learn to mend the runners when they appeared. Clothes were not discarded just because they were in need of repair.

Thursday was laundry day again, when the bed and bath linens were changed. Laundry that needed to be starched was not done, but all of the linens were done then. Also, Thursday was cleaning-upstairs day. The third floor and the whole second floor were cleaned. During the winter, any kind of quilt and the flannel blanket sheets were hung out to air. The way they cleaned in those days was that the covers were taken off of all the dressers, the windows were dusted down, and the baseboards were dusted. By the time we got home from school on a Thursday, mother usually had the whole upstairs fresh and clean.

After we moved to Boyertown, we walked home from school every day for lunch. Mother always had to cook the noon meal as well.

Friday was cleaning-downstairs day and that meant taking everything out of the ice box. We got a new block of ice two or three times per week delivered by truck. It wasn't till I was perhaps fifteen that we got an electric refrigerator. When I say we took everything out of the ice box, I mean everything. Every Friday. The ice box was totally emptied and cleaned and things were then put back. Mother cleaned all the windowsills and trimmed and watered all the plants. She had many plants in every windowsill during the summer. She usually did that while we did the rest of the cleaning.

We always had large kitchens and I don't remember a wet mop ever being in our family. We got down on our hands and knees to scrub the bathroom and kitchen floors. When I was about eight years old, I was introduced to the scrub bucket, Octagon soap, and a scrub brush. My chore was to scrub the steps going from the kitchen down into the cellar. I was supposed to scrub and wipe one step at a time from the top to the bottom, and then clean the bucket out in the drain in the cellar. The wooden steps were not finished and I saw how the water soaked into them. To get through faster, I scrubbed the Octagon soap into all the steps with the brush and then wrung my rag out and came to the top of the steps and merely wiped the residue soap off. Mother caught me one day, and I didn't do that again!

By having to scrub the cellar steps for so long, I really felt quite important when I graduated to scrubbing the kitchen floor by about age ten or eleven. Here again, mother made sure I just took reasonably small patches rather than taking too large a scope at a time. Also, the front porch had to be washed off every Friday. It always felt good on a Friday night to know that the scrubbing and cleaning were done.

On Saturday morning we always awoke to the aroma of the weekend baking. Mother baked for the weekend and for the early part of the next week every Saturday morning. While she baked, my dad went to the grocery store to get the fixings for vegetable soup. When he returned, dad got busy preparing vegetables for a huge pot of vegetable soup. We had fresh-baked goods on a Saturday night with a pot of vegetable soup. The pie that we all liked best was apple tart, and she did bake the best apple tarts! Of course, she'd had a lot of practice at the restaurant.

Mother loved to bake and she loved to cook, but I don't think mother loved to wash dishes too well because we were always standing on hand to wash the dishes as she cooked and to clean up the dishes after she was finished. We would ask her to let us help her bake cakes, but she would say "No, if it isn't a success, we can't afford to lose the ingredients in that cake."

I remember one time mother's mother (Ida Weil) in Philadelphia became ill. Mother went away for a whole week. My granddad was supposed to bring her back on a Sunday. I was only about eleven at the time. Nina and I got into the kitchen and we played "Mother" the Saturday before mother returned. We got out her recipes and we baked all day. And you know nothing was a flop. We did really well. Primarily, just watching my mother, I learned a lot of the basics.

In Junior High, Home Economics was mandatory at our school. Early on, I started working in the cafeteria just to be able to learn more about cooking. I also took all the dietetic courses the school offered.

Mother was excellent at baking shoe-fly pie. Of course, that is Pennsylvania Dutch and the Pennsylvania Dutch people like to take a breakfast cake and dunk it in coffee. (Also, being Pennsylvania Dutch, no one can necessarily agree on the spelling. Shoofly, shoefly, shoe-fly, and shoo-fly are all acceptable spellings if you want to find the recipe) She usually had a good supply of shoe-fly pie. She occasionally made raised cakes, which was a yeast breakfast cake. But shoe-fly pie was usually a weekly affair. My favorite breakfast cake was "funny cake," which was a white-cake in a pastry over a chocolate bottom.

I think my favorite Pennsylvania Dutch dinner was "schnitz un knepp." Mother first boiled a smoked ham shoulder for quite a long time. They didn't have pre-cooked hams in those days. When the ham was nearly done, she added dried apples to the broth. In that good, sweet broth from the cooking of the dried apples, she put dumpling dough. Then, when the dumplings were fluffy, she got it all out on a platter and served it with a platter of ham. That was my favorite meal. Of course, about once a week we had sauerkraut with pork and mashed potatoes. I really enjoyed that, too.

I don't remember any time in my whole life that I ever felt free to go to the ice box or the refrigerator to get something out without asking mother's permission, even up until I was married. It was just a respect that we showed our mother, because she knew what she had in there for meals and what could be eaten for snacks. Even a piece of pie or piece of cake was served only after a meal. Things from the refrigerator were never eaten between meals or at bedtime. They were to be eaten only when mother served them.

I would like to mention something about our mealtimes. Breakfast was usually a bowl of cold cereal, eaten when we woke up. We ate a lot of Shredded Wheat in those days. My dad, of course, went to work early and we children had breakfast on our way out the door to school. I am sure mother had her coffee and shoe-fly pie after we were all out the door. On days when we were all home, mother often cooked yellow corn meal mush. She served it with molasses and milk. I *never* enjoyed mush and milk breakfasts! All in all, breakfast was much as it is in many families today with people eating on the run.

Our main meal was always a family time. We always had a large dining room or kitchen table, depending on where the large table was situated wherever we were living at the time. We always had a white tablecloth on the table for the evening meal. Mother believed strongly that although we were poor, she couldn't teach proper manners if we ate on anything other than a white tablecloth. So, on would come the white tablecloth before the evening meal. We were taught to set the table properly. Everyone gathered around the table and no one was permitted to start eating till we were all there and grace had been said. Mother had her place to the right of dad, who sat at the head of the table. We each had our assigned places and we took that place and we were expected to be at the table when mother and dad sat down. We were also required to be excused before we left the table.

The conversation at the table was always fascinating to those of us who were younger, especially when my older sisters were working and still coming home for meals. Mother and dad always spoke Dutch to each other at the table and English to us, while we talked English to one another. Even in passing food around at the table, mother would address dad in Dutch and then turn to one of us and offer something in English. It was just an accepted way of my parents turning the Pennsylvania Dutch on when they talked to each another and off when they talked to us children.

I wanted to mention something more about the evening meal. We always had the white tablecloth on our large dining room table. The table had matching chairs and a large matching sideboard. After the evening meal, we cleared the table and shook the crumbs out of the white tablecloth. If there were no stains on it, we folded it up and put it in the sideboard drawer, out of which we would take a large, red and white tablecloth that was then put on the table in its place. There was always a white, flannel-lined oilcloth tablecloth on the table and over that was placed the red gingham cloth. For breakfast in the morning, the red tablecloth was taken off and we had our breakfast on the oilcloth. During the years we ran home from school for a sandwich, we had our lunch on the oilcloth as well. The red gingham tablecloth was only on the table between meals.

I am trying to differentiate our meal times. It was only in the evening that we used the white tablecloth, and, of course, for Sunday dinner. We had our main meal in the evening during the early years of living in Allentown when the girls were working at Hess Brothers and everybody was just home in the evening. In later years, after the older ones were married and all of us younger children were going to school, our noon meal became our main meal. Boyertown was a small town and we children had an hour and a half off for lunch while dad had an hour off from the factory. We all walked home to have our noon meal. A lot of the families in that town did the same thing and walked home at noon. The sidewalks were full of people scurrying home from the two elementary schools, the high school, and the factories for dinner, and then back again for the afternoon school or work. In almost every block while walking home from school, I smelled sauerkraut and I thought, "I hope that's what mother has today." It was more than a mile home and we had to walk back and forth quickly and we couldn't spend much time. A lot of the families in the town had the same types of meals that we had.

After the evening meal, we always had to get our books out and study. We all studied together around the dining room table. We couldn't go to our rooms to study because that would have required the use of electricity. Water wasn't the only thing we had to conserve. We also had to conserve electric. To do that, we all studied around the dining room table. Each house that we lived in had a large, hanging, glass-domed lamp that really shone over the whole table. Mother always had her sewing machine at the dining room window and sewed while we did our homework. If we went to the kitchen for a glass of water, or if we went to any other darkened room for anything, we could turn on the light only for as long as we were in there. Then, we had to put it out when we exited. It was extremely important for light to be on only in the room that we occupied at the moment.

After my father came home and had his evening meal, there were a lot of little things that he had on his agenda that he wanted to keep up. He kept the cellar clean and he was in different parts of the house doing various things that he saw needed to be done. As far as my mother's daily chores were concerned, after the dishes were put away from the evening meal, there was no more cleaning, there was no more ironing, and there were no more chores like that. That was the time when my mother quietly darned stockings, sewed, or mended so she could be around during the evening activities. After dad did the things that he needed to do, he sat and read the newspaper. He'd either find a chair, if one was empty at the dining room table, or go in the living room to his reclining chair. Dad never had any activities at all outside of his family. All his evenings were spent with the family. Things changed dramatically in our home from an economic standpoint after the Depression. Dad never again had a job that paid well. We always struggled after that. We had no car at all after the Depression. He didn't have a car the rest of his life.

Dad did all the grocery shopping. Mother made the shopping list and dad walked to the grocery store and carried the groceries home. However, it was customary in our town for us to have a baker and a milkman who delivered our needs every day. They collected their money once a week. We also had a butcher who stopped two or three times a week with his truck. Mother would go out, step up on the back step of the truck, and get the meat she wanted. Usually, this was the least expensive meat. Mother would get a few pounds of hamburger and she would buy her Sunday roast off the truck. She also bought a good bit of sausage and scrapple.

Scrapple was very popular on the Pennsylvania Dutch menu. This is a form of ethnic food at its finest. Scrapple is made up of various parts of a pig that remain after it's been butchered. To avoid offending the reader's sensibilities, I will not detail which parts these are other than to say it's what's left over after removal of all the parts that you can imagine eating such as the hams, shoulders, various roasts, and fat for lard. The remaining parts are ground and made into a sort of mush with the addition of other ingredients such as cornmeal and buckwheat flour. This mush is cooked in a large vat, poured into loaf pans, allowed to congeal, and is then sliced and fried.

Most of the more affluent Pennsylvania Dutch homes and the farmers who made their own used scrapple as a breakfast meat. They sliced it, fried it, and ate it as their breakfast meat with their eggs and potatoes. Poor folks like us used it as the main meat dish at the main meal. We ate it about once a week with ketchup. Potatoes, a vegetable, and a piece of pie completed a dinner. Sausage was a dinner meal as well. Often, mother bought a small piece of ham shoulder from the butcher wagon and cooked it with string beans and potatoes. She also cooked cabbage and potatoes with a small piece of ham. All of her meat came from the meat wagon.

In other words, dad had to walk to do all the grocery shopping because we had no car, but we got our meat, milk, and bread from the trucks that stopped out front and made their delivery. Also, about once a week, a produce truck stopped. Any fresh fruits or vegetables came from the produce truck. Most families did their grocery shopping this way.

Many people in those times did not own a car. Some families did have a car that was generally kept in a one-car garage in the back yard facing an alley. People walked, for there were no buses in our town. They walked to work and they walked to school. Most of the housewives didn't know how to drive.

The dairy, bakery, and meat businesses were very competitive. Even in our small town, there were two or three dairy and bakery trucks that came through our town and through every town around there. There were numerous individual entrepreneurs. There wasn't a conglomerate that owned all of the dairies or the bakeries. There were just a lot of families that owned these businesses. My uncle Arthur Kranzley in East Greenville had his own creamery, but there were other creameries around. You could choose the brand of butter, the brand of bread, the baker you wanted, and the dairy you wanted to serve you and they would come to your door. It was quite competitive, which was good for us. Grocery shopping at the store was primarily for obtaining the staples. Milk served (delivered) at the door was often cheaper than milk purchased at the store.

Many people owned orchards and came around to sell apples by the bushel. We never bought apples or potatoes by the pound. We always got a bushel at a time. It was cheaper, because we ate a lot of apples and potatoes. I don't remember us ever, or very seldom, being without apples in the cellar. We could go down and get an apple when we wished.

Candy was a luxury. If we had candy, it was homemade. We had taffy-pulling parties sometimes, and we made our own fudge. The only time I ever remember us having any "bought" candy in the house was when dad brought Green Leaf gum drops home to surprise mother. She was crazy about them. Sometimes we had horehound drops in the home for medicinal purposes. Mother and dad were such lovers all of their lives that any candy he brought home was with her in mind. He would hand it to her and she doled it out piece by piece as she pleased.

I never had any spending money. We were not given an allowance. Our daily household chores were expected of us and we never received any money for doing them.

The Depression was still on and we continued living in poverty. My dad did have work although not really enough to take care of the family. We all had to do what we could. Even though we were poor and had to move several times to find cheaper rent, through it all with my parents, there was a dignity there that I never felt inferior to other people. A lot of my classmates had more than I did, but there were others who were struggling as well. Mother always took the attitude that you didn't have to have money to be clean and have proper manners.

Even when dad was out of work, I never heard any talk that the government had any responsibility to provide for our needs. There was no welfare department. I remember there was a food line that we would hear about, long food lines where people would go for food. My father was so proud he never stood in the food line. He just worked daily, even if it was washing dishes for money for food.

I remember when I was older that I asked my mother whether she and dad always had enough to eat. I didn't ever remember missing meals or ever going away from the table hungry. She confessed to me one time when we were talking about the Depression years when dad was out of work that there were times that she and dad would not really finish their meal until we children were excused and away from the table to make sure we all did have enough. Learning this really grieved me because I had no knowledge that they ever did that.

I mentioned the fact that it never occurred to us that the government had any responsibility to provide for our needs. I guess that's why I feel so strongly in social work that people ought to help people and churches ought to help people. We never had an income tax in those days. Even when we worked, there was no income tax. The United States government, during my years of growing up, consisted of people who were paid by tax dollars to run the government. The government was not responsible to pay the people. The people were responsible to pay the government to create laws and keep peace.

It wasn't until the election of Franklin Roosevelt when I was twelve that the New Deal came into being and the whole thought of the government giving money to the poor people came into being. This was a total switch from the United States ideology up to that time.

The United States wasn't the only country going through a time of crisis and Depression. The Great Depression was worldwide and the New Deal and all the Civilian Conservation Corps (CCC) camps and the National Recovery Act, all that started in 1932 when I was twelve years old.

I want to mention my dad a little bit. From the time I was very young, I was just so excited every time I saw him come home from work. In Lansdale, I was allowed to stand at the window and watch for him to come home from the restaurant. I was in first grade then, and my mother gave me permission to run and meet him at the corner and hold his hand and walk back to the house with him. I was so proud to be able to do that. I remember when I was very young, too, I just followed him around the house watching him do his daily chores such as going to the cellar to tend the furnace. I followed him when I knew he was shaving or sharpening his razor. I sometimes sat on the closed toilet seat and watched him shave while telling him all the day's news. I learned later that I was very much a daddy's girl. Not that he preferred me, but I was very much to follow my dad around. He was a real sweetheart. I must have been pretty old when he still let me jump up and he would hug me. I remember the day he came home from work and said, "Elsie, you're getting too big for me to do that any more." I remember how upset I was when I thought my dad could never ever let me jump up into his arms again and how traumatic that was. I was fortunate to have this kind of a father. It was just so easy later when I read scripture verses to relate my relationship with my earth father to my relationship with my heavenly Father.

My mother was very talkative. She told us stories like I tell about my childhood. I learned a lot about her childhood because she was very, very talkative. She is the one who read to us. She sang a lot and taught us songs. She is the one who talked to us. She is the one who disciplined us and who communicated with us. I suppose mother communicated on a superficial level, but she created the atmosphere of our home life, which was a lot of chatting and a lot of sharing our days' experiences and a lot of singing. In our everyday living, regardless of what we were doing, we always had a sense of being loved and we always felt secure.

My three older siblings, Mildred, Iva, and Linwood, took piano lessons from the time they were quite young. They could all play the piano very well, especially Linwood and Mildred.

My mother and dad always had a piano. With the three older children around, there was a lot of piano playing. Mildred learned all kinds of music. She loved to play jazz and she loved to dance. We gathered around the piano and mother would get an old hymnbook out and we would sing a lot of hymns. I still remember Mildred playing "Whispering Hope," and mother, Mildred, and Iva singing a trio. I used to love to hear that. That was during the Depression years too. When all the girls were home in the evening, we did a lot of singing.

In her older years, after dad's death, mother was not that singing, happy person any more. Her grandchildren don't remember my mother the way that I do.

In looking back over my earliest childhood memories, all seven of us were quite different, even in appearance. Four had brown eyes and brown hair, and three had blue eyes. I was the only red head and my eyes are blue. While still very young, people called me "Reds." Mother told me that my hair was not really red, that it was golden, and that I should say so to them. This gave me the feeling that it was an insult when someone called me "Reds." Hence, I would quickly say what my mother told me to: "My hair is not red. It is golden." If I became angry and lashed out verbally, even as a little child, people would say I was showing my red-headed temper.

I was also dubbed the chatterbox of the three. I loved to talk and express myself. At the table one time, the older ones weren't there. I was just chatting away. Everyone started laughing because I just went from one subject to another. Now, when I go from one subject to another, strangers think it is my age. My family knows differently. I have been that way from the time I was a very little girl.

There were times when I was outside playing with other children that I felt guilty laughing and having fun. My guilt would be so strong that I'd go in the house, find a quiet place, and start doing my Christian Science lesson.

"God is Love" is the heart of the total Christian Science theology. One of the rituals I was compelled to repeat over and over was "God is Love." I said this to myself as I walked to school.

After moving to Boyertown and away from the Christian Science influence, I did the lessons less religiously, but became more compulsive in some repetitious rituals. During the times I was quiet, my fear of death became almost unbearable. I shared this with no one.

I loved to supervise and to take part in little plays when cousins visited. At these times, I could pretend to be someone else. Someone with no worries.

In school, I was always absorbed in my studies and I always excelled academically. I was also very competitive. In the one-room country schoolhouse, the grade the teacher was testing sat in the front of the room. As she called out a question, the first to answer could move to the first seat. This was called "trapping." I felt I had to know my lessons well enough that no one could "trap" me out of my seat. Even though there were just five or six students in my class, I didn't like anyone else to be sitting in that seat. However, I wasn't one to do my homework ahead of time. I liked to cram and just get the tests out of the way.

After being in a one-room school, I was now an eleven-year-old girl going to seventh grade. The Junior and Senior High were in the same building.

I soon had some close friends, but I preferred walking to school alone so I could say "God is Love" every step or repeat the Scientific Statement of Being several times or else repeat some Psalms.

In ninth grade, we had to choose between pre-college or commercial courses. Although my big brother was the only one so far to graduate from High School, I had dreams of going to college. I decided on the pre-college curriculum and took my first year of Latin. My electives were dietetics and drama.

I thought if I could just keep busy, maybe I could get rid of this awful, driving fear!

Looking Both Ways from 13

A new phase of my life started at about age 13 years. In looking back, though, I see the need to tie some other things together. I have to go back to when I was eight years old. Remember that I'm thirteen now, but it was when I was eight and my girlfriend died that I started my spiritual search and got into Christian Science because of my mother's own spiritual search. Having been in Boyertown now for three years, I was no longer reading the *Science and Health with key to the Scriptures*. I kind of left Christian Science behind me, but the ideology, the desire to some day get back to it, was still there because I liked the quietness, the simplicity of it, and the non-threatening part of it. I had felt a great discomfort when my mother went to Mrs. Peters' prayer meetings, when we lived on Franklin Street. My feeling was that religion was such a personal thing. I thought that since I preferred Christian Science, I felt satisfied that I could ignore to some degree the things that made me uncomfortable when I was around Mrs. Peters. However, when we moved to this third place that I am speaking of now, Mrs. Peters was invited by my mother to start coming to our house for prayer meetings and to bring her friends.

Now Mrs. Peters was an elderly lady. I'm not sure how old she was, but to me, at that time, she was *old*. The two friends she brought with her were even older. Mother told Nina, Bud, and me that she expected us to come into the room and listen to them and get down on our knees while they prayed. We didn't have to pray, but we had to respect that they were her invited guests and get down on our knees. I was very uncomfortable with this part of Mrs. Peters' religion. This was a part of religion I didn't accept for myself. Nina, on the other hand, although she went to Sunday School, didn't seem to be very sensitive spiritually. It didn't really matter to her one way or the other. As an obedient child, as we all were, she got down on her knees. Before we went in, though, Nina would kind of make fun of it and giggle about it and try to get all the fun that she could out of it.

I was dutiful, of course. It was all part of my being this religious, good person. But I was miserable. I felt terribly uncomfortable while they were praying. I remember Mrs. Peters praying one night, "O Lord, thank you that we are one day nearer to the summons of death." That really wasn't something I'd wanted to hear. Afterwards, I just dreaded prayer meeting night because it was so depressing. I thought I never wanted to be that kind of a Christian. I wanted to be another kind of Christian, the kind that I saw in the Christian Science Church, the kind that just talked about God's love. Because of hearing my mother call someone fanatical, I felt like I had a right to feel that way myself. I kept this inside me. Bud, however, was indifferent. He was just ten years old and he was dutifully on his knees. I think Ida Jean must have been spending some time with my dad, either in the cellar or in the kitchen.

One evening, while everyone was praying, Bud fell sound asleep with the cat, also sound asleep, on his back. Nina got a big kick out of that and really giggled. Of course, the old ladies didn't think it was too funny that she laughed about it.

Camp meeting time came and we were all supposed to go. My father was very quiet. We never heard his responses one way or the other. I learned later that he thought, too, that this was fanatical. Mother and he talked about it on the side. He didn't come into the prayer meeting. Mother was the one who was spiritually inclined. I think he just let her take the leadership role in this.

My mother made the commitment that we would all attend the camp meetings in the summertime. This was a well-known camp meeting. When it started, people came in from other states to take up their cabins and go to the camp meeting grounds. We walked up there, of course. It was up on the hillside and everyone was very emotional. They didn't speak in tongues, but they did a lot of shouting and a lot of singing and a lot of testifying and a lot of preaching hell, fire, and brimstone.

Of course, I was very uncomfortable. I thought this was fanatical. This was not the way I wanted to worship God. A God of love as I had learned to think of Him was not the God that I was worshiping with these people. Perhaps I just knew God in a different way. I spoke to mother about the invitation time, and she said, "Well, that is how they believe, but it is rather fanatical." So she just passed it off. Mother kept going, however. In her own mind, she was going through the same thing that I was and appeasing herself that this was fanatical and as long as she was listening and tolerant, she was a good Christian and that was what she was supposed to do.

I want to mention that at this time I was still dutifully reading the Bible, still dutifully doing some of the same things that I had decided in my own conscience that I had to do to keep in good favor with God in case I died. Now that I was thirteen, I no longer felt that my death was imminent, but I still had a terrible fear of death, and knew that whenever the time came, I certainly wanted to know I had gained enough favor with God to go to heaven after I died. I was still constantly figuring out what things I could do so I wouldn't die that day. I don't know at this point how many chapters of the Bible I was reading a day, but I was still very religiously doing the things that I was so compulsive about, saying "God is love" in my own mind when I was walking alone, feeling that if I would keep saying "God is love" or even repeating some of the Psalms I had learned, like Psalm 91, that I had to constantly be either memorizing some of the Psalms or saying "God is love." It became quite a superstitious thing with me.

I was still going through this emotional and spiritual torment when I was invited by some friends to attend a series of revival services at a little church in a nearby village where an evangelist was speaking. His name was Rowan Pierce. He had been a Methodist minister and God called him into evangelism. It was in a little community church in a nearby village called Colebrookdale that we went to hear him. He was an extremely intelligent and well-educated man. The service was very proper. The hymns were sung without much emotionalism. When he stood up to preach, he said he was going to preach on the text (Hebrews 9:27-28 KJV) "…it is appointed onto men once to die, but after this the judgment: So Christ was once offered to bear the sins of many; and unto them that look for him shall he appear the second time without sin unto salvation."

That sermon sent me to the depths of despair. The emotional turmoil I felt as God's judgment on me was indescribable. My mother said the camp meeting folks were fanatical. Yet, this was a quiet, well-educated preacher who believed the very same thing: we could *know* that we were going to heaven. I was so frightened that I talked to my mother about the service. I said I really liked the Christian Science Church better because I never felt scared there. I told her how I felt and she again reminded me that this was also fanaticism and there was no way we could know for sure that we were going to heaven. Because I loved and respected my mother, her comments again appeased me and I tried to put that aside. Mother still kept with her prayer group while reading her Bible more and more.

One day, when I came home from school, mother excitedly greeted us with: "Something wonderful happened to me today. I was listening to George Palmer on the radio, out of Philadelphia, and he said that we *can* know that we are going to heaven, that we *can* know that we are Christians, that it is *not* guess work, that the Bible *is* God's handbook, and that we *can* know. He told us to get down on our knees. I got down on my knees and prayed for Christ to come in and dwell in my heart and I surrendered my life to Christ and now I *know* I am a Christian."

Well, I was totally distressed when I heard this because hadn't this been what Rowan Pierce said at the little Colebrookdale Church? He said we could know, and mother had said it was fanaticism, and now she was saying the same thing that he said. I think that was one of the darkest days in my life, at least up to that point in my spiritual search. Now my mother was going the way of this fanaticism and further and further away from the comfort zone I felt with the Christian Science Church. I was quite distressed, but, of course, I didn't let her know.

About this time, three businessmen in Boyertown, a Mr. Renninger and two Trout brothers, started what they called the Layman's Bible Conference. These three men traveled, at times, to Philadelphia, to hear some of the great Bible teachers of the day. During their travels there, they had a spiritual experience. Before that, they had been very worldly and not religiously inclined. One of them was quite a reprobate in the town. Consequently, they became really concerned that the people of Boyertown would become able to hear some of the great Bible teachers and speakers who either lived in the Philadelphia area or who periodically came to Philadelphia for some of the great conferences. They often attended those meetings in Philadelphia before starting their own conference. There were enough people in Philadelphia that honored their concern and would let them know what speakers were coming into the city and at what times, and then they would make contact.

As a result, the Layman's Bible Conference in Boyertown became a monthly occurrence. For three to five days every month, these three men acquired the Odd Fellows Hall. This was on the first floor of an apartment house where the Odd Fellows had their clubroom and auditorium. The Odd Fellows was a service club something like Kiwanis Club. The committee acquired this auditorium for their Bible Conference services.

Because they did not want to interfere with the schedules of any of the churches in town, they started their Bible Conference on a Wednesday or Thursday during the week and continued on Friday night, Saturday night, and Sunday afternoon. If the Bible teacher or evangelist could only come on a Saturday and Sunday, they sometimes they ran it into Monday and Tuesday. However, they never had a service on a Sunday morning or Sunday evening, honoring the regular church services' times.

Mother was always a happy, good, person, but now there was a difference. Her search was over and she had a joy and a peace that she had never experienced before. She started attending the monthly Bible Conference meetings and shared her newfound faith with anyone who would listen. Before long, she insisted that each of us attend at least one of the services during that weekend each month. Dad never went with us but didn't object to us going.

The concern for the little religious Pennsylvania Dutch town was shared by the evangelical contacts the Conference Committee had. As a result, we heard men like Donald Grey Barnhouse, Harry Ironside, Percy Crawford, O.R. Palmer, Anthony Zeoli, George Palmer, and other well-known Bible scholars of the day.

I sat through one service after another, just dreading the end when the invitation was given. The invitation was not given in an emotional manner, but was given calmly and reverently like Billy Graham does today.

I always resisted. I simply didn't see myself as a sinner! I had my own agenda. I was going to Sunday School faithfully and reading my Bible daily. In fact, by now, I was reading ten chapters a day! This made me feel like I was really keeping up with all those people that chose the kind of religion they had at the monthly Bible conferences. I was glad it was only once a month that I was expected to attend.

The year we moved to Boyertown, one of my neighbors, by the name of Jean Lambert, started seventh grade with me. She continued to be my very closest friend through the years. Jean was one of seven children. Their family was going through hard times financially too. I had four or five other girlfriends. I was never one to just have one friend. I had a group of friends that were morally and academically in the same circle in which I found myself. Changing houses in Boyertown didn't change my friends because we all went to the same high school, which was a real advantage for me and my enduring friendships.

There was another girl in my class, Jeanette Hartman, who was not in my circle of friends. Jeanette went to the Layman's Bible Conference and was trying to become friendly. It bothered Jeanette that I liked to dance. My older sister, Mildred, liked to waltz and taught me the waltz steps. I just loved the waltz step and to dance around while Mildred played the piano. In gym class, the teacher asked me to help her teach the waltz step to the other students. Jeanette came up to me one day and said, "I'll be so glad when you come to the Bible Conference. Then you'll know that it is a sin to dance and you won't do it anymore."

The truth of the matter was I enjoyed dancing. Jeanette knew that my mother was a faithful attendee of the Conference and she just couldn't understand how I, as her daughter, could be helping the teacher instruct the class in these waltz steps. Well, that disturbed me because I didn't want to ever get to be a fanatic because then I couldn't even dance anymore. So, I became more resistant than ever and tried to close my mind to anything I heard at the required monthly service.

In February 1935 my mother said, "Well, the Bible Conference is coming up and I want you children to go."

It was on a weekend, of course. Linwood and Esther's first baby, Billy, was only six weeks old. They had set up housekeeping in an apartment, of all places, above the Odd Fellows Hall. The windows to their apartment overlooked the street. We could look up and see their apartment lights as we went into the Hall.

Linwood and Esther wanted to go out this particular Saturday evening, the first evening of the Bible Conference, and had asked Nina to baby-sit. My mother said Nina could do that, but she announced that Bud, Ida Jean, and I would be going to the Bible Conference with her. I was so distressed that I pleaded with her to let me go babysitting with Nina. I promised that I would not interfere but I wanted to go with Nina so she would not be alone. Mother relented and let me go with Nina that evening. Bud and Ida Jean went with mother.

When we all got home that evening, mother proudly announced: "I want to tell everybody that Bud was saved tonight. He went up and talked with the minister and he prayed with him and he is a Christian now. He has trusted Christ."

My heart sank. I thought, "That's another one that has gone fanatical. I don't know what is happening to my family."

Well, that was on a Saturday night, so Sunday morning I went to Sunday School, as always, and I knew what was in store for me in the afternoon. I would be going to the Sunday afternoon service, which was called the Conference Rally because folks came from afar to hear the speaker. So, in Sunday School, I asked my friends if they would like to come over to my house and go sledding after Sunday dinner. We'd had a lovely snowfall, and we lived across the street from a large cemetery on a long hill. There was good sledding down toward our house. They said they'd love to go.

Of course, at the family dinner on Sunday, my mother said, "Well, children, this afternoon is Bible Conference and I want you all to go." Although we had been taught to be honest and not lie, it showed the desperateness I felt in the way things were going spiritually in my family and with my mother, that I said, "Oh, mother, I already promised my girlfriends I'd go sledding this afternoon." Now, I didn't lie. I did promise them, but what I didn't tell her was that I got up the sledding party myself. So it shows a little bit of my personality, too, in wanting a lot of fun and trying to appease my own discomfort with what was going on. Because mother was very much for honoring promises, she said, "Now Elsie, you knew better than to make a promise like that on a Conference afternoon. I'll let you do it this one time, but don't ever do that again."

So I went to the sledding party that afternoon. Of course, Nina, with her big black eyes, gave me a dirty look because I had beaten her out on that one. I hadn't gone the night before. She kept me out of that by babysitting. And she wasn't in on my sledding party. So she was stuck in having to go with mother, Bud, and Ida Jean to the Bible Conference.

Suppertime came. It was getting late in the afternoon and I went home. They trudged home through the snow from the Bible Conference. What do you think greeted me then? Nina said, "Oh, Elsie, I was saved this afternoon and it was the most wonderful service." She started telling me all about the sermon the whole time we were washing the supper dishes. I might have mentioned before that Nina loved to sing and that she had a beautiful voice, but the whole time we were doing dishes, she not only told me how she had enjoyed the service and that she had made a commitment to Christ, but she also told me she had learned a chorus. Now, the speaker not only was a student of Princeton Seminary, but he was spending a long weekend on an evangelistic assignment from the seminary. His song leader was a fellow by the name of Sy Nelson who played the piano beautifully and taught them the song:

"I'm saved, saved, saved;

My sins are all taken away;

I'm saved, saved, saved;

I'm happy in Jesus each day."

She learned that song and she sang it the whole time we were doing dishes. I just didn't know how to handle it. Here was my sister and my brother and my mother, happy in their newfound faith. I felt very much alone.

When I went to bed that night, I lay there and tried to go to sleep. I'd already sat through enough messages during the many months I had been going to Bible Conference to hear about the return of Christ and the Church being caught up to meet Jesus in the sky. At that point, I wondered if Jesus would come if only my dad and I were left. This really added to my distress.

I went off to school the next morning knowing that this conference started on a Saturday night but wouldn't end until the following Tuesday night. I knew that my mother would be expecting all of us to attend on Monday evening, and, of course, I knew Nina and Bud would be eager to go. In school that day, I had a good bit of homework and I brought every bit of it home. I was just loaded down with books that Monday as I came home from school. It had rained some during the day and the sun had shone at times. The snow was melting and the snow that wasn't shoveled off was quite sloppy.

As soon as I walked in the door, my mother said, "Now, don't forget, we are all going to the Conference tonight."

I said, "Oh, I have way too much homework." I saw there were also my regular Monday chores to be done. I said, "I can't do all my homework and all my chores and still have time for the conference."

She said, "I'll excuse you from your chores. You do your homework right now and have it done before dinner. You *will* be going to the service tonight."

With that, I really got in touch with my own innermost feelings. Because I was desperate and felt so trapped, I started to cry. I said, "Frankly, mother, I don't want to go."

"Why not?"

I couldn't think of any other reason besides the one that was really bothering me the most that day. That was my fear that Jeanette Hartman would be spreading it around at school that both Nina and Bud were now part of her little society and that soon I would be too. After that, I wouldn't be able to dance anymore and I'd be sitting on the bleachers with her. So, when my mother asked me why I didn't want to go to the service, I said, "Jeanette Hartman said that if I was saved, I couldn't dance any more."

My mother was surprised and she said, "Oh, that's not true. You're a good girl. That's not going to make any difference in the way you live. You go along with us tonight and after the service you just ask that young minister whether it is a sin to dance."

So, I dried my tears, did my homework, and went, knowing that I wouldn't have to actually respond to the invitation, but just ask the preacher about something that was bothering me because my mother had suggested it.

I mentioned that the weather wasn't very pleasant but we went anyway, through the slush and muggy weather, all of us, mother, Ida Jean, Nina, Bud, and me. The preacher was L. David Cowie, a student at Princeton Seminary. He later became quite a well-known Presbyterian minister on the Northwest Coast. Sy Nelson was also there from his home church, which was the Hollywood Presbyterian Church. Sy Nelson, together with others, is the gentleman who later started Scripture Press Printing Company. These were the young and very zealous men who ran this evangelistic weekend.

When we got there that Monday night, there weren't many people, maybe two dozen, in the Odd Fellows Hall. Because it was also a ballroom where dances were held at times, all the chairs in the auditorium were folding chairs, set up in three sections. Everybody was sitting in the middle section of the auditorium. The lectern was up on a platform that stood at the front of the hall. The song service was first, and Sy led with the song Nina had learned the day before. When it was time for David Cowie to start speaking, he picked up the lectern from the platform, brought it down, and asked everybody to move forward. I was in the third or fourth row in the middle section with my family. As he put the lectern down, he said, "Since I'm sure there are only believers here what with the weather being so bad, I'm going to speak about the promises of God, what we believers have in Christ that unbelievers don't have." He turned to Psalms 37:5, a verse that says "Commit thy way unto the Lord; trust also in Him; and He shall bring it to pass." KJV

He talked about the joys a believer has, that they don't need to worry, and that when they do worry, they take upon themselves a burden that the Lord Jesus didn't want them to have. He took the word "commit" from the Hebrew. As you remember, from the time I was eight years old, my main thing was to worry and take so many burdens on myself that I couldn't do anything about. Here he was, speaking about the joys of being a Christian and, of course, since I was a Christian, I thought, well, I'm glad to hear this because I want to learn how to not worry. He took the verse about "committing our way" and told us the Hebrew word for "commit" was a strong word for rolling our burdens onto the Lord. He said it was the same word that ministers use when they commit a body to the earth, ashes to ashes and dust to dust, and you didn't go back and remove a body after it was committed. It is the same word that is used when a church burns a mortgage after the debt is paid off. They commit the mortgage, the debt, to ashes because it has been paid in full. Believers have the same privilege, of committing their way to the Lord, trusting in Him, and having faith He will bring it to pass. Cowie also mentioned the fact that the first thing believers do, the first act of belief, is to commit their lives and their souls and their future to Christ. In just the same way, they have to commit their paths and the things that they worry about. The joy that this would bring! If I did worry, all I needed to do was confess to God in prayer that I had removed my burdens from Him and confess that they weren't really committed and just roll them back over on Him and ask for grace and strength to keep them where I had committed them. This was the most welcome message I'd ever heard and a message I just longed to make a part of my life as a believer.

I don't believe he even gave an invitation. He may have. I don't remember that part, because all I had in my mind was that now I knew how to take care of my worries. I only had to ask God to take them and tell Him I wanted to roll them over on Him.

And so I went up to him after the service. I thought I was just going to walk up to him as my mother had advised me and ask him the question about dancing. After one or two people had talked with him, I was the next one in line. He looked at me and he said, "Young lady, would you like to be a Christian?"

I don't know how he knew that I had never made that step, unless during the service I had shown my deep interest, my hunger, and my longing. That would have been all the more noticeable because there were so few of us there. Nevertheless, when he asked me that question, I said, "I surely would." Up till that moment, I had convinced myself I already was a Christian.

At that point, we sat down on the front row. We didn't even get down on our knees. He had the Gospel of John (KJV) and he opened it to the fifth chapter, verse 24, and he read to me, "Verily, verily, I say unto you, He that heareth my word, and believeth on him that sent me, hath everlasting life, and shall not come into condemnation; but is passed from death unto life."

He read the verse another time, and then emphasized "...He that heareth my word...."

He again read Ps 37:5 "Commit thy way unto the LORD; trust also in him; and he shall bring it to pass." (KJV)

He said "You are hearing his word." "Do you believe that God sent Jesus into the world?" I certainly did. He read again: "He that heareth my word and believeth on him that sent me, hath everlasting life, and shall not come into condemnation...."

We went over the verse a few more times.

He asked, "Do you believe that Jesus was the Son of God and that he came in the flesh?" He asked me some questions about my faith in Christ and certainly I believed intellectually. It had never been explained to me that He took my place, my penalty. I knew that He was the Son of God but I never saw him as my Savior.

"And would you trust Him to take you to heaven?"

I said, "Yes, I would."

He led me in a prayer to receive Christ as my Savior. Then he asked, "Young lady, if you should die tonight, where would you go?"

I said, "To heaven."

He asked, "Why?"

I said, "Because the Bible says I have eternal life."

He started questioning me. I was to give the answers from John 5:24 (KJV). "He that heareth my word" (present tense) "has" (present tense) "everlasting life and will not" (future tense) "come into condemnation but is passed" (right at that moment) "into eternal life."

Though he led me in a prayer to accept Christ, he said, "Would you thank God now in your own words, that He has come into your heart, that you do have eternal life and you will live forever with Him from this moment on?"

And, I did.

On the way home, I wasn't emotional. I didn't laugh, I didn't cry, I just felt this tremendous burden of having to work for my own salvation was gone. The tremendous uncertainty about death and about eternal life was lifted from me.

He gave me the Gospel of John that he was reading out of and said, "Now I want you to read the whole first chapter of John before you go to sleep tonight. Tomorrow, read the second chapter and the next day read the third chapter and so on until you have read the whole book of John." I told him that I would.

That night, instead of opening my own Bible and finding the Psalms, I wanted to fulfill my commitment to read the first chapter of John and use this Gospel that he had given me. I came to John 1:12 (NIV) "Yet to all who received him, to those who believed in his name, he gave the right to become children of God." I thought, "That's what I did tonight. I received him." Then, I came to John 1:29(NIV) "Look, the Lamb of God, who takes away the sin of the world!"

And it was Jesus! I thought, "That is so wonderful," and I knew that even though I had read this before, now it was like God's personal love letter to me. The first chapter was so exciting and so fulfilling and so revealing to me about the part that Jesus took in my eternal destiny that at the end of the chapter, I closed the small Gospel of John, turned out my light, and went peacefully to sleep.

I have often wondered since then just how many days I read the Gospel of John before I realized that I was no longer reading ten chapters a day out of the Bible. I can only say that, truly, the bondage that I was in, the phobias that I had, the impulses that I had, and the slavery, really, that I was in for all those years from the age of eight, the fear that I had, was gone, and I was free. I was totally free from this bondage of religion. This was my spiritual journey up to that time. I was now embarking on what proved to be an adventurous Christian life.

Embarking on the Adventurous Christian Life

You might wonder how my dad responded to all of this, because he never discouraged any of us. He never encouraged us or discouraged our going to the Conference or the things that happened after that. I learned years later, in talking with my mother, that it was during this time that my dad said to her, "Do you mean to tell me that all my relatives, all the people who have gone on before, are in Hell because they don't believe like you do?"

She said to him, "No, I think we have come to the knowledge of Christ because of the prayers of your mother." Then she proceeded to tell me what kind of a mother (Alvesta Gehris Barr) my dad had. Now, my grandma Barr, my father's mother, passed away just two months before I was born. She died on the steps of her church on Good Friday, after a Good Friday service. My mother said that although grandma Barr went to church with the rest of the family, she also went to an old-fashioned camp meeting service at the Methodist church in East Greenville. The townspeople, especially the people of their church, called these meetings "fanatical." I think they liked that word in those days. Grandma Barr would just quietly get herself dressed and go off to those meetings. Her children were grown and she went alone. This was during my mother's young married life. She remembered grandmother's adult children teasing her for going off to the Methodist camp meeting. Grandma Barr only responded quietly, "I get something there that I don't get anywhere else." Traditionally, from the time of John Wesley, the Methodist church has taught the assurance of salvation. My mother said dad's mother was such a sweet, happy person, always smiling. She always knew there was something so different about grandma Barr, even though she passed away at quite a young age, and my mother felt strongly that she was praying even then for her married children and her grandchildren.

I don't think dad ever went forward publicly during an invitation. He did make a confession of faith in later years and started going to church regularly. As a matter of fact, he was very diligent about quietly giving portions of scripture to others. Every place he went, he left Gospel tracts. In his own way, he had a quiet testimony. My mother witnessed verbally to everybody she saw.

The day I received Christ as my Savior and embarked on my Christian life was my sister Nina's seventeenth birthday. I was fourteen going on fifteen but I wasn't actually baptized (in Swamp Creek) till I was seventeen. I guess I wanted to make certain that was the right thing to do. Nina had already quit school (at 16) and was taking care of children and doing housework. She had looked forward to quitting school for several years because she had quite a weight problem. Although she was a good student and loved her English classes, she was very self-conscious about her weight. She received a good bit of teasing in school, and more and more disliked going. She looked forward to the time she could quit, as her two older sisters had.

Another reason she wanted to quit was that she had only two school dresses. This was because of our finances but also her weight. Those two school dresses had to be bought by my parents because she was too large to wear hand-me-downs. They were not very youthful-looking and made her appear quite matronly. Nina was extremely self-conscious about that.

On the other hand, I had some nice clothes because I could wear hand-me-downs from my mother's youngest sister (my aunt Ada) who dressed stylishly. If they didn't fit, mother altered them. Though I had a limited wardrobe and I never had anything new, I did have a larger wardrobe and some cute dresses. We couldn't afford new yard goods for my Home Economics class, so my teacher permitted me, as she did others, to obtain larger garments and take them apart at the seams, press them out, and put patterns over and make new-looking clothes out of them. On one occasion, I was even asked to model a jumper I made from a larger garment. I did a lot of sewing because if I wanted nice clothes like some of my more affluent classmates had, I had to remake or alter them myself.

Nina and I were certainly always close and especially after we were both Christians and attending a Bible fellowship church in the country. There were people who picked our family up so we could go. I knew the personal grief that she felt and how timid she had become because of her weight problem. I don't remember that she ever tried to seek employment other than taking domestic work in people's homes. However, she strongly encouraged me to continue school. Because you couldn't quit school in those days until you were sixteen, and because I had skipped a grade, I was not going to turn sixteen until the beginning of my senior year. So I really had only one year after I turned sixteen, and I continued with my college prep course.

As I look back, I see that it was Nina who really made it possible for me to get through high school, even through that last year. Once I turned sixteen, I got a job at a department store. I earned $1.30 for working eight hours all day Saturday. There was $1.29 in my pay envelope. One penny went to Social Security starting in 1937. Nina only earned $5 or something like that for working for a family for a whole week, but she helped me financially, making it possible for me to get through school. She saw to it that when she got hosiery for herself, she got some for me. If she got any other items that young ladies needed, she got me a supply as well. She was just as anxious for me to get through high school as I was. We were very proud of each other.

We had always been a happy family, but now that mother and my younger brother and sister were Christians, there was a new and deeper level of communication. We enjoyed talking about our experiences and about the things we were learning. I looked forward every month to the next Bible Conference and didn't want to miss one meeting. Jeanette Hartman, her older sister, Edith, and a younger sister, Lillian became close friends with Nina and me.

One gentleman from the committee that started the Bible Conference, Charles Trout, had a daughter, Rhea Trout, who became my very dearest friend. She was one year younger than I and played the piano. Because of other people that were beginning to trickle into the Bible Conference, even from out of town, we girls always had a good time every month when we gathered together. When there were special services, we were always sure to go.

The following summer, the Bible Conference committee requested of the Church of God camp meeting that they be able to have summer Bible Conferences on their grounds when their denomination was not using the facility. So, the whole summer of 1935, after we all became Christians, we enjoyed walking up to the camp meeting grounds for our conferences. We also attended the Church of God camp meeting.

For six weeks of the summer, the Bible Conference had nightly meetings. We heard men like Culbertson from Moody Bible Institute and Anthony Zeoli, and Donald Grey Barnhouse. It was a wonderful time because as a new child of God, as a babe in Christ, it was a time of real spiritual discipleship and hunger for the Bible and we got to meet many people. We learned the importance of prayer. The Hartman girls, Rhea, and the Barr girls (Nina and I), all got together and had times of prayer and with a simple faith just really started praying for one another's individual needs.

The radio became a very important part of our Christian growth as well. When I woke up each morning, mother had the radio on. There weren't Christian stations like we have today, but there was always a morning Bible service on. Especially on a Sunday, we looked forward to hearing the Sunday Breakfast Association out of Philadelphia, which was a rescue mission that always had good speakers. The men from skid row who had gone to the Mission for something to eat would give their testimonies and it was just amazing to us to hear of the transformed lives.

I knew there were some folks that were driving out of town to a small Bible church in Neiffer, Pennsylvania, ten miles from Boyertown. Since my family didn't have a car the first year of our Christian experience, we couldn't get to that church. I just grew in my faith through the means that I have just mentioned. It was probably the summer of 1936, as I finished my junior year, that some folks that came to the Bible Conference invited the Hartman girls, Nina, and me to drive to Neiffer, to visit this tiny Bible church with its young pastor and very small congregation. We went with these friends and had a delightful fellowship.

It was a very small community chapel, typical of the old-fashioned community churches of those days. A potbellied stove in the front provided heat in the winter time. There were even electric lights, something that was less common in the country at that time. The pastor was Brother Didden who was a very young man in his early twenties. He had a real gift for Bible teaching and had a heart for God. Many of the members of his congregation were young. This church provided a wonderful experience for my family and me. We visited the church whenever friends could pick us up. It was ten miles away, so we were completely dependent on others to get us there.

Our Neiffer church was growing pretty rapidly in membership. They had a small Sunday School department and the pastor's wife was the Sunday School teacher. A young married man was asked to be youth leader. He and his wife lived on the other side of Boyertown. They had to go through Boyertown to get to the church and provided transportation for those of us who wanted to attend church more regularly. There were also prayer meetings on Saturday nights. Mats were placed on the floor and everyone who came to the prayer meeting got down on their knees in front of the pews and prayed. Sometimes the participants were on their knees for an hour and a half to two hours, praying for God to bless the services of the following day. Interestingly enough, many of those who came to the prayer meeting were also young people. Many from the original group of young people that came to pray eventually went into full-time Christian work.

Another big event occurred in the life of the Barr family at the time we were living in our third rental house since moving to Boyertown. A florist wanted to buy the house from our landlady after she sold her millinery business. The florist needed the whole house for himself and his business and we were asked to move.

Because our Christian life and the experience of Christian growth had meant so much during the time we lived there, we girls started praying for the next move. This kind of prayer was exciting because it was the first time that we believed that God was interested in our daily affairs and that he would direct us step by step. Nina and I took our need to our close-knit group of Christian friends, and we all prayed about it diligently.

The only available and affordable rental house was in a very bad section of town. The area was regarded as a rough neighborhood. As a group, we took the matter to God in prayer. This was our first big step of faith!

Shortly afterwards, dad learned of a vacancy in a lovely duplex in the very nicest section of town where all the houses were well-kept. The owner of the house owned a box factory and had lived in the house himself at one time. Dad said this was a place he would be proud to move his family into but he was sure he couldn't afford it. We were now paying only fifteen dollars a month rent. Dad was getting desperate because these were the only two houses available anywhere. Mother and dad went to the owner's house to talk with him and make him an offer. Nina and I asked our three Christian friends to pray with us. As soon as mother and dad were out of the door, we rushed to a little room upstairs, got down on our knees, and started to pray around the circle. We talked to God as simply as little girls talk to their daddy. I guess we got to begging God to make Mr. Koons rent that house to dad! I know we kept right on praying until we heard them come home. We saw by their faces that God had answered our prayers! This resulted in a time of real thanksgiving.

Mr. Koons' actually made his decision during his conversation with mother and dad which was during our time of group prayer. He had planned to ask a rent that was higher than dad could afford because of his experience with previous renters. They had always been very demanding and he'd often had to put more money into the place than he'd planned to. Dad's offer included keeping the place up and making repairs at his own expense.

Even though this was the same type of house we were used to living in, it was of finer quality. There were the basic rooms that we were accustomed to, but the third floor was sealed beautifully. There was a screened-in back porch on the second floor. Other features included a built-in China closet in the dining room and beautiful hardwood floors throughout the first floor. The living room was larger than any we'd ever had before, and there was a beautiful dining room. We saw

God honor our faith as we believed Him for miracles. This was the most beautiful house since the one we lost in Allentown.

Dad always had steady employment the rest of his life, but his wages remained low. As a result of his low wages, it was difficult for me to anticipate any possibility of there being any money for me to be able to realize my dream of going to college, barring a miracle.

My senior year in high school was very busy. I carried a heavy class load at school and became increasingly involved in the Neiffer church. I was asked to be the Sunday School teacher of children six through eight years old. This was a tiny, one-room church, and I took my five children behind the piano in the corner of the room. This was the start of my career in Sunday School teaching. I was so proud, and I loved these precious children.

My greatest desire was to become a missionary nurse in India. In my planning, I was uncertain whether I should get my Bible training first or my nurse's training. I applied to a local hospital. As a matter of fact, I applied to two hospitals, one in Philadelphia and one in a nearby town and was told in both instances that I could not go into nurse's training until I was eighteen. I was sixteen when I graduated from high school. I knew I needed to get a job but gainful employment was still so difficult to find. My friends were headed directly to college or nurse's training because they were a year older than I was.

Because I knew it was important for me to earn more money to help out my parents and also to save for my own future, I applied at various offices and found the starting pay to be very, very low. I started pursuing different job opportunities, and found that if I were working in a hosiery mill, I could double my wages and earn money more quickly. The work at the hosiery mill was tedious. They were selective in who they hired and one criterion was that their employees had to be high school graduates. Consequently, I was able to get employment there and start with a decent wage.

As I listened to missionaries speak at my church, my burden to be a missionary to India grew stronger. A woman visited our church who later became a member. She was already a missionary in India and our church had taken on her support. I was moved when I learned of the religious practices in India and the bondage of those religions because I already knew of the curse of the bondage of religion. I wanted to shout to all religious people that Christ had died to set them free! I longed to go to Bible School and also to get nurses' training so as to be prepared to meet these people at their point(s) of need.

If I couldn't get into nurses' training directly after high school graduation, I desperately wanted to begin my Bible training. However, not having any funds, I hoped that I'd be able to work my way through. Because the missionary I mentioned had graduated from Moody Bible Institute in Chicago, I sought all the information I could from them. I wrote them a letter pleading to be admitted. I admitted up front that I had no funds but was willing to work in the kitchen washing dishes or doing whatever they found for me to do, if they would just accept me as a student. I quickly got a letter back saying that they respected my request but that I had to have the funds for at least the first year and they would then consider my request to be a working student the second year. Brokenhearted, of course, I continued to work in the factory and tried to save money. However, I did have my own expenses such as my room and board. When I did manage to save a little bit, I would see needs at home and would meet those needs to make the burden a little lighter for my dad.

Bud was coming along through high school but he wasn't yet old enough to work. Ida Jean was only nine years old. Dad's expenses were not getting any less. Fortunately, we had a nice home where we could at last feel settled. It seemed like the struggle of the Depression days was behind us. Our whole future seemed more optimistic as we watched God at work in our lives. We could rest in Him by faith knowing that He would supply our needs for whatever His will was for us in our lives. The struggle no longer seemed hopeless. Each of us knew that we were comfortably led by His Hand. Through Christian growth, I came quickly to the realization that when God said "No" to a prayer, or when He closed doors, it was because that was His will, even when we wanted so badly to do things that were good. I was not very clear about what sort of education was in God's future for me. As a result, I became very active in church, teaching older children, taking some correspondence Bible classes, never missing any Bible study classes with the good teachers that were coming to the church, and never missing an opportunity to go to the places that our youth director took us to do Christian service. Though I had quite steady work, I knew by faith that work was merely a means to an end and that the Lord would direct me.

This continued longer than I thought it would. I got the factory job when I was seventeen. When I turned eighteen and could have gotten into nurse's training, the financial situation was really no better at home, so I continued working. My eighteenth birthday went into my nineteenth birthday and I was nearing my twentieth and I was no closer to getting into school to further my education.

About October 1937, Howard Holman (who was Stauffer's age) walked over (about five miles each way—he didn't have a car) to our house and told me God had told him I was to be his wife. I took this seriously as I was praying for the direction of my life at that time. He explained that I was *very* spiritual because I never missed a Saturday night prayer meeting and because I'd been chosen to teach the six-year-olds. He had me on an elevated spiritual plane and a lofty pedestal although I didn't see myself that way. Howard was *so* heavenly-minded.... He didn't say anything about my good looks or anything else. He thought I'd make a good pastor's wife and therefore a good helpmeet since he planned to go into the ministry. Eventually, God found someone else for Howard and he had a successful ministry for many years.

In my social life, I did have some dates but it was at about this point when I first met Stauffer Moses, the young man who was to become my husband. He was the brother of some of my friends down at Neiffer church, but he wasn't going to church at the time. His family lived on a dairy farm.

I graduated from high school in May 1937 and was not married until 1940. During the last two years of high school, after I had become a Christian, my sole interests, of course, turned toward my Christian life and the excitement of my Christian faith and my new friends. All my extra-curricular activities were devoted to things that really were of vital interest to me: going to Bible studies, being with Christian friends, taking part in services at rescue missions and in old peoples' homes, singing in a girl's trio, and giving testimony.

During that time, perhaps toward the end of my senior year, the speaker in a youth meeting asked for those who would to surrender their lives for whatever God wanted them to do and for wherever God wanted them to be. He called for a total surrender for Christian service, for saying, "Lord, I just want to be what You want me to be and to go where You want me to go and for You to be Lord of my life." I made that commitment at that time. Although I already had the assurance of salvation, I now felt definitely that there was a place of service for me and that I was really telling the Lord that I was willing to go into full-time Christian work if that was His will for me.

Perhaps that was the reason I tried earlier to get into schools for further training. Perhaps I was more determined through making this commitment that the Lord did want me in full-time Christian work and so I wasn't quite as willing to stay at home. After struggling so hard to get into schools, I think that I had to come to the point that I was willing to say "Lord, if you want me to just stay at home and raise a family for you, I am willing also to do that." I had to come to that point as well, which helped me to direct my life from then on.

During the three years between graduation and getting married, I worked at the hosiery mill performing two highly skilled procedures that I had to learn, first "topping" and then "looping." As a result, my income was even more than my father was earning and I was able to be of more help, then, in the home situation.

During those three years, however, my father's wages did increase some. Meanwhile, he continued to keep the home in mint condition and just do everything he could to make his landlord happy.

My sister, Nina, continued to do domestic work, sometimes living with a family and working by the week and only coming home on weekends. Since she did domestic work, her income was very limited, not much more than enough to take care of herself. Nina had been dating a young man from our church by the name of Alton Weiss and she planned to be married in September 1939. Because she always desired a nice wedding and couldn't afford it and she knew that my mother and dad couldn't afford it either, I took this opportunity to happily plan her wedding with her. She had a very small church wedding and I took care of the expenses. I guess it was one of the joys of my life because I felt I owed this happiness to her. She had made it possible for me to get through high school with dignity. Now I was able to give her the kind of wedding that she had always wanted.

During the following year there was a change in the hosiery situation. The industry was starting to shift from rayon to nylon. For some reason, my work became rather irregular. Some weeks, I just worked two or three days. Of course, I then put more time in studying and in my Christian work, while earning less money.

At the time Stauffer and I started planning to get married, my salary had gone down because of my irregular work. I felt that since I could no longer be the support to my father that I had been, it was not such a hardship when I left home and got married. Maybe I took too much feeling of responsibility because Bud was still in high school and my little sister Ida Jean was just in junior high and I felt very responsible to help them financially so they wouldn't experience the hardships I had during my High School years. However, at the time that I got married, I felt that I was no longer that help. In the providence of God, I suppose I needed that kind of a push to know that I wasn't indispensable at home. At some point after that, my dad was able to change jobs and work in a truck body works, something that was a little lighter for him and that paid a bit more money.

At about this time, the owner of our house wanted to sell it and offered it first to my father. He said that he would take all the rent dad had put into it through the years as the down payment, and he sold it to him for much less than he would have asked of a stranger. At long last, my father and mother were proud owners of their own home. So, the children, my children and the other grandchildren, always regarded 328 W. Philadelphia Avenue in Boyertown as "the old homestead." God honored their Christian life, as they trusted Him implicitly for their provision. In their older years, when all of the children were gone from home, dad still worked as he always had up until the very day the Lord took him home at age 72 with a heart attack. He came home from work one day and simply passed away there. He was a dear man who knew the Lord his last days. God honored his trust in Him.

As I look back now and reflect over those six years from the time I became a Christian until I was married, I realize that had I gotten my wish to go immediately from high school to an institution of higher learning, I probably would not be the person that I am today. I would have had a formal education, it is true, but God in His providence gave me a broad-based education with much of the same kind of training through my individual study driven by a hunger for knowledge and further education through reading. I wanted to be a nurse with a thorough knowledge of the Bible, and I sought after anything that had to do with dietetics and nursing. All the books that I purchased had to do with those very subjects. I had a real passion for learning in the areas in which I had longed for a formal education. I continued to read and study in those areas, hoping that some day I would have further opportunities for that type of education in a more formal setting.

I digress at this point to answer the following: I have been asked many times, since I was so compulsive and rather phobic in my younger years about the fear of death and religion, how that was different after I became a Christian. I can say with full assurance that the day that I received Christ as my Savior, the burden of religion was broken and I was free *in* Christ. On that day, the Bible became like God's love letter to me. I dearly loved the Lord Jesus and wanted to walk with Him. While I had many doubts along the path of faith, I can't remember a time that I ever doubted I was a child of God. It no longer mattered whether my death came when I was fifteen or sixteen, or fifty, seventy, or one hundred. I **knew** that whenever it came, I would be with Jesus. I never again felt that I had to work for my salvation. Rather, I was possessed by a longing to serve the Lord Jesus in such a way that others who were in some kind of bondage (as I had been) might know Him too.

These were the days before Christian radio stations and also well before the days of television. Early in the morning, in preparing for the day, we tuned into Christian radio programs for an hour that were on secular stations. On a Sunday morning, and all during the day on Sunday, there were Christian broadcasts. The one that attracted our attention, of course, was the one beamed out of Philadelphia, the Sunday Breakfast Association, where they provided breakfast for the men who came in from the streets. Then the church service was broadcast. They had notable Bible teachers for that. The men who had been redeemed from a life of alcoholism gave their testimonies.

That is what attracted the young people's attention, and why we originally started to go down to witness the Gospel in Philadelphia. Going to these men on skid row and also those that were coming in to give testimony was the earliest evidence to me that the power of the Gospel could break any bondage. It could break the bondage of religion for those of us who were so religious and were going to church and trying to be good in order to earn our salvation. The power of the Gospel extended to those people who were in bondage to the addictions that were destroying their families. This new experience was a real challenge to the young people and to me personally.

And now, I un-digress. When I started dating Stauffer, all of our dates were to the various rescue missions and the places of ministry. He played the trombone and I sang in a trio as we led the services. Also, because I had taught myself to play the piano, I was able to play for many of the services when the pianist wasn't there. We also had meetings on the streets of Philadelphia which you don't hear too much of today. For those, we purchased a folding organ that we set up on the street and which I played. There were several other people in our group who played musical instruments. Two people in our young people's group played the accordion. We didn't take the folding organ when the accordions were there. A young man played the trumpet. We had a pretty good little band that attracted passers-by who would gather around to listen. They were given the Gospel and we handed out Gospel tracts. We had a zealous group of young people who ministered whenever they had an opportunity. Each Saturday night, they also gathered in our little church for a time of prayer, asking God's blessing on the Sunday services.

The church grew. We moved from the little community chapel in Neiffer to a larger church building in Limerick several miles away. Our new church had been a beautiful Mennonite chapel, and had a great deal more room. Of course, the church quickly filled up there because of the good preaching of our young pastor and the zealous group of young people who were the life of the church. Because the pastor was so eager to disciple his young congregation in the faith, his preaching was always expository. He took a book of the Bible and went through it verse by verse, or he built a sermon on the basic doctrines of the Christian faith. Those were precious years as I grew in knowledge of the Word of God and in my personal walk of faith.

Stauffer Henry Moses

Stauffer Henry Moses was born on August 1, 1914, the son of Ida Stauffer and Harold Moses. He had one brother, Bob, who was two years older than he, and three younger sisters. They were Martha, Kathryn, and Helen. Stauffer was born into a hard-working, dairy-farming family in Chester County, Pennsylvania. The family later moved to Montgomery County to a large farm, also acquiring adjoining farms. They retailed the milk that they produced, primarily in Pottstown, Pennsylvania. From the time Stauffer was eight years old, he was awakened early every morning to help milk the cows. Then he ate breakfast, changed his clothes, and went on to school. Chores began again upon his return from school. His formal education was over after the eighth grade which was common in those days. Stauffer's uncle, Henry, was in charge of the retail end of the business. As a teenager, Stauffer helped him every Saturday on the milk routes by both serving milk and collecting money. Stauffer enjoyed the business end of the dairy business more than the farm end. By the time he was eighteen, his father had put him full time in the retail end with his own truck. Even at that age, Stauffer saw the need to acquire both retail and wholesale customers. He built up the route by stopping at restaurants, factories, and other places where he could sell the milk wholesale. Stauffer had grown up in the protected environment of the family farm. Now he was exposed to the business world. He quickly developed a love for gambling in a small way in the slot machines that he found in the various wholesale stops that he served.

His parents were members of the Reformed Church of America. When Stauffer and his siblings were youngsters, they were taken to Sunday School regularly. At the age of fifteen, Stauffer took the Heidelberg Catechism and was confirmed. After that, he felt that he had learned as much about religion as he needed to and he went to church less and less frequently.

Stauffer was "saved" at age 18 years, but when he was "stood up" by a girl he was dating, Helen, he went to a dance hall, met Elsie Upthegrove, and dated her for three years. His gambling became heavier and he didn't go back to church. However, he made a real and total (i.e. "no turning back") profession of faith with Brother Didden at about age twenty-two when he came to the end of himself with his gambling and running with an unsaved group. The first Elsie subsequently broke up with him.

His mother, Ida, during these years, was seeking peace of mind and a more meaningful reason to go to church. By listening to the radio, she acquired increasing knowledge of the Bible. The more she learned, the greater her hunger to know more became.

The family farms were located within ten miles of the little country chapel in Neiffer. Stauffer's mother, her oldest son, Bob, and the three girls, started going to that chapel and getting involved in the activities of the church.

Stauffer was indifferent to all of this because he was busy with his life. He had a steady girlfriend (not me!) and was building up the milk routes. He also followed a lifestyle that was not the kind his parents had modeled.

By the time he was twenty-two, he did more gambling than just with slot machines. Often, his whole salary went to gambling. He had become a compulsive gambler and started borrowing his salary ahead of time, wanting to retrieve some of the money that he had lost in the week's gambling. Finally, when his salary was gone, he started borrowing out of the milk money that he collected. His big collection days were Mondays and Saturdays. If he gambled some of that money, he wouldn't mark in the books that they had paid, thus padding the books. When his father approached him about poor collection days, he was not honest with him. Stauffer finally came to the point of despair when he realized that he was out of control with his gambling. He also realized that he was stealing from his father as well as lying to him. Stauffer came from a very moral family and he knew the difference between right and wrong. At one point, he felt that life was not worthwhile. It was like there was nothing to live for. He really did not want any part of his mother's or his sisters' religion. Because of his pride and not knowing which way to turn, he decided to go visit the pastor in the church office and talk with him.

It was during this visit that the pastor gave Stauffer the plan of salvation. He told him how Christ could break the bondage of addiction in his life. At that moment, Stauffer turned his life over to Christ and became the new creature and the person that I knew. I had never known him in the days that he was going through this struggle.

Stauffer's conversion was almost like that of Paul's when he was saved on the road to Damascus. His hunger for the Word of God and his zeal for others to hear the Good News made him the zealous person of vision and zeal that I knew for all the years we were together. He put gospel tracts and portions of scripture on his sun visor. While he served milk and did his day's work, he memorized whole portions of scripture. He had almost a photographic memory. Stauffer memorized quickly, and soon became a person who gave personal testimony of his own deliverance from compulsive gambling. In his zeal, he wanted to go to the missions with the young people from the youth group and witness to the people that had an addiction problem.

Stauffer eventually replaced the church's first youth director who went onto the mission field. His was not a paid position, but he was a zealous young man who was eager to influence the youth of the church to care about those who were down and out. He felt strongly that the young people should have recreation time and fun together, but that they should take the Word of God to needy people on a regular basis. Under his leadership, we went to the rescue missions of Philadelphia every month. We also went monthly to a rescue mission in Reading, Pennsylvania. An old people's home in our area was a favorite place of service as well. Eventually, I started dating him. He was six years older than I. It was hard for me to even realize the kind of life he had lived before his conversion, but I admired his zeal. I admired his burden for souls and his desire to get the gospel out.

It must have been sometime in 1939 when Stauffer had a close encounter with death. This was a life-transforming experience for him. While working on the farm, he cut his hand. Within a week, it was clear that he was developing blood poisoning. Red streaks spread rapidly up his arm. This was in the days before antibiotics. Stauffer prayed for the Lord to spare his life now and he would give himself completely to whatever and wherever the Lord wanted him. This was the point of complete surrender. From this time on, Stauffer sought the Lord's will in everything he did.

Notwithstanding, I still struggled with a desire for more education. I believed that I would be able to go on to college or nurse's training school if I broke up with him. So, I broke up with him for six months. I just pursued my own interests but I kept seeing him in church and found that I really missed him. However, if it was God's will for me to go away to school, I wanted Stauffer to get on with his own life. Another September passed and I still had not made any progress in my own endeavor to get an education. Finally, I realized that Stauffer was not the roadblock to my getting more education. We started dating again. All of our dates were to rescue missions—preaching on the streets and sharing his simple faith.

I occasionally helped Stauffer's older brother Bob and his wife by babysitting for their two little children. One weekend while I was at their home, Stauffer came by to pick me up for a date. When we got back, we were standing at a gate by the barn. The moon was shining brightly. Stauffer proposed to me and I surprised him by saying "Yes!" Immediately, we started planning our life together. By this time, Stauffer had been youth director of our church for two years. Our young people's group was growing. We knew that if we had a church wedding, it would bring us a good bit of expense. We decided we should be married April 6, 1940. Stauffer and I wanted to be married by the pastor in the chapel. To avoid the demands that would be placed on us by a big wedding, we wanted it to be quiet and a secret with only our parents there as witnesses. Out of respect to my brothers and sisters, we did tell our siblings.

Jokingly, my sister said, "You are getting married in a church and that is a public place. We can come whether we are invited or not."

Stauffer, being a big tease, kidded around about that. Well, nonetheless, we were surprised and excited when we arrived at the church and found my brothers and sisters and his brothers and sisters at the wedding. So, we had a very inexpensive wedding, but we had the very people there that we would have wanted to be there. They came armed with rice and we were bombarded on our way to the car. The next day, when the folks came to church, they asked who was married. We were in a little bit of trouble with our young people because we pulled one over on them!

Stauffer's parents' homestead was very large. They had several hired men living in the home. Stauffer's mother got up every morning and prepared a big breakfast while the milking was going on. When the folks came in from chores, they sat around the big family kitchen table for a large country breakfast. I really enjoyed the excitement of living on the farm and I loved the country and the prospect of farm life. We stayed there in a large bedroom in the old homestead for some months and eventually went into housekeeping on the adjoining farm that his father had recently purchased.

Early in our marriage, Stauffer and I talked about commuting to Philadelphia to attend night school at the Philadelphia College of Bible. The plan was to work toward a degree to be better equipped to lead our young people. Neither of us had a clear understanding of what God's will was for our lives together. However, we both had a burning desire to serve the Lord and to win souls for Him. Because we had dated a few years with us breaking up for six months and all the trauma that goes with a romance like that, our first year was extremely happy. We just did not have that tough first year that so many couples have.

After only thirteen months of marriage, Eileen, our first little girl, arrived. She was born at home on May 26, 1941. The doctor came to the house and her daddy helped with the delivery.

World War II was already going on, although the United States was not yet involved. Many young men were being drafted. Because of the size of the dairy farms, the draft had not reached Stauffer, his brother, or any of the hired men. It was vital for the farms to keep operating with the threat of war. Eileen was six months old when the United States entered World War II.

Our second little girl, Audrey Jean, was born thirteen months later, on June 28, 1942. Stauffer continued working on the farm and with the youth of the church. Because of the babies, I couldn't accompany him to all of the services that the young people had. He continued to go to Philadelphia to the various places of service that the young people had scheduled.

Stauffer became increasingly aware of his need for more Bible education and talked often about going to Philadelphia for further theological training. He knew my desire for the same kind of education. In order to fulfill this desire, we requested some help with the children. A staff member from our church came two afternoons a week and took over the care of our two babies. We started traveling to Philadelphia for evening classes to study the Bible.

Those were difficult days. Stauffer awoke early in the morning to take care of his milk routes and the day's work. Then, late in the afternoon, we would head for Philadelphia, forty miles away. There, we sat through classes. Finally, we made the trip back.

Because of the war, gasoline was rationed. Sometimes we just had enough gas to go part way and then we would have to take the train the rest of the way into the city. We generally arrived back home around 11 o'clock at night. Stauffer went immediately to bed because he had to start his day again the next morning between four and five o'clock.

Our third daughter, Diane Marie, was born on July 11, 1945. Of course, my participation in school ended several months before her birth. Stauffer continued to go to school and continued with his leadership of the youth. When he went to the Philadelphia Rescue Mission with the young people, I waited up late for him. When he came home, he was always excited about the service and the number of men who came forward to accept Christ as Savior. He always preached the message, or most always, and he had a real message of Salvation that showed his sincerity. The superintendents of the different missions always enjoyed having him preach. His presentation was straightforward. Stauffer presented the gospel with a simple, childlike faith. He presented the Lord Jesus Christ as the Only One who could redeem people in all walks of life from their sin and give them freedom from the bondage of sin. I taught our girls simple little songs. Often during the summer we went along with him. He proudly put his two daughters up on chairs or something higher and told them to sing loudly so the men could hear them.

One day, he said "Now sing really loudly because one of the men in the back row can't hear very well."

Eileen replied, "Tell him to move up front, daddy."

Of course, when he relayed this to the men of the auditorium, they enjoyed that and they laughed. This broke the ice for that evening's service.

It was customary in the rescue missions of Philadelphia for the leader of the service and the young people who accompanied him to sit in several rows of chairs that were placed behind the speaker. When the invitation was given, for any men that came forward, the young men in our youth group went down and talked with them and prayed with them. The little girls and I seldom attended these services, except on very special occasions when we had other errands to run in the city.

Stauffer was very enthusiastic about the results of the services and increasingly enthusiastic about Christian work. When he came home from collection days on the milk routes, I would ask, "Did you have a good day? Are we going to be able to meet all our expenses?"

He would reply, "Yes, I had a good day, but what do we have? We just have an income. We are just making a living." His heart even then was toward serving Christ full-time, especially in the field of rescue mission.

Before Diane was born, it was decided that Bob, Stauffer's older brother, would assume total responsibility for the main dairy farm. Stauffer would officially be responsible for the milk routes, the plant, and everything involved with retailing the milk that he and his brother and the other farms produced. With that responsibility, we realized that some changes needed to be made. The hired hand that drove the truck on the milk routes would no longer be able to live in the homestead. We had to make room for him in our bungalow. So, in our small home we had not only one of the truck drivers, but we also set up the office to take care of the business part.

September 9, 1948, the Moses family celebrated the birth of our first boy, Larry Harold. It aroused a lot of excitement throughout the family and the church that the Moses' finally had a son.

Increasingly, I saw Stauffer struggle with his desire to go into Christian work full-time as opposed to continuing in the business. He finally rationalized that if we could make the business prosper, he'd encourage young people to go to Bible School and we'd help support them. Upon graduation, they'd go onto the mission field in our stead and we'd send them support checks. This thinking didn't remove his personal burden and his own restlessness, however.

Many times, I came before the Lord and put it before Him in my own devotional time. I loved my four children so much. Stauffer and I had been married more than ten years, and I just pleaded with the Lord to gently lead us and to protect our children, that however difficult a time he was having in letting go now of the prospering business, that our children would be safe and he wouldn't have to face a crisis in his own family before he would just let go of everything worldly and launch out into the field that he loved so well.

Stauffer's father was not a Christian. Stauffer spoke to him several times about the possibility of selling out the retail end of the business. His father remained very much opposed. We just kept going the way we were going. One day, Stauffer had a long talk with his father. He poured out his heart to him and told him the struggle he was going through. He acknowledged that his father wanted to make a big name for them and to see the Moses Dairy name go on. He also recognized his father had put his confidence in him to build up the business. However, Stauffer was now asking to be released from the family enterprise to go out into areas unknown.

His father was grieved, but said, "If that's what you must do, Stauffer, you have my blessing."

When Stauffer came home that day and told me, we had a time of rejoicing. We knew that our struggle was over and we would now launch out and see what God had for us. Because neither his father nor his brother was interested in retailing the milk they produced, they urged him to find another dairy that would buy their milk and sell it for them.

Little did we know when we took that step what tests of faith lay before us. However, we had one thing that we held very close and dear to us. That was the sweet peace and the joy that we had as the parents of four young children. We knew that God's hand was upon us and that we were finally stepping out by faith, trusting Him to lead our steps. Certainly, if God had indeed called us to a life of Christian work, He had a perfect plan and we had to seek that plan day by day.

Some years before, Stauffer and I had moved off of one of the farms and onto a little corner plot with very few trees where a young neighbor had built a small and inexpensive house. Stauffer's father had purchased it for us as part of our taking over the retail end of the dairy business. This was to allow other farmers to live in the various farmhouses. We felt sure that wherever God led us in Christian work we'd have the proceeds from the sale of that house to purchase new quarters.

Before long, Stauffer found a dairyman not too far away who wanted to increase his retail business. He looked over our plant, the trucks, and the assets that we had. He wasn't interested in the equipment that was in the plant, the pasteurizer, the homogenizer, the bottle washer, and that sort of thing. He was only interested in the trucks. So, we had to find buyers for all that equipment which by definition was all used

Of course, to our way of thinking, there was a great deal of value in the good will of our customers. As a result, we believed that we'd cash out and be able to pay off the notes that we had acquired on some of the equipment that we had purchased and have money left over. Our first test of faith was when the sale was made to the dairy, our equipment was all sold, and everything was settled. We paid our debts and had no money left over. Nothing. Not a penny.

Besides going to the rescue missions of Philadelphia, once a month we went to a rescue mission in Lancaster, PA. When the director of that mission found out that we were praying about rescue mission training, he asked Stauffer to come up to Lancaster and be his assistant. Our training thus far had just been in preaching the gospel. Stauffer recognized the importance of obtaining on-the-job training for really being with the men, knowing how to handle them when they came in, and all the details regarding the administration of a rescue mission.

This was a very welcome opportunity for us and it was only fifty miles from our home, going the opposite direction from Philadelphia. Stauffer had to be there for the Sunday night service and he couldn't come home until the following Friday afternoon. This meant that I was alone with the children from late afternoon Sunday until the following Friday. Although we had our house to live in, we didn't have any income except the small amount that they gave him to be the assistant-in-training at the Lancaster rescue mission. This, of course, was not sufficient to care for a family with four children and pay for the cost of transportation back and forth from our home to Lancaster. Since we only had the one car, Stauffer took it and I was without for the entire week. This meant we had to do our shopping and whatever else we needed to do on Saturday when he was home. If I needed the car, say for doctor's appointments, he left it for me and hitchhiked to Lancaster.

After six months of commuting to receive that mission training, he felt that he had to come home to provide for the family. Our needs weren't being met and we still didn't have clear direction on what God wanted us to do. Stauffer took a job with a friend who was a member of our church. He worked in a glass shop installing windowpanes in storefronts and in automobiles. Additionally, because he had business experience, Stauffer also collected some of the bills. This supplied our needs for a little while. Subsequently, a relative who was a boss at the Firestone Tire Company gave him a job there for a period of time. Stauffer and I were very conscious that we were in God's "school of spiritual training" and that there were things that He needed to teach us. We searched the scriptures and we recognized that our waiting on the Lord was very vital to our preparation for what He had in store for us.

As the year went by, we became very much concerned about the next step. Stauffer said to me one day, "We planned for the money after the sale of the routes to wholly supply our needs so we could live in the way in which we were accustomed until we went into Christian work. That didn't work out. What if dad says, 'you know, I still haven't given you the deed to the house and I don't want you to sell it.'"

I said, "Surely he won't do that."

And he said, "No, I don't think he will, but are we willing to let go of everything here?"

I hesitated because I had to do some praying about that. We took it to the Lord in prayer and asked Him to remove every bit of confidence we had in possessions and to totally trust in Him. We committed the house to the Lord as well. In rescue mission work, we knew that we had to either live in a part of the mission, something we didn't want to do with the children, or have a house away from there. We knew as trainees, as a family in training, we wouldn't get the kind of salary that would allow us to live away from the mission in our own home. I realized I was depending on the money from the sale of our house to provide housing for us in the mission field.

Not too many days after we surrendered to God the house and all that we had accumulated through those eleven years, his father said to him, "Stauffer, I think this is all foolish. I believe that you'll come back some day and you'll want that house. I don't want to sell it. I want it to be right there for when you get this out of your system and you come back. I'll rent it out until you return."

Well, our hearts were prepared for this but probably not for the fact that we were not even going to receive the rent money. Stauffer's father planned to use that to keep up the taxes, insurance and other expenses of the house. So, once we moved out, the house was no longer ours. Not the house. Not the rent. Nothing. We had to say goodbye to that totally. We faced that reality also as we continued to wait on the Lord for our future.

It was around this time that there was a district meeting of the International Union of Gospel Rescue Missions in our area. We had been attending these meetings already for several years at the invitation of various mission directors.

That is how we got to know and have fellowship with and came to pray for a lot of the rescue missions in the Philadelphia district.

In May 1952, the national convention was held in Trenton, NJ, which is in north Jersey and not too far from our home. We went every morning and returned home in the evening. It was there that we got a sense of what was going on throughout the country, not just in the Philadelphia district. It was a good few days. Our little girls even attended with us one day.

At that convention, we met Mr. and Mrs. George Akins from Savannah, GA. George was attracted to Stauffer's sincerity and told him they needed an assistant in the rescue mission in Savannah. The Akins' invited us to come down and look the mission over. If agreeable, we were to move down there with the family. Stauffer and I spent only a few days with them in June. After much prayer, we decided this was the next step of faith for us to take. This was actually the first step in Christian work that we took by blind faith.

In August, we packed our furniture into a rented van and took our family of six to the rescue mission in Savannah, GA. Because we had no money to pay rent anywhere, we had to move into the Mission itself.

Our church, by this time, had grown to quite a large congregation, perhaps four or five hundred members, and the Sunday School department was also quite large. They had a farewell service for us. There was just a lot of excitement that Stauffer and I were launching out and going into Christian work. At the same time, some of the other young people who had been with them through the years were also launching out.

The rescue mission was in downtown Savannah. The chapel, dining room, kitchen, and offices were on the first floor. There was a stairway going up to the second floor and there was a door going into another area there but then the stairway wound around and went up to the third floor. It was planned that the Moses family would have the entire second floor in which to set up their home. There was a large recreation room. Along the side of the recreation room were small rooms and a little kitchen. It wasn't really an apartment, but it could be fixed up very comfortably. I saw instantly when we visited, before we moved down, that there was a lot of work to be done. This wasn't really an issue since I was used to hard work.

We agreed that I would make up the menus for the men's meals, that I could use the services of the cook to cook for the men, and that our family could have our evening meal in a side room down on the first floor. Since this was the way the missions in the Philadelphia district did it and the Akins' were used to seeing missions in other parts of the country, we believed they'd want us to bring some of the ideas that we had to the Savannah mission.

The Akins' didn't actually live in the mission or even in the city. They lived in the country on beautiful land where they had started a Christian day school for children in the area. Mrs. Akins taught some classes and was also personal secretary to her husband in his Mission office. Mr. Akins was in and out of both places as well.

Stauffer's job description was to take full charge of the rescue mission. The Akins' requested that I work in the office with Mrs. Akins.

The year was 1952. Larry was almost four years old, Diane was seven, Audrey was 10 years, and Eileen was 11 years old when we moved to Savannah. We had been married 12½ years and were, for the first time, going into full time Christian work and learning literally that God was our provider.

We had a whole year of seeing God take complete control of our finances and all of our material possessions. We were stripped of virtually all of our previous financial assets. Our fantasy had been that everything would be under control and that we would be comfortable because of the financial cushion from having lived and worked on the farm. The reality was that we were just simply living from the Hand of God. We were to learn more about that within a few days of arriving there.

A few promises were made to us before we moved to Savannah. We had a washer and dryer and were told that we would be able to hook them up so as to be able to use them. The mission was to provide food for our meals whether we ate in the dining room or in our own living quarters. There was to be a cook for the men and I would supervise him.

My brother-in-law and another friend from Limerick drove the big truck down ahead of us and were waiting for our arrival to unpack the truck. We unloaded the whole thing into the large recreation room because nothing had been cleaned up to prepare for us. There were four or five small rooms to the side of the recreation room. One of these was a kitchenette. A very large corner room with many windows adjoined the recreation room. We looked out over the busy downtown street. Adjacent to the mission was a used car lot with lots of intense lights. At night, even though the upstairs was darkened, it was quite bright from the business lights outside.

Prior to our coming, the director had allowed some of the mission men to occupy this area. They were supposed to be sober and were in need of a place to stay while looking for work and a more permanent place to live. He didn't require them to clean up when they moved out. The first thing that greeted me was stacks and stacks of filth in each room, including unbelievable numbers of empty liquor bottles under the piles of dirt. The rooms were in terrible condition and the kitchenette was not fit to cook in. Obviously, the supposedly sober men were still doing a bit of drinking. The large room on the other side of the kitchen was not in such bad shape, relatively speaking. Stauffer and I went about sweeping and scrubbing that area. We set up our double bed and the four children's beds all in the same room. We pulled the dressers out of the recreation room and placed them in our "family dorm." Fortunately, the older girls were used to carrying their weight and were good at helping me by making up beds, cleaning up, washing and drying dishes, and even Diane at seven had her chores. Finally, we all got to sleep that first night.

The next morning, we awoke excited. We were on our mission field! The children felt our excitement that we were going to tell the boys and girls in the neighborhood about Jesus. Daddy was going to tell the men that lived on the third floor about Jesus, too. We were now missionaries! We were full of song and excitement, and happy to be on our mission field at last. It was an exciting time because we weren't just a young couple going to the mission field. Here was a couple married 12 years. Our four children had been raised in the church and knew well the songs that they learned in Sunday School. They could quote scripture as well as sing to the people we would minister to.

So, the first full day we were there, we awoke in the morning and the girls helped make up the beds. We couldn't locate the bedspreads right away, but we did have sheets on the mattresses and we straightened out the beds and pillows and then decided to find the local park that was just a few blocks away. The children went there to play because there was no safe play area for them at the Mission. There were still a few more weeks until school started. The older girls watched over Larry and Diane at the park while I worked in the office. The windows in our bedroom and in the large recreation room had no screens. The recreation room windows came all the way down to within a foot of the floor. When those large windows were open, you could almost walk out and fall to the street below. With an active four-year-old boy, I was extremely concerned and made the two older girls responsible for watching him every minute when I didn't have him with me.

It was now the second day we were there. I was just beginning to scrub the other rooms. We were eating out of boxes of food that we had brought from home. We still weren't ready to eat from our mission's kitchen. Nor was I even remotely organized in the kitchenette.

The director's wife, Mrs. Akins, called up to me and said, "We have a ministry among the children. A woman from Australia is here in the States. She is going to be doing some Bible clubs for us. You don't have to, but if you would like to go with her today, you can. But don't take the little fellow with you."

"Well," I said, "I still have a lot of work to do, so if it isn't required of me, I won't go."

The next day, Mr. Akins saw me in the hallway and said "Now you're a missionary and you didn't go to the Bible club yesterday."

I said, "Well, I'm still not settled. I've only been here for two days and I'm just not yet settled. Besides, we have to talk about having some protection at the upstairs windows so that I can leave the children upstairs while I go about my duties."

He said, "You are a missionary now. You mean you can't trust the Lord to keep your boy from falling out of the window?"

My response was, "God gave him a mother and I am responsible for his protection insomuch as I can provide it."

He then started telling me all my responsibilities. He said, "I know we just have one son and he is 13, but my wife always learned to put the Lord before the children and you have to learn that, too."

That evening, after the evening meal, we gathered the children around for family worship. Somebody knocked at the door at the top of the steps. When Stauffer opened it, there was a jolly-looking man with a very pronounced accent. He proved to be an Australian evangelist by the name of Reverend Joe Carroll. He was in town to visit his sister who was doing the Bible Club work at the time. He said, "I hear you are newcomers. The reason I've come is that I found a man on the street who is very inebriated. I brought him in. He's downstairs now and they are taking care of him."

So we welcomed Reverend Carroll and talked with him about our first week in Christian work. I had a very serious question. Even after just two days, I already felt a lot of pressure. We told him about the Akins' expectations of me and their attitude toward the children.

I know God sent him to us that day because he said, "Now, Mrs. Moses, let me remind you that God gave you these children. He gave you a Christian husband who is the father of these children. There are going to be a lot of people making a lot of demands on you. But, for you to put God first, you put your husband first. You are his helpmate. You help him where he wants you to be, and you put the children next. If anyone wants to give any orders about your children, they need to go through your husband, especially if things are different from what was presented to you before you came."

With that, we approached the school year, which was only another week or two away. We had to enroll Larry in day care. He was going to be four in September and it was now the end of August. When his dad took him to day care the first morning, he cried and I cried. This was so different because I had always been with my children all the time.

I finally got all the rooms along the side of the recreation room scrubbed and cleaned and we set up the children's beds in those rooms so we could have some semblance of order.

I started a Bible Club in the Mission and my girls and I went around the neighborhood inviting the children to come. We conducted those Bible Clubs after school one day a week in our recreation room. That gave the children a ministry as well. My children were trained to assist me. I had come to Savannah fully prepared to hold weekly Bible Clubs for local children in the Mission as well as in a downtown housing project at the Community Building.

Only a few of the neighborhood showed up the first week because we had not advertised it properly. The second week Stauffer went with us, taking his trombone. He walked through the streets of the project, playing his trombone, while the family walked behind him. By the time we reached the Community Building, there was a crowd of children following us. Word spread quickly after that, and by the third week we had all the children we could handle! We were really excited about having a place of service where we were made so very welcome by the men in the Mission as well as by the children in that neighborhood and in the housing projects. We indeed felt like missionaries to the inner city.

There were some disappointments during those first weeks. We found out that there was no connection for the washer and dryer. When we spoke to the director about it, he said, "It would cost too much for your large family for me to allow you to hook up your washer and dryer. Your wife can take your clothes to the Laundromat. She'll be too busy to iron your shirts anyway. You can take them to the cleaners."

I must mention that Stauffer was on salary of only $125/month. This wasn't much more than minimum wage which at that time was 60 cents/hour. I wasn't getting anything, though I was more than willing to do whatever I could. His salary was our only income. With that, we had to make car payments of $25 a month and take care of all our other needs. We didn't have money for Laundromat expenses and this was contrary to what we'd been led to expect.

The second day we were there, Mrs. Akins was in the office and she was ready to go to the grocery store. She called up to me and asked, "Do you have a minute? I want to show you the grocery store where you can do your shopping."

I said I'd go with her, so she and I went to the supermarket. I thought she would introduce me to them and let them know that I'd be picking up groceries there for the Mission. Our salary was supposed to be the $125/month cash, our apartment and groceries. Our food was supposed to be included. She didn't introduce me to anyone. She told me to pick up the groceries I needed. On this first occasion it was less than five dollars. She paid for it and we got back to the office. She gave me a petty cash pocket book with ten dollars in it and said, "Now here's the cash to buy things you need for the Mission kitchen for the men."

She didn't mention anything about our need for food and that was it. The ten dollars didn't seem like much for the needs of the men and didn't include us at all. They totally ignored the fact that our food was supposed to be included as part of our salary. In God's provision though, we had in our freezer a variety of vegetables that I had frozen from my garden in Pennsylvania. We also had different kinds of meats. Several men from our Pennsylvania church had meat-packing plants and had given us some beef. We had our freezer filled with roasts. Fortunately, there was enough food there for us to have vegetables and meat for quite a while.

Now, we were used to having Golden Guernsey Milk on the farm in Pennsylvania. We knew that the Akins' had Guernsey cows on the farm where their school was. We were real happy to think that we'd be able to give our children some good fresh milk. Upon inquiring about that, they said, "No, we want to sell our milk. We don't even give the school children that milk. After all, there is government powdered skim milk in the store room behind the Mission kitchen. You can use that."

Well, I went over to the storeroom and got the government commodities out. The skim milk had been in storage for so long that it was as hard as a rock. We had to use a hammer to break it up into pieces small enough to dissolve in water to make milk, and then it tasted like chalk or worse. The children couldn't get accustomed to it and neither could we, so we also had to buy milk. Of course, we just didn't have any food money. We also didn't have any money for clothes. The little bit of cash we did have had to go into the needs of our car, plus I don't remember how much I spent for the many loads of laundry every week. In those days, you had to wash and starch things and then iron them. Drip-dry synthetic fabrics did not yet exist. There were also more things you needed to dry clean. Our weekly bill for laundry and dry cleaning wasn't something we'd expected.

Here we were, a thousand miles from home and no way to do our own laundry unless we used some of our small cash allotment. There was no way to buy food either. I remember how desperate we were and how we just cried out to the Lord and said, "Lord, you know where we are. You are the supplier of our needs. The Akins' are not. When man's promises fail us, you don't fail."

We continually cried out to the Lord to supply our needs. We knew that our Pennsylvania church supported missionaries in the field. However, they had made no specific commitment to send us anything. Fortunately, we hadn't been in Savannah very long when we got a letter from the pastor saying that they would send us a check every other month for $50, which would amount to $25 a month. That was the amount of our car payment. Anyway, that was a big help, but the total amount still didn't even cover our basic survival needs. There was no way that we were going to write home to ask for help. Hadn't the chapel family given us a nice farewell celebration? They also took an offering and that is what we used to pay the moving expenses as well as our early living expenses. We couldn't write home and say, "Please send us money." It was just something that never dawned on us to do. We were very conscious that God was putting us through His school. We thought of the verse (Matthew 18:7 NIV) Matt 18:7-8 "Woe to the world because of the things that cause people to sin! Such things must come, but woe to the man through whom they come!"

So, we asked the Lord to just prove Himself faithful in this time of testing.

We got a letter one day from my sister, Nina who was married the year before I was. Her husband Alton had taken a job at the dairy farm and had worked for us in the milk plant. When we sold the milk routes, he was out of a job. He took a job in a foundry. He couldn't make a go of it in the place they moved to, so he took two jobs. I guess perhaps the neediest people among our relatives and in our church family at the time were Nina and Alton. Yet, we got the dearest letter from them. They told us how much they and their children missed us. Our children were about the same ages as their children. Included in the letter was their tithe. They said, "We prayed about it and we both feel strongly that our tithe from both jobs should go directly to you. This is the amount of our tithing from the sum of the two jobs that Alton is holding down."

We wept. These were the neediest people both in our family and in the church and yet God was using them to take care of our needs. I feel like crying when I tell about it now. Their tithe didn't only show up that month, but a check came from them each and every month from then on.

We were constantly disappointed at the way our lives were going in Savannah and the things that we saw happening around us at the Mission absolutely shocked us. As we came before the Lord with our needs and with our complaints to Him of the injustices that we saw happening to the men we were supposed to be serving and to us as a family and in so many areas, we again acknowledged that we were in God's school and that He was giving us the training that we needed and never mind the methods that He was using. We just needed to lean on Him and trust Him to lead us each step of the way.

The most heartbreaking thing to me was that I couldn't supervise the men's cooking. They didn't have any real food to cook. Our family ate in our own kitchenette and Stauffer worked with the cook. In the morning, they had grits and lard gravy. At noon they had rice and tomato gravy. In the evening, they had the same thing. The man who did the cooking prepared large pots of the government commodities we had on hand.

The men in residence were alcoholics from the area who were sober at the time and needed a place to stay. After their breakfast in the morning, they walked several miles to the Akins' farm where they were hand-digging a lake for the school that was part of the Mission. The Akins' did not provide them with transportation. Late in the afternoon, they walked all the way back, arriving completely tired and worn out. They were greeted, of course, with rice and tomato gravy for their evening meal. In retrospect, it seems to me that the Akins' were taking advantage of these men in the form of a sort of slave labor.

Stauffer still felt that Mr. Akins knew the situation was bad and that his purpose in having us move in was to make it a really good Mission. However, when Stauffer tried to make recommendations regarding the men's nutrition, he was met with the attitude that these men would soon be drunk and that rice and tomato gravy were good enough for them.

As a result, Stauffer visited the different canneries and said, "I'm from the local rescue mission and I wonder if you have any contributions you could make, any unlabeled or dented cans."

He brought back truckloads of canned goods in all sizes in the pick-up truck that he had available to him. Of course, the cans weren't labeled. However, we soon noticed that every can had a number pressed into it. The cook quickly figured out what was in the can from this number. Since we got that food in from local places, we were permitted to use some of it in our own kitchen upstairs. I remember in the very beginning when our supply of food got very low. I'd open three cans and whatever was in those cans is what we had for dinner. Sometimes it was corned beef hash, maybe a can of corn, and maybe a can of spaghetti. After a while though, I got smart and started labeling them myself when I realized that the spaghetti can was stamped with a certain number and so was the corned beef hash. We ate a lot of corned beef hash in those days!

Stauffer had another grave concern about the men. They slept on worn-out mattresses without sheets and without enough blankets. He said I should request single bed linens and blankets from the local churches when they called, asking how they could help. He said "If we can get the circles to bring linens in as they do in other missions, we can start having nice, clean beds for the men to sleep in and they will take some pride in their surroundings here."

Already, church circles were learning that there was a director living in the Mission. This resulted in an increased number of calls to see what they could do for us. It was autumn and we particularly needed their help because winter was coming. When a circle leader called, I told them we needed linens for cots or single beds. Stauffer gave me a list of things he wanted the men to have in their dormitory and I started telling the church groups what they should bring.

One day, I got a call from a circle woman who asked if her group could take a tour of the Mission. I was just so excited because I thought the men would want to scrub and clean and get the place ready for the tour. I worked it out with Stauffer and told her when she could bring her group. Up until that time, I hadn't been up to see the main dormitory. Stauffer challenged the men to get the place clean. Because we now had enough linen, their beds were fixed up. When the church group came, Stauffer took them up and I accompanied them. Despite all the cleaning and the linens on the beds, one of the women in the tour group was completely stunned by the poor condition and the state of disrepair of the men's dorm. She told one of the Board members how shocked she was about the place she had been sending contributions to. The Board member called the director and his wife. Of course, we didn't know all of this was going on. That evening, the Akins' called us. They both came into the office and called me on the carpet in my husband's presence, saying "You have done a terrible thing in showing the Mission to the women's group."

My husband defended me. He said "Why, I was in on that as well. She didn't initiate it. They requested it."

They replied, "Well, she is the Eve in this case. She didn't know she was doing evil and you fell right in line with it."

We went back to our second floor apartment very confused and very concerned about the situation. Our grief wasn't as much any more for ourselves as for the attitude toward the men and their spiritual, physical, and emotional needs. This was something that was just beyond our comprehension. We had talked with numerous mission directors in our district and had toured their facilities and had goals that we wanted to achieve in Savannah. We believed that reaching those same goals here is was what was being required of us.

I need to tell something about one of our Mission men, Mr. Saturday. He was usually at the desk by the Mission door. When transients came in, he admitted them. If anyone brought any old clothes or had any business there during the day, he met them and took care of them. He received everyone and helped in any way that he could. However, for several weeks at a time, he was periodically in the local jail serving time for public drunkenness.

One day, two well-dressed women came to see Stauffer and they asked, "Must our brother die on skid row?"

Stauffer replied, "Who is your brother?"

They said, "Mr. Saturday. He is usually at your desk but he is in jail right now because he got drunk."

They went on to tell Stauffer that Mr. Saturday was the father of eight children. He had lost his family because of his drinking. He had been in and out of the Mission for some years. He was either at the desk sober or on the street drunk or in jail.

They said, "After he is sober in jail, Mr. Akins, the director, goes and gets him out, puts him back at the desk, and it is a vicious cycle. This has been going on for several years."

Stauffer said, "Well, he really needs to be taken out of this environment, then. I know of a place in Bel Air, Maryland, outside of Baltimore, where they have a rehabilitation home that takes men from the Baltimore Mission who want rehabilitation and a new lifestyle. They take them out there and give them eight weeks of rehabilitation. I have never been there, but I know the gentleman from attending our district meetings, and I am confident that he has a real concern for the men."

They said, "We are willing to pay the bus fare if he has room for our brother."

Stauffer called Mr. Manderson in Bel Air and was told to send him up. He picked Mr. Saturday up at the jail and put him on the bus. Mr. Manderson picked him up in Baltimore. Eight weeks later, he returned to Savannah. He had gained weight and was just as happy as he could be. He gave testimony of the Grace of God and said he was convinced that his life was changed.

Stauffer, of course, said, "Now, Mr. Saturday, you don't want to come back here again. You find a place to stay and get some meaningful work to do. Go to church, get into Bible study, and keep up the Bible study that you started in Maryland. In fact, tonight I'm going to a Bible study. I'd like to take you with me."

Stauffer had a group coming into the chapel that night. He asked me if I'd come downstairs and play the piano and introduce the speaker for the evening. Then I'd be free to go back upstairs to the children and help them with their homework and get them off to bed. That was the arrangement. Stauffer picked Mr. Saturday up from wherever he was staying at the time and took him to prayer meeting and Bible study. I did as we had planned. I saw the service through and went up and got the children to bed. Stauffer still wasn't in, so I went on to bed. I awoke a little bit later and he still wasn't home. With concern, I walked across the recreation room floor and looked out the front window. The Akins' car was there and also Stauffer's was in its parking spot. I knew something was wrong. I waited for him to return. When he did, he was visibly shaken by what he had just gone through. He said that when he got home, he saw the Akins' car. When he stepped inside to go up the steps, they were in their office. They said they needed to talk with him.

When he went back to their office, they said, "Now, who gave you permission to send Mr. Saturday to Baltimore?"

He said, "I didn't think I needed permission. His sisters asked me what could be done to help him get his life straightened out. I'm running the Mission and it was the right thing to do."

They said, "Well, we were embarrassed." They happened to be at the same prayer meeting. It was a large church. They said, "We were embarrassed to see him there. If you want to take him to a prayer meeting, pick another church besides ours. He was our best deskman and you have spoiled it. We don't want you to send anyone away for rehabilitation any more unless we give you permission."

At that point, Stauffer said, "If I didn't believe that God could change a man, break his addiction, and return him to his family, I would leave, go back to the dairy farm, and tell my father I was wrong. But I believe in the power of God and that he can change men's lives and send them back to their families."

He said, "Elsie, I know that we love Savannah and we love the people here, but I see the handwriting on the wall. I don't think they are going to want us around much longer. People contributed to our Mission because they had a heart for the mission men and thought they were feeding the transients. Instead, the funds are going to beautify the grounds and the farm. The men are actually being exploited."

Disappointed and grieved, we put all of our concerns and all of our worries in the Lord's hands and went off to sleep. A day or two later, we got a telephone call from Mr. Manderson. He said, "Reverend Moses, I'm calling to tell you how much we enjoyed Mr. Saturday when he was here. During the entire two months, he kept talking about how different the Mission was since you and your family were there, and how you care about the men, and how you just talk with them and encourage them, and the difference that has made in the lives of many men, and how much your family is involved in your ministry there. You probably won't want to do this, but I need somebody to run my rehabilitation center here. With the good report from Mr. Saturday, I want to ask if you would please consider leaving there and coming here to run this center."

Of course, Stauffer told him that we would pray about it. Then, he came to me with the news.

Now, there was another little matter that was happening at the same time. I felt ill for a week or two or three before this. As a matter of fact, I felt quite nauseated. I wasn't too worried, Larry was now four years old and we hadn't planned a larger family. One day went into the next, however, and we had to face the reality that we were going to have our fifth child. I was still going down to the office every day. Often, I had to leave the office to go upstairs and hang over the commode! I didn't want to share this with the director's wife because I knew they felt we had three children too many already. I thought they would put a lot of pressure on me, or on both of us, if they knew we were expecting another child.

In praying about the invitation to come to Bel Air, we might have weathered the storm in Savannah a little bit longer but we definitely saw that God was allowing us to have the blessings of yet another child. He was preparing even ahead of time for this and providing a place in Bel Air just about ninety miles from the farm in Pennsylvania.

Early in February, 1953, we moved from Savannah to Bel Air, Maryland and started them in school there. Bethany Acres (the name of the farm that was being used for rehabilitation) was a beautiful farm in the rolling hills of Maryland. The director and his wife lived in the farmhouse. We began the process of moving into one of the buildings that had originally been a chicken house. It was now a cute but modest cottage. We had pretty organdy curtains at the windows and it was just a real homey building now that it had been renovated. It didn't look at all like a chicken house, but that's what it had been earlier when this was a regular working farm. The barn had been converted into a dorm for men.

Mr. Manderson was the son of a minister and was a wonderful musician. Through his teenage and college years, he was rebellious and got into drinking and playing in nightspots. He got to the point where he was pretty much in the advanced stages of alcoholism and couldn't get sober until he went into delirium tremens (DT's) and finally got some help. He was in bad shape before he had a wonderful conversion experience. Now, he was an evangelist and God was blessing his time spent in evangelism in various churches in the Northeast. His wife developed a burden for women in jail. She was trying to help him run his rehabilitation center for men, but they both saw the need to have a man run it because he was increasingly away from home. When Mr. Saturday was there, they felt that the person that he talked so much about, Stauffer, would be the right one.

Although Stauffer didn't receive much salary, the board also offered us board and room. Everything that we negotiated for, all the promises, all the agreements that we made, they fulfilled. We believed that we were being led there. The children were enrolled immediately in school. We got them bikes so they could ride over the rolling hills of Maryland to a one-room school. We settled down once more. I felt more like I was back home. We were again in the country and I loved my new surroundings. It was easy to go home to Pennsylvania for visits. We were only ninety miles from the farm.

Mr. Manderson was excited because Stauffer was a farmer in addition to having the gift of evangelism and a real heart for the men. Stauffer and I were very happy with our new ministry. He and Mr. Manderson had a really close relationship. Mr. and Mrs. Manderson and Stauffer and I often prayed together when Mr. Manderson was home from the evangelistic services. Sometimes he was gone a week and sometimes two. Mrs. Manderson occupied her time by going into Baltimore every week and visiting women in jail.

It was in the setting of this new ministry that Stauffer really saw the value of discipling these men in the Word and teaching them of the victorious Christian life and living for Christ. Merely winning them to Christ (salvation) was not sufficient. He spent a great deal of time with the men teaching and encouraging them (sanctification).

Everything a farm needed was there, enough to keep the men occupied during the day taking care of the grounds and following their own program. No crop farming was done but there was a tractor to keep the lawns mowed. Neighboring farmers worked the fields. There was one cow that had to be milked. Stauffer usually found among his men someone who could do that.

Calls came from the two rescue missions in Baltimore for Stauffer to preach there as well. Stauffer loved to preach the gospel. When a man at a Mission was in need of rehabilitation, the director either brought him out or Stauffer went in to get him.

We ate well and so did the men at the farm. There were about a dozen men in the converted barn. The food here was a major improvement over the unlabelled cans in Savannah.

Initially, we thought the Lord was leading us into rescue mission work. Now, we began to realize he had different plans for us. We saw the extreme necessity for rescue missions when a man was in urgent need of a bed. Beyond that, we saw ever more clearly the need for rehabilitation. The experience with Mr. Saturday had shown us the need to remove a man completely from his environment and to provide him with a place where he really felt cared about and where he could be nurtured in the faith. This was the answer for people with an addiction problem.

Stauffer spent the day with the men in the out-of-doors and in the dorm. He came home at lunchtime at the same time the children returned home from school. We all had dinner together in our cottage. He quickly determined what a man's physical, emotional, and spiritual recovery would require. Schedules were set up and responsibilities for work were delegated. The men arose early, ate a nutritious breakfast, and went to work outside for the morning. After lunch, the men had a rest period. They were allowed to stretch out and take a nap for an hour. Work details then resumed until the evening meal. One man and a helper were always assigned to prepare the food. Stauffer referred to them as his "little kitchen crew."

One day, the director's wife came home from visiting women in the Baltimore jail. It was after lunch and she didn't see the men out working. Instead of finding Stauffer, she walked into the men's dorm where she saw a dozen men sleeping on their cots. When it came to dealing with the men and their alcohol problem, she was very stern and strict. She awakened them all and told them to get dressed and ready for a trip to town.

She came down to our cottage where Stauffer had just had his lunch and was relaxing a bit and she said, "Reverend Moses, I want you to take all these men down to the city. They are just a lazy bunch of men."

He said, "No, they were resting."

She said, "They don't rest here, they work here. Resting can't be part of the program."

He tried to reason with her, but she was adamant and ordered him to take them. She said, "You might be the assistant director running this place, but I am the director's wife and that's what I want you to do."

Of course he obeyed, but he reminded her that they had no money.

She said, "They are resourceful; they can always sell their blood." So, that's what Stauffer did. He took them to the city. It broke his heart to let them off to sell their blood and be back on the streets drinking. He came home, grieved, and said, "What kind of training are we getting now?" We took it to the Lord.

A few days later, Mr. Manderson returned from an evangelistic tour. Stauffer told him what had transpired during the week. He fully understood, and was in complete agreement with the daily routine that Stauffer had set up.

Mr. Manderson said to Stauffer, "This is why I wanted a man to direct. My wife just can't handle it. These things shouldn't happen. Brother Moses, I don't know what to do. She is zealous, but I can't go on like this. To complicate it more for me, I believe God has called me to evangelism. What should I do?" Stauffer said, "I suggest that the four of us pray about it separately, the two couples separately as well as individually."

Mr. Manderson was going away and would be gone a couple weeks. Stauffer said, "I won't take any more men in while we pray about it. In the meantime, consider this suggestion. Your wife loves working with the women in the jails. When they come out, she has no place to take them. You could redecorate your barn and make it into a facility appropriate for women from the jail. She could run the place and be totally responsible for that ministry. You would still have your evangelism and she would have the fulfillment of her vision. Otherwise, she leads those women to Christ in jail and then has to watch them return to the street. That might be why she feels some of this anger toward the men."

I had some feelings about this. We were very happy there and my pregnancy was progressing. I said, "So you advised him that we would move on so she'd have a place for her women...."

He said, "Well, I don't see any other solution. She's going to continue to interfere with what Reverend Manderson and I believe is vital to the rehabilitation of these men."

At the end of two weeks, we all agreed this was the way to go. Only four months had passed since our arrival and we were on our way again; to where, only God knew. The Mandersons were both very kind and apologetic for the turn of events.

Reverend Manderson took Stauffer aside and said, "Reverend Moses, you know that my wife and those women can't run this farm. I wonder if you would agree to stay here, run the farm, and have a ministry in town at the rescue missions."

Stauffer and I talked about it. This wasn't really a crisis and we didn't have to leave right then. We could take our time, not take any more men in, and wait on the Lord to see what He was doing in our lives as well as in the Mandersons.

This was about the end of May or the beginning of June. The country school was just getting out for the summer. All the children wanted to go home to grandma and grandpa. Grandma and grandpa wanted the children to come as well. We packed them up and took them to the big farm to be with their aunts and uncles and grandma and grandpa.

Stauffer's father, Pop Moses, was not a professing Christian but he was a very caring man and had a lot of good psychology about him.

Pop said "Stauffer, we have this big house here and I am really short of help. We're just beginning to make hay. I'd truly appreciate it if you'd come home for the summer and help me out. Elsie could help grandma in the house and the children would be free to enjoy a summer on the farm."

So we had two options. He and I could stay in Bel Air for the summer or we could do what his father suggested. Stauffer and I had good communication skills and we talked things over and prayed them through. Nonetheless, there were times when he became quiet and withdrawn. I knew that he was going through a spiritual battle and that he was deep in prayer. Despite our excellent communication and the many years of being together, he was going through things that were new to both of us…things that perhaps I didn't know anything about. Here he was, the father of a family with the fifth child on the way. We had been so sure that we were in the center of God's will with each step we had taken. Yet, Stauffer pretty much bore total responsibility as father and provider. Some years later, he was sharing with a group what he was going through at the time. He lamented that with all the men gone from the Bel Air farm, there was no one left to milk that one cow. It was summer time and the children were home with grandma and grandpa. He took the milking stool and a pail and just decided to milk her out under the stars. It was evening, and as he was milking the cow, the tears started to flow and he started to pray. "Lord, a year ago I left a dairy farm with hundreds of cows. I enjoyed the farewell service of hundreds of people. We headed for Savannah to go into rescue mission work and tonight I am alone in the middle of a field on a farm in Maryland milking this one solitary cow. If all you can trust me with Lord is to milk this one cow, then let me to do it to Your glory."

Since the children were happy on the farm and Pop Moses did need us, the decision was made to spend the summer there. Certainly our time of training was over. Reverend and Mrs. Manderson were most gracious. We all recognized the need for a ministry to women in Bel Air and that Mrs. Manderson was the person who should head this up. As I look back now, I think even then, God gave Stauffer a vision for the special needs of women that weren't being met by anyone else.

Thinking our baby would be born in Baltimore around mid-September, I had been going to an obstetrician there. I had a lot of packing to do. The Mandersons had no one to move into our house and they agreed that we could store all of our furniture there while we spent the summer in Pennsylvania waiting for the Lord to direct our path from here. By the end of June, we were all settled in at grandma and grandpa's farm. Because it was a large place, there was plenty of room for all of us. I took my medical records from the doctor in Baltimore to the doctor back home who had delivered our first four children.

It was wonderful being back on the farm. Everyone worked well together and we all had fun. We all baked, we all did dishes, there was just…from morning to night there was a busy-ness that the adults were involved in and that the children took part in as well. We shelled peas under the big maple tree in the back yard. We did many loads of laundry and the girls helped me hang it on the clotheslines. The iron was kept busy when we took the clothes off the lines. There was just something wonderful about being back on the farm. The folks there always made hard work a lot of fun. It was really a very good summer. Stauffer helped bring in the hay and with all the other farm work.

Stauffer made a visit to our home pastor, who, of course, knew we were back. We had come full circle. Stauffer returned from that visit very discouraged and said, "We are either called or we aren't, Elsie. The pastor said some people think they are called when they aren't."

The discouragement from the home pastor was almost a worse blow to him than all we had gone through during the past year. In our family worship time, we took our burden to the Lord. We knew that God had indeed called us. We knew that and believed with all of our hearts that going to Savannah was not a mistake. We believed that going to Bel Air was not a mistake. Stauffer said these experiences were like Marine boot training camp. In Savannah we learned what to do more by what not to do than we could have learned in several years with a good director. The experience with Mr. Saturday and the fruit it bore with his rehabilitation in Bel Air had widened our scope. By now, we knew that the Lord wanted us either in rescue mission work or in rehabilitation. The rehabilitation part of it had not yet really been firmly fixed in our minds. We thought God was still leading us in the direction of rescue mission work.

Stauffer was majorly concerned about our finances and knew that he might have to go back to work until the Lord revealed our next step. He got in the car one afternoon and started toward Pottstown to see if he could get a job in a place with a good hourly wage, perhaps in the tire factory. On the way, he became increasingly burdened by his lack of peace. He was convicted to turn the car around and head back to the farm. He just cried out to the Lord and said "Lord, I can't be Demas the quitter." (2 Tim 4:10 NIV) "for Demas, because he loved this world, has deserted me and has gone to Thessalonica."

To me, he said, "Elsie, I know if I'd have taken a job it would have been the wrong thing to do. I knew absolutely that I couldn't do that. The Lord is about to do something for us and for me to take a job would be to turn away from walking in faith."

Additionally, we shared a concern with many of the rescue mission people that there were countless cities without a rescue mission. In talking it over, we believed that there was undoubtedly a city that would be open to having a rescue mission started. We got out our rescue mission directory and our map of the United States and looked at all the principal cities with populations over 50,000. There were, indeed, many cities that didn't have rescue missions. For example, we noticed that Louisville, Kentucky and Knoxville, Tennessee didn't have one. There were many cities in Pennsylvania that didn't have one.

Stauffer asked, "Would you be willing to stay home on the farm while I go to a city that we both agree on together? I'll get a job there, become acquainted with the people of the city that would know the need, see if we can't get something started, and, at the right time, I'll send for you."

I agreed to this arrangement. This way, Stauffer wouldn't have the responsibilities of the family and he could start earning money and send it home. I could keep helping grandma Moses on the farm and the children would be back in the schools they'd attended except for the past year.

However, shortly after that, in our family worship, we came to the place in Acts where Paul wanted to go to Bithynia and the Holy Spirit forbid him and he wanted to go to Mysia and again the Holy Spirit restrained him and then he was in Troas and he had a vision, a dream, and in his dream a man from Macedonia said "come and help us." So, Paul had gone to Macedonia.

The Holy Spirit used that portion of scripture to speak to both of our hearts. We recognized that we both wanted to go to Louisville, Kentucky. We actually wanted to go somewhere, virtually anywhere, and we were going to pick a city almost at random and say "Lord, bless us, they need something there." So, we came before the Lord with this burden that we had and the fear that we might step out of His will.

We said, "Lord, we are going to trust you now. We are on the farm. You know where You want us. Help us to wait quietly before You."

We claimed Isaiah 40:31 (KJV): "But they that wait upon the Lord shall renew their strength; they shall mount up with wings as eagles; they shall run, and not be weary; and they shall walk and not faint."

We knew that there was a certain place God had for us and that we should wait quietly before Him until he showed us where that would be.

Albany

As we waited on the farm, we believed there was a specific place where the Lord wanted us to serve Him and that He would reveal His plans to us in a very definite way. Consequently, we carefully considered all doors of Christian ministry as potentially leading to this place of service. During the next weeks, Stauffer kept in touch with the headquarters of the International Union of Gospel Missions. Through that organization, he learned that there was an opening for a director of a rescue mission in Jamestown, New York. He went there for an interview and felt encouraged. Stauffer received the verbal acceptance of the Jamestown Board. They showed him the house where the director and his family would live. It was comfortable and it was ample for a family of our size.

Upon returning home, he said, "I believe we've found the place God is leading us to. The Board voted me to be their next director. They're going to mail us a formal offer to consider."

In addition to the Board's favorable reaction to Stauffer, it appeared that we were receiving other guidance from the Lord as well. An incident occurred when we moved to Savannah that we felt was not coincidental. Before the move, we sold the player piano and the sofa that were in our living room. The girls had been taking piano lessons but it was too large and heavy for us to move. Our sofa needed to be reupholstered but we didn't have the money to do that and pay our moving expenses as well. Would you believe that in the living room of the house where the director would live in Jamestown were…you guessed it…a piano and a sofa!

With anticipation, we waited several days for the written confirmation of our acceptance so we could start making plans to move. We hoped it would be before the second week of September when the baby was scheduled to arrive. We also hoped we could move and get settled before school started so the older children could get enrolled. Finally, one afternoon, the telephone rang. The operator asked for Stauffer. When he answered, I could hear that he was accepting a Western Union telegram. Out in the country in those days, telegrams were relayed first over the telephone for quick delivery. The written telegram came later by regular mail. Stauffer repeated the words on the telegram as he heard them. The telegram read:

> Dear Reverend Moses. Sorry. New England man called.
> Sincerely. Board of Directors. Jamestown Rescue Mission.

He hung up the phone, dropped his head, closed his eyes, and said "Thank you, Lord." That was it. This was a closed door. In times of disappointment, Stauffer accepted that God was in control. He only wanted God's will for him.

I was not so spiritual. Another little one was on the way and I wanted my brood settled before then. This news sent me upstairs where I lay across my bed and sobbed. I had the desperate feeling of being totally abandoned by God. After our on-the-job training experiences in Savannah and Bel Air, I felt confident that Jamestown was the place God had been preparing for us and that He had been preparing us for Jamestown. A year before, we left the dairy farm with the full assurance of God's direction. Now we were back on the farm, with no sense of direction at all. I wondered if we were really "called" after all. I felt despair and hopelessness.

Stauffer came into the bedroom. While my sobs subsided, I was aware of his own deep anguish even as he tried to comfort me. As we lay silently in each other's arms, we heard voices in the next room. His mother and his sister, Becky, were praying for us, crying out to the Lord on our behalf.

Looking back, something funny always happened when we were the most confused or when our path was the most obscured. There was always some assurance from the Lord that He was walking right there with us. At this dark point, I remembered I had some yard goods. I wanted to make maternity gowns to take to the hospital when our little one arrived. My sewing machine was still packed up in storage in Baltimore so I went to Nina's house with my pattern and materials. I told the family on the farm that I was going to spend the day with her getting my suitcase ready for the trip to the hospital. As one sister does to another, I just poured out to Nina all of the pent-up feelings I'd had for the last twelve months. This included the rejection that we had just received a day or two before. She listened to me patiently. Then she started laughing. She said, "You know, this is going to be like a boil coming to a head. You are so pregnant you're not fit to move your family. Look at you! Here you are, crying because you can't move. There's no way you could move. That baby is going to be born and a door is going to be opened and God's timing will be perfect. You wait and see."

I returned that evening encouraged and looked forward to seeing just what the Lord did have in store for us.

Because my baby was due in another couple weeks and the older children had to start school, we found it necessary to make one last trip to Bel Air where all of our possessions were in storage. Since it wasn't much further to go into Baltimore, we decided to do some shopping in the city for school clothes. There were no expressways, and driving over the brick streets and trolley car tracks in Baltimore was more than an eight-plus-month-pregnant woman should have had to bear. That night, I awoke and realized I was in labor. The doctor told us to go to the hospital immediately, knowing that number five child was going to arrive quickly. While the children slept, we informed Grandma Moses and left for the hospital.

My pains subsided by the next morning. The doctor said it was false labor caused by the previous day's trip. Nonetheless, he wanted me to remain in the hospital another day for observation. All day Friday I walked the long halls on the OB ward. Friday night, I was told I could go home Saturday morning. I slept well that night knowing that our little one would be born in God's time.

Saturday morning, August 29, 1953, I awoke knowing that I wasn't going to be leaving the hospital that day after all. When my doctor arrived, he announced that my baby would be born before the end of the day. I called Stauffer and gave him the news. Because my contractions were not close together, I told him to come later in the day. He said he'd be there after lunch unless he heard that he should come sooner.

The morning dragged on. I walked the halls and finally decided to take a nap. When I awoke, I was in active labor. My doctor had to be called so he could be present for the delivery. Stauffer arrived minutes after our baby was born at noon. By then, I had fallen asleep again.

On Stauffer's way to the hospital, he picked up the mail from the box at the end of the long lane leading from the farm. He read it while he was waiting to see me. One of the first things he said when I awoke was, "We have a little girl, and she might be a Georgia peach after all." He had received a letter from Albany, Georgia, requesting he come down for an interview.

My response was, "Not Georgia!" I couldn't have cared less about that faraway state. I didn't even know where Albany was. Only minutes after my baby, Susan, was born, I didn't share in his enthusiasm about her being a Georgia peach.

I remained in the hospital for ten days, as was the custom then. No children under the age of twelve were allowed to visit and the time went by slowly.

Stauffer brought the children by the hospital daily so I could wave to them from the second floor window.

At last, Susan and I went home to the farm. What a reception her brother and three sisters gave her! They were so ecstatic about having a tiny baby in our home that we all decided to make her middle name Joy. She not only brought joy to our family, but we were aware that she was a special gift from God in His plan in guiding our steps as we walked by faith towards our next place of service.

I was only home a few days when a telephone call followed the letter from Albany. I was sitting at the large kitchen table in the farmhouse with the family and everyone else that gathered for meals at grandma's house. The telephone rang in the next room. Everyone became quiet while Stauffer talked. It was a call from Albany. I heard him say, "No, my wife won't be able to come to talk to the Board with me. Well, we have a two-week-old baby. No, she isn't the first one. We have five in all now."

Impulsively, I said, "Well, that ends that. There is no Board that is going to want a mama, daddy, and five children."

He finished the telephone call. When he came back to the table, he had a smile on his face and a look in his eyes that suggested something was really going to happen with this prospect. The fellow on the other end of the phone was involved with starting a ministry in Albany. We were being invited to come for an interview. When Stauffer told him that we had five children, he said, "Oh, God has been so good to you. We only have one child. We wanted others, but we couldn't have any more. Five children will not pose a problem at all. We just wish Mrs. Moses could come along down for the interview."

Several days later, Stauffer went to Albany for his interview. Everything started moving us in that direction now.

All during that summer, Stauffer and I had been praying for the door to open to our next place of service. He commented that he would like to know what it would be like to have two doors open and then have to wait for one to close. That was just about to happen. Before he left for Albany for the interview, he was called by the Baltimore Rescue Mission where he had preached many times during the months we were in Bel Air. They needed a director. Theirs had resigned and they wanted Stauffer to come down and talk with them about becoming their director. That caused both of us much concern because the Rescue Mission in Baltimore was old. It had been founded several generations before and was one of the oldest rescue missions in the country. The members of the Board of Directors were all godly men. Many of them preached at the Mission. To have a part in and to be the director of a well-established and well-financed Mission was something that would have been ideal for us at this point. By comparison, the Albany Board was just getting organized and didn't know exactly what it wanted. He told the Albany Board he would talk to me about the opportunity but explained that he had another offer that he would have to take into consideration as well.

After the trip to Albany, Stauffer went to Baltimore to talk with the folks there. He was able to go down to Baltimore in the morning and return that same evening. Overall, he was very much encouraged by his visit. This was a well-organized mission and the Board of Directors wanted him to come. They knew Stauffer well and they had seen the results of his preaching and his zeal and sincerity during the months he worked with the ministry in Bel Air. The position came with a large home that would allow us to live in the city without having to live in the mission itself.

The opportunity in Georgia was six miles out in the country from Albany, a city of 56,000. Everything there was unorganized and nothing had yet really been started. The ministry there was just in the form of a vision at that point, the dream of a small group of people.

Now it was up to us to wait upon the Lord and ask Him to show us where He wanted us to go. Both opportunities seemed wide open and the doors to each ministry seemed to be opened equally wide. The practical choice for us at this point would have been to go to Baltimore. This ministry was only ninety miles from home. The mission was well-established and well-financed. We had the promise of a good bit of security with a comfortable income and an adequate home. There was also a children's ministry at that mission besides the Rescue Mission for indigent men.

On the other hand, the opportunity in Albany was with a group of men under the leadership of Judge Malone. Malone was a Bible teacher at the First Methodist Church and as well was the Juvenile Court judge. Additionally, he was also the Executive Director of the Albany Housing Authority. He was concerned about the addiction problem among the men of the city. The children of these alcoholic men appeared before him frequently in Juvenile Court. His concern led him to challenge his Sunday School class to do something about this problem.

During World War II, The Royal Air Force (RAF) used the land across the road from the Albany airport as a training base. The land and buildings were now available to the Albany Housing Authority. Director Malone formed a Board of men who visualized having an alcoholism rehabilitation center on the RAF grounds. They were determined to see that dream become a reality.

Roy Blanton, the President of this fledgling board, called several meetings to organize the rehabilitation center. In one of those meetings, **The Anchorage** was chosen as the name and the project was incorporated with that name. The logo was an anchor with a cross.

The Board then decided their next step was to seek the right man to turn their vision into reality. Roy Blanton was the person who made that first call to Stauffer.

Stauffer and I had now gathered all the data. All the information was in. In simple faith, we asked the Lord to close one of the doors. We were open to going to either place, knowing that God would surely direct our steps. Our most crucial prayer request of God was that we be asked to our new place of ministry as a result of a unanimous decision of the Board of Directors with no dissenting votes whatsoever. We wanted the full confidence of the Board. In praying, we also asked the Lord to provide a place for us to live. Additionally, we prayed that the Lord would lay upon the hearts of whichever Board of Directors to pay the expenses of moving our furniture from storage in Bel Air. It looked like it would be too great an expense for the newly-formed Albany Board to move us long distance and provide a place for us to live. In a sense, our prayers were very practical ones. It did seem more likely that these prayer requests would be answered favorably by the Baltimore people. Perhaps we were leaning a bit more towards the Baltimore situation. It seemed that the things we were asking for were already taken for granted by us and by individuals on the Board in Baltimore. Possibly the men in Albany weren't even thinking of these things and might even deny our requests if we made them. On the other hand, our personal burden lay more with the need for providing rehabilitation than for rescue mission work. However, we were open to working with men on the streets if that was where the Lord wanted us.

By now, the previous director of the Baltimore mission had already left. That Board requested Stauffer serve as interim director for a week while we considered both opportunities. Stauffer bid us good-bye and left for Baltimore. During that week, he became acquainted with the staff. His desire to accept the Baltimore position was definitely increased.

However, in our desire for God's will, we continued to pray about the position in Albany. When Stauffer left Baltimore at the end of the week, the Board tried to press him for an answer. Stauffer told them he would give them his answer within a week. He returned home and we continued to pray earnestly. Because we were asking God for a unanimous decision by the Board, Stauffer called the president of the Baltimore Board and said, "I have a very personal question to ask you. Was the whole board unanimous in their decision or was there even one dissenting vote?"

The president said, "Well, to be honest with you, we did have one dissenting vote. The only reason he dissented was because of your children and the fact that the ministry to the children…he felt it might be a conflict of interest on your part, having to work with other children as well. While I have you on the phone, Reverend Moses, I must tell you that we decided to use the house that we intended you to move into for another purpose. We still want you to come down and find a place to live, though, because we do want to provide living accommodations."

Suddenly, we were in a different ball game. God was answering prayer. That one dissenting vote on the Board indicated to us that door was now closed. In addition, they were apparently not going to provide us with the quarters they had originally offered us.

Meanwhile, the Board of Directors in Albany met again. The president of their Board sent a letter by registered mail so we would be sure to get it quickly. They said, "You have been voted in unanimously as the first director of The Anchorage in Albany. We want you to take one of the buildings on the RAF grounds and pick as many rooms as you want for your family. We will paint it any color you want. Also, we will bear the total cost of your moving expenses."

Within a period of one day, what we thought was a sure thing in Baltimore was not. God allowed two little things to change. The assurance of the very things that we thought the most important in our prayers was guaranteed a thousand miles away, in Albany. We had received a definite answer to prayer!

Many times in the ensuing months, we praised the Lord that we had that experience of the two doors opening and the one closing. We had God's assurance that he had allowed these little miracles in order to demonstrate that he had answered and would answer our prayers concerning our needs. After we made the move, we never doubted that God in His providence had led us to Albany. We had truly received the Macedonian call: (Acts 16:9 KJV) "And a vision appeared to Paul in the night; There stood a man of Macedonia, and prayed him, saying, Come over into Macedonia, and help us."

The people in Albany who were so burdened about the addiction problem in their community had almost used the words, "Brother Moses, we are praying for you to come our way because we really need your help." When Stauffer and I asked God many months before to give us a Macedonian call, we never dreamed that it would almost literally be that way in a city that we never even knew existed. We didn't have a clue where Albany was when we lived in Savannah. God was so good and so gracious in reassuring us that His hand was on us all the time and that we were truly in His school.

It was just fourteen months since we had moved to Savannah. We were now preparing to go back to Georgia, this time with an addition to our family. When Susan was eight weeks old, we once again bid farewell to our loved ones at home and set out for the Deep South. We arrived there the last day of October, 1953, excited about the freedom to establish whatever program we felt was needed.

Our initiation into Rescue Mission work in Savannah had been intense. During the winter and spring months in Maryland, we had seen the results of rehabilitation. Given the experience of the two places, we accepted much of the program from Maryland because of its proven effectiveness. We believed a man should commit to a minimum of two months of rehabilitation, and more if possible.

1953 was just eight years after the conclusion of World War II. Many of the young men who returned home from the service turned to alcohol. During the ensuing years, those who were addiction-prone had increasing problems. Judge Malone saw growing numbers of the juvenile delinquent sons of these men in his court. He was concerned about the lack of spirituality in their families. When he faced a young man who presented with his father or his family in court, Malone put him on probation instead of holding or detaining him. He also sentenced him to attend a certain number of weeks in a Sunday School of the father's choice. The father was required to accompany him. As a result, many of the families started going to the First Methodist Church, where the fathers attended the judge's Sunday School class. This class grew rapidly. There were older men in the class who had some years of sobriety through the program of Alcoholics Anonymous. They encouraged the younger men who came into the class. Alcoholics Anonymous was less than twenty years old and still a fledgling organization in 1953. Because of our church background, we really didn't know anything about the A.A. program of recovery. When Stauffer had his initial interview in Albany with the newly-formed Board, several of them were members of Alcoholics Anonymous while many weren't. Nonetheless, they all kept talking about the Alcoholics Anonymous program and how important they thought the 12-step program was as an integral part of a center for alcoholics to get away from their environment and to get help.

When Stauffer interviewed in Albany, he wasn't totally convinced that was the right place for us. The Board wanted to see a strong Alcoholics Anonymous program in place and they told him what their idea was and how Alcoholics Anonymous would fit in. Stauffer, with his uncomplicated faith and pure honesty, said, "Gentleman, I think you are interviewing the wrong person. I am simply a preacher of the Gospel. I know that God can transform lives. My congregation would be people with an addiction problem. My message would be one of salvation and victory in Christ. I think you'd better seek out an expert in Alcoholics Anonymous to run your center."

After Stauffer was done with his analysis of the situation, Judge Malone rose to his feet, went over to him, shook his hand, and said, "Reverend Moses, that's really what we want, but we didn't know how to say it."

In retrospect, it was precisely because of the fundamental programmatic issue of an A.A.-based program on the one hand as opposed to a program of salvation and discipleship (sanctification) on the other that we were prompted by the Holy Spirit to ask the Board for a unanimous decision. It simply would not have worked to have that as a basic conflict at the Board level. I used to tease Stauffer later that when we had prayed, the likelihood of a unanimous decision from Albany seemed pretty bleak while a unanimous decision from Baltimore looked like a sure thing.

Judge Malone was a man who wore many hats. Besides being the Juvenile Judge, he was director of the Albany Housing Authority. At that time in U.S. history, housing projects were rather scarce. However, the need for housing became great as American soldiers returned from the war after 1945. When the British left the grounds across from the airport to return home, the city of Albany had the entire air base at their disposal.

Judge Malone chose to be an advisor rather than to be on the Board of Directors of The Anchorage. He told the Board that they could have all the government buildings, which included ten acres of land, for one dollar per year. The Board was to bear the expense of making everything suitable for our new center.

On one side of the highway was the airfield. On the other side were twenty acres of buildings with two huge dormitories, a big mess hall, a PX, and an infirmary. All of this was surrounded by fields. The city partitioned off the dorms and even the PX and infirmary. Every available square foot of floor space was made available to military people as they came home and were in need of apartments. The Housing Authority also built a lot of very inexpensive dwellings next to the government buildings.

By 1952, most of the buildings were empty. It was like a ghost town. By and large, the previous tenants had gone on to nicely-built housing projects or to places of their own. The twenty acres were nicely landscaped with beautiful lawns. The government buildings were situated at least fifty feet behind the road, which was maintained by the State of Georgia. There was a wide walkway from the main road to the buildings. Parallel to the main road was another walkway which ran in front of all of the buildings. The cement walkways were twenty feet wide. This provided safety to children on the grounds. They had what amounted to a street inside of the complex where they could ride their bicycles and roller-skate. They didn't have to go out on the highway.

The two huge dormitories were two stories high, several hundred feet in length, and thirty feet in width. A wide porch ran along the side, both downstairs and upstairs. We planned to use only one of them which was large enough to house fifty men on the second floor. In addition, there was still enough room to keep other men that had completed the program and wanted to remain a little longer.

As you entered the front area downstairs, there was a reception room and several offices. Behind this was a large room that was made into the chapel. Eventually, we obtained pews. Behind the chapel were game rooms. After passing through the game rooms, there was what had originally been a big lounge with a tremendously large fireplace. To the back of that were more small rooms where staff could sleep. The cook and several of the staff members could be downstairs and didn't have to stay upstairs with the men who were in rehabilitation. Beyond that was a large dining room. Finally, there was the kitchen and then a large pantry. It was a very large and attractive building that was perfect for our needs.

There was one problem. As families moved out, many of the windows had been used as targets. Perhaps two hundred windowpanes had been knocked out on both floors. Other damage had occurred as well. The facility really needed a lot of work.

The building where they planned for us to live had been the infirmary. It was to the right alongside of the dormitory as you faced it. The length of it ran parallel to the highway. There were many rooms that could be made into bedrooms. It was a cheerful-looking building that didn't look anything like an infirmary. Knowing that I had the luxury of designing our new home, and having five children, I decided on plenty of bedrooms. I asked for a guest-room, a master bedroom, and three or four other bedrooms. We had a full bath and there was another area we could make into a half bath. A long, narrow porch ran across the front. Also facing the front were the kitchen, living room, master bedroom, and two other bedrooms. Everything else was in the back of the building. It was a very pleasant building and we knew that it could be fixed up to be completely cozy. The Board anticipated that the building would be ready by the time we arrived.

Roy Blanton was one of the most active members in Judge Malone's class. He was a very committed Christian man who had never had an addiction problem himself. He made his living selling International Harvester equipment. He was the newly-elected President of the Board of this new rehabilitation project. It was he who made the calls to us and who encouraged us to come. Stauffer and he shared the same faith and the same vision. Roy's mother was a devout Christian. She always dreamed her son would be a missionary. When we met her, she said, "Now, at long last, he is a missionary. I see him as a missionary working together with you." We felt a real kinship with him. He remained one of our steadfast friends for years.

The trip to Albany by car consumed several grueling days. There were no expressways. The seven of us traveled in a sedan. I wished that we'd at least had a station wagon.

Upon our arrival, the Judge and Roy Blanton took us all to a quiet dining room in a nearby restaurant. You can imagine the tension I felt sitting in a restaurant with a Judge, the President of the Board, and my five children, after just spending three days on the road. I was totally frazzled. Before we got our food, the baby started fussing. By the time our food arrived, she demanded all my attention. Roy finished his meal quickly, came over, and said, "This baby needs her uncle Roy." Roy held her on his shoulder while I ate my dinner. Susan went right to sleep.

Just as I was starting to feel comfortable, they broke the news to us that the Sunday School class had not yet gotten our building ready. The floors had not been completely laid down. The asphalt tile had not yet been put down over the cement floors. The van with our furniture arrived the day before as planned, but our things had to be stored next door in the old PX. I had really been looking forward to setting up our beds and gradually getting our place straightened out, but that was not to be.

We were presented with a couple options. One of the Board members had a large house and we could stay with them. Alternatively, we could stay in one of the little houses that the renters had left when the housing project was closed down. It had a stove and refrigerator. We could camp out for as long as it took the Sunday School class to finish the floors and have the building ready for us. There really wasn't much of a decision to make. I just didn't want to move our family into the beautiful and well-furnished home of total strangers and be so far from where Stauffer would be supervising and working during the day.

Stauffer set to work and painted all day long. The members of the Sunday School class came out to help him evenings and Saturdays. He was there when the contractors laid the floor. In the middle of November, we were finally able to move our furniture over from the PX. After setting up our beds, we finally felt that we were at home.

Soon after we arrived, there was a Board meeting. When Stauffer returned, he said, "This is truly a venture of faith. We not only have to trust God for our needs and believe the commitment the Board made as to what our income will be, but we have to start raising all the funds ourselves for the whole project."

The treasurer was one of the bankers in town and a member of the Sunday School class. His report was that they had three hundred dollars in the bank and eleven hundred dollars in unpaid bills! The unpaid bills, of course, were the expenses of moving the Moses family south.

Here we were, finally settled in a comfortable, freshly-painted building with plenty of bedrooms for all of our children. Right next door was a large, run-down, two-story dorm and the new organization was eight hundred dollars in debt. The news that we were starting out with an eight hundred dollar deficit was shocking and made the challenge to both of us even greater. While we knew on the front end that we'd ultimately be responsible for raising the operating funds, we'd anticipated that there would be up-front capital that was already raised by the board for operations before we took on this responsibility. This, despite the assurance that God had taken us the pathway He had to get us to this place of ministry. Nonetheless, with full assurance we prayed, "Lord, thank you. You brought us here and you promise to supply all of our needs." On the other hand, what we did have going for us was a unanimous Board who were really excited that we had arrived. We had the full confidence that not only the Board of Directors, but an entire men's Sunday School class, was 100% behind us.

Stauffer said, "It was a challenge to give up our successful dairy business and just trust God to supply our needs as a family. Now we have to believe and trust God for the financial needs of a large ministry as well."

Judge Malone had carefully selected his Board. Most, but not all, were members of the First Methodist Church. He saw the need for this to be an interdenominational project. There were men on the Board from a variety of businesses and professions. This was the first interdenominational para-church ministry started in Albany. We recognized, as did the Board, that the community and churches had to be educated as to what we were about. There was a real need to educate people about our project right away.

Immediately, a little office was set up in our living room. A folding table became our work area. Information from various Board members and from the area telephone book and from the city directory was compiled into a mailing list. This was the start of regular bi-monthly newsletters that we sent out. Calls were made by Board members to various churches to solicit speaking engagements for Stauffer.

Stauffer and the Board hoped that we might be able to admit perhaps a dozen men in one section of the building by the coming March. We needed the help of the Sunday School class and other volunteers to replace all the window panes. After that, there was still a great deal to be done.

The first week of December we got a telephone call from a woman whose husband was a member of Judge Malone's class. She asked Stauffer when we would start taking men in, saying that her brother desperately needed a place and that she couldn't handle his drinking any longer. She said that he was sober at the time, but she knew he wouldn't be sober long because of the pattern of his drinking. Stauffer told her we would be ready to accept him in March. She begged Stauffer to just take him right away. He told her he'd call her back after he talked it over with me. The woman sounded so desperate that we started trying to figure out what we could do to help him.

Our apartment in the infirmary only took up two-thirds of the space in the building. Our quarters were fixed up very comfortably. At the other end of the infirmary was an entrance facing the front that looked almost parallel to our two-thirds of the building. There were several rooms where a family had lived during the days of the Albany Housing Authority. We reasoned that perhaps we could put this fellow in there. As long as I was already cooking for our family, I could just cook a little more and send food down to him. Stauffer called the lady back and told her to bring her brother out. The first week of December, John, the first resident of The Anchorage, arrived.

A day later, another woman called about her brother. She had heard what Stauffer had done for the first woman and called to ask if we would take her brother too. We figured this would provide John with some company so we told her to bring him in. After all, it wasn't that much of a burden to cook for only a couple more people.

A few days later, Stauffer admitted the third man. By this time, the first man acknowledged to Stauffer that he was an experienced cook. He couldn't stand keeping that a secret any longer. There was already a kitchenette down at that end of the building. We set up a stove there and I started sending food down for him to cook.

The week before Christmas, we started decorating our home. We got a Christmas tree and the children and I were decorating it when we realized the men at the other end should have a Christmas tree too. So, the children put up a little Christmas tree for the men and trimmed it with some decorations I provided.

More men came. We hadn't planned to take any more men in until after our open house in March. Here we were on Christmas Day with eight men! They had their own Christmas tree and they cooked their own turkey at their end of the building.

Each Sunday night during that month, Stauffer took my folding organ to the other end of the building and set it up. He led the singing while I accompanied on the organ. The men were given paper-back hymnals that we had obtained. They picked out their favorite hymns. To our surprise, they were all men who had Sunday School and church experience when they were little boys. Maybe we shouldn't have been so surprised. These men had grown up in the Bible Belt, after all. For an hour, they kept me pumping that organ and playing for them. They just bellowed out and sang. Stauffer then gave a short message and they said, "We want to do this again." So, we did. I took the folding organ down once a week, every Sunday night, for our regular "formal" Sunday evening service. I set up the organ and we all sang our hearts out. Stauffer also had an informal time of worship and fellowship with the men every evening of the week. There were other planned times for study when Stauffer spoke with the men.

During the day, he taught the men how to put window panes in the dorm building and assigned them other tasks. Many evenings, and always on Saturday, the Sunday School class came out to help these eight men as they worked on the large dormitories. There were quickly nine men, and then ten. They got the first part of the building that they had planned ready and continued even further. By the time the date came for us to have open house in March, instead of looking to take on a dozen men, we already had twenty-four on board. We continued like that, with the men doing all the work under Stauffer's supervision, until the place was filled and the building was all completed. Our final capacity was fifty men.

Before the office was completed in the main building, a young woman named Mary Rex offered to come and work with us for very little salary. Mary was a college graduate who wanted to do mission work. We met her in Savannah and had kept up correspondence with her as she was very eager to work with us. The other end of the building from where our home was, where we had started with the first men, was made into a cute apartment for Mary. While this project was underway, Mary stayed in our guest room. She relieved much of my burden with the office work that we were trying to do out of our living room.

So, by the time the large dorm was complete, we had a secretary and we had an apartment for her. The project was way ahead of its original goals.

The chapel behind the offices was equipped with beautiful, conventional pews donated by a church. A platform was built and a traditional altar rail was placed on top of it near the front. Behind that was a prayer room. Whenever Stauffer gave the invitation, he asked the ones who responded to come forward and kneel at the altar. From the beginning, the Sunday night services were attended not only by the men there, but by A.A. members. The room was crowded with men from the Alcoholics Anonymous meetings who heard about the old-fashioned gospel services that were being held at The Anchorage.

Our congregation increased by more than just the men who were residents at the time. By the time we moved our services into the chapel, many townspeople came out every Sunday night to hear Stauffer. This included the wives and children of the residents, the Judge, and men and women who were members of Alcoholics Anonymous. Because there was an interest on the part of the men of the Alcoholics Anonymous group, they often sent men to us who were in need of help. To reciprocate, the residents were allowed to attend Alcoholics Anonymous meetings in town one night a week.

The warm climate of southwest Georgia presented an opportunity for Stauffer to raise two crops of vegetables a season instead of the usual one. Stauffer saw our five acre garden as a means of feeding the fifty men and the staff. Men were assigned to garden duty. Stauffer supervised the planting of rows and rows of corn, beans, onions, potatoes, peas and other vegetables. By the first reaping of our garden the first year we had a bumper string bean crop. We had been praying for a freezer to store our extra vegetables for winter eating. Stauffer came to the house to ask if I would supervise the kitchen crew in blanching this large crop of beans to freeze. I had been planning to can them because we still didn't have a freezer. When I got back to the kitchen a group of men were already cleaning and breaking the beans and were ready for their next orders from me.

We started blanching and bagging the beans in preparation for the freezer. The men and I were well aware that we still didn't have a freezer in our possession, but it was in our prayers. Before the end of the day, the telephone rang. The man on the other end of the line, a brother of one of the residents, introduced himself to Stauffer and said, "I sell meat cases to grocery stores and I took as a trade-in a large ice cream freezer cabinet like they use in ice cream stores. I'd appreciate it if you'd take it off my hands. It could be used as freezer storage for vegetables." He came back to the kitchen and told us all the good news. We observed the disbelief and excitement of the men witnessing the power of answered prayer before their very eyes.

I asked Stauffer later how he knew that the freezer was coming *that* day.

He said, "I knew that God was going to answer our prayer and I figured if He didn't, I'd take the beans down to the city cold storage until the Lord did supply the need of the freezer."

Stauffer rejoiced that God saw fit to answer the prayer the very day that the freezer was needed because of the impact it had on the men who were just learning the walk of faith. He didn't realize also that his wife needed this evidence of faith and answered prayer in her life as much as these new believers. God continued to strengthen my faith as I walked side by side with my husband in his walk of faith.

There were no detoxification units anywhere in those days. We became a place for men to sober up before going into the rehabilitation phase. A doctor on our Board gave us an open-ended prescription for Paraldehyde (a very potent sedative used in days of yore for alcohol withdrawal) that we got from the local pharmacy a gallon at a time. Neither Stauffer nor I were medical people. The doctor told us to start out giving them a teaspoon at a time and just go on from there. We were to give it to them before meals, in order to calm their stomachs so they could eat, and at bedtime.

Stauffer had this Paraldehyde locked up in his office. One day he had to be gone and he told me somebody would be knocking at the door to get his medicine. He told me where the Paraldehyde was, and he said, "Right before the meal, give him a teaspoonful." He failed to tell me to mix it with water. I gave the poor guy the teaspoon of straight Paraldehyde and almost blew his head off!

Stauffer appointed the men who had been there the longest or who came in sober to assist him in giving medication and helping him sober the men up. Most of the men came because they wanted to sober up. We had little trouble with anyone denying that they had an alcohol problem. The men experienced Stauffer's kindness to them and his patience in getting them sober.

We had a short Bible study every morning in the chapel before the men began the day's work schedule. There were also services every evening. I am sometimes asked if we made them mandatory. I don't remember that attendance was ever a problem. We always started our chapel services in the evening with a local minister or Sunday School class teacher, or someone else who gave a chapel service that lasted anywhere from forty minutes to an hour. The men loved to sing. Our secretary, Mary Rex, was an accomplished pianist. Someone gave us a piano. The men looked forward to gathering in the chapel in the evening and singing for about half an hour and then hearing a message. New arrivals who were sobering up often heard the singing and sometimes wanted to attend chapel services before they were well enough from a physical standpoint. They really looked forward to the services.

Men were referred to us in various ways. Most came to us through a wife or a son or daughter calling us. Ministers and doctors also sent them to us. In those days, the 1950's, alcoholics weren't very welcome at the local hospital. There was only one hospital in the town. We had a struggle if a man came in physically sick, possibly dangerously ill, and in need of detoxification. The hospital didn't want to accept a man in the hospital in that condition. Apparently alcoholics were looked on as if they were just really "sorry" and that was all that was wrong with them. Sometimes Stauffer had to be really firm with the hospital staff to get their support. Then, he'd say "I'm not a doctor, but I know there is more wrong with this man than the alcohol that's in him and he needs emergency treatment."

The doctors at the hospital recognized the immense burden that Stauffer was under with fifty alcoholic men at The Anchorage. His visits to the hospital were increasingly welcomed. There was one incident when a man was in the hospital that Stauffer didn't even know. Stauffer went to the hospital to visit someone, but the nurses ushered him into another room instead.

They said, "We're so glad you are here, because we don't know what's wrong with that fellow."

Stauffer had to diagnose that the man was actually in DT's. This is a serious and potentially fatal manifestation of alcohol withdrawal and constitutes a medical emergency. Many truly unusual things happened in those days.

The ministerial association asked Stauffer to become a member and have his regular visitation time at the hospital for those who weren't churched. He always looked forward to the week when he was responsible for visitation at the hospital, reaching the unchurched for Christ.

Increasingly, invitations came into the office for me to speak to different church groups. Women's groups wondered what they could do for The Anchorage. They supplied us with bed and bath linens. One group came out once a week to mend the men's clothes. Even in the first year, it was becoming an institution that most of the churches embraced. They were very open to providing for our needs through Sunday School classes and women's missionary circles.

At the end of the first year, we had a large rally. The men who had left came back to give their testimonies. We had a special speaker. Several hundred men arrived. The Board of Directors planned that the treasurer would give a report and then take an offering, hoping to get a good collection from the rally for our expenses.

When the treasurer took the platform, he said, "I'm on the Board of Directors. I'm a banker, and I was elected as treasurer before the Moses family ever arrived. Our first report a year ago was that we had three hundred dollars in the bank and eleven hundred dollars in expenses. I tried to resign after that meeting and the president (Roy Blanton) wouldn't let me. I knew that this project wouldn't work because it wasn't working out on paper. The numbers just wouldn't add up. With all my banking experience, I knew this was never going to work. One year later, we have fifty men over there and hundreds who have successfully completed rehabilitation. We have a positive bank balance." He gave the amount of the bank balance and then broke down and wept, saying, "What didn't work on paper worked by faith. We do have a faithful God who supplies all of our needs."

Word spread throughout the state about The Anchorage. Men began to come in from surrounding towns and from southeastern Alabama. We always had a full house and a waiting list.

In the beginning of our ministry, it never dawned on us that there might be alcoholic women in the homes in Albany. In those days, as today, alcoholic women were hidden. The only women who we knew got drunk were those that frequented the saloons, which wasn't very common. Those women were definitely looked down upon by society.

There was the rare occasion when a man would come to Stauffer's office after several weeks and say, "I'm worried about my wife and I'd like to go home because she has probably been drunk ever since I came and she needs help as badly as I do."

He had become aware of his responsibility to her after he got the alcohol out of his own system. At that point, Stauffer and I would visit her and I would bring her back to our guest room if she was willing. My older daughters helped me sober her up. Then she attended the evening services with our family.

The first woman alcoholic we brought into The Anchorage was put in our guest room. My older daughters assisted me in caring for her through her withdrawal.

When she arrived, Stauffer said, "You are going to have to search her pocket book and suitcase for any alcohol or drugs."

I objected, saying "I have never looked in another woman's pocket book in all my life."

Stauffer said "Just as I search through a man's clothes, you will have to search the women's."

Upon opening her pocket book, I felt rewarded for my boldness when I found a small bottle of pills. I took them into my possession. After serving her a cup of coffee, I carried a breakfast tray to her. She greeted me with, "I declare, Mrs. Moses. I remember telling my maid to put my saccharin in my pocket book. I have searched and searched and I just can't find it."

I quietly withdrew to hide my embarrassment that I didn't know the difference between saccharin and pills! This was my first lesson in realizing how different it was going to be working with women rather than with men.

In reflecting on that incident I am aware that this was my first object lesson in meeting the special needs of women. I had to depend on the experiences that God was teaching me. There were no degrees after my name and no "how-to" books written on the differences between the emotional and psychological needs of women and men for recovery from addiction.

For the first five years of The Anchorage, the occasional women that I took into our home were the wives of the men who were in residence at the time. I realized from the experience of having these women that their husbands and children kept their addiction a secret. The neighbors were simply told, "She isn't feeling well." In the event of her death, heart failure was the reason given. In most cases, only the immediate family and the doctor knew her secret. Coming to The Anchorage for assistance to obtain sobriety was her first step past her secret and towards the hope of finding sobriety.

I learned that profound shame was felt by the woman, her husband, and the children. For example, one of the mothers who came to us for help had a feisty daughter who was the age of my children. Judy confided to me that when she came home from school, her mother often lay passed out drunk on the kitchen floor. She had to step over her to get her lunch. When Judy was at camp with my children, she went out of her way to brag about her wonderful Christian mother. She kept her mother's secret from her peers and trusted that my girls wouldn't tell anyone about it. (Years later, despite two alcoholic parents, Judy succumbed as well and had real difficulty getting sober herself).

In the same way, husbands wanted to be proud of their wives and they didn't acknowledge their problem. The men who had alcoholic wives were often several weeks into sobriety before admitting that their wife also had a problem. They frequently admitted this because of fear that she could possibly be at home dying in her drunken condition while he was getting help.

Four years after the start of The Anchorage, more board members were added. After one of their monthly meetings, Stauffer told me that a matter had come up that involved me. A doctor had been one of those added to the Board and he asked why we were serving only men. Another Board member had replied that we didn't want "sorry drunk women on the grounds."

The doctor said, "Women are dying that never leave their homes when they are drinking. Only their family and their doctor know their secret."

Stauffer told them of my occasional "house guests" over the previous four years. They asked him to have me attend the next board meeting. In the meantime, I was to get in touch with some of the women's groups to determine if there was enough interest among them to start a Women's Division.

A large group of women came the following week from the Porterfield Methodist Church. I gave them a tour of the men's facilities. In the chapel, I explained the accomplishments of the past four years. I told them about the "hidden women" that I had taken in as houseguests. My question to them was, "Do you think the women of our city would be supportive of serving the needs of alcoholic women as they have the needs of alcoholic men?"

I was met with complete silence. Finally, one woman asked, "Mrs. Moses, just how successful is this program for men?"

What she really wanted to know was how many of the several hundred men who had left The Anchorage had returned to drinking. It was a question I hadn't anticipated or I would have searched the files for statistics.

Before I realized it, I found myself saying, "How successful is our program? It is 100% successful! Let me explain. We are missionaries. This is a Christian Rehabilitation Center. The commission given to us by Christ was to 'go up into all the world and preach the Gospel.' Every man hears the Gospel. That is our commission. How many believe? How many never drink again? I don't know. God keeps those records."

Before the meeting was over, the women made a commitment to spread the word to women's organizations all over the city. They said, "If the men of First Methodist are the fathers of The Anchorage, we want to be the mothers of the Women's Ministry."

I had a favorable report for my first Board meeting. It was not my last.

There was a vacant building on the grounds unused for many years. It was located up the road on the other side of the men's dormitory. It had been the Royal Air Force officer's quarters. Most of the rooms were beautifully paneled. Because it wasn't included in the ten acres the city allowed The Anchorage, we acquired special permission from Judge Malone and the city of Albany to include the building in The Anchorage ministry. With the help of the male residents, that building was repaired for use as the Women's Division. The churches and business people encouraged us with their involvement in the expanded ministry. The Furniture Dealers Association completely furnished and professionally decorated all the rooms in the building. Each furniture store in town took the responsibility of providing for one room. The church groups brought the bathroom and bath linens and the household items for the kitchen.

In 1958, five years after The Anchorage started, the Women's Division was ready for admissions. We had a large dining room and kitchen and recreation room and enough space for eight women. We entered a new phase of having room not only for fifty men in the large barracks, but now we had room for eight women in the Women's Division. There was a great day of celebration when we had the open house and a special service of praise and celebration for God's past blessings and the new ministry just beginning. The official opening of the Women's Division was also evidence to all that the ministry was there to help women who had been hidden before now. The woman secret drinker, protected by children and spouse, was now being openly acknowledged as someone in need of help. We became increasingly aware of the need to offer education to the public and to the churches about the hidden women alcoholics.

We acquired a housemother to supervise the Women's Division. I went daily to support and help her as needed. Most of the women who came to us still had intact families. They were sent by doctors, or they came at the request of their husbands. Many were on the verge of divorce.

The reason we enjoyed the work so much was that many of the men and women still had homes to go back to and people who cared about them. As a result, the success rate was very high. The drug of choice in those days was almost always alcohol. Virtually the only other drugs that we encountered were the barbiturates.

We had extremely strict rules. There could be no fraternizing between the Men's and Women's divisions. I look back now and I really appreciate Stauffer's wisdom in the rules that he made. He told the men that if there was any violation of our stringent rules, the women wouldn't be asked to leave, but they would. It made them extra cautious to avoid being flirtatious with the women. Of course, there were some incidents. He stuck to his threat and it was always the man who had to leave.

Initially, we were the only rehabilitation home for men in South Georgia. Another one for men started later in LaGrange, Georgia. Other places began as well. There were, I think, two along the Carolinas. To our knowledge, there was nothing for women.

The person who taught the Bible study class at the Men's Division in the morning at 8 o'clock went from there to the Women's Division and had the same Bible study class at 9:00. I had one morning a week and Stauffer had one morning a week. Some town folk came out who each had one morning a week. Stauffer's assistant also had one morning a week.

For the Sunday evening chapel services, the housemother and the eight women were in attendance. They sat in the first row on the left side as you faced the front. My family always sat in the second row. The men and the visitors from town took the rest of the chapel. When the service was over, the housemother and the residents of the Women's Division left immediately and went back to their quarters to have their fellowship. They never came into the dining room to have the after-service fellowship that we had with the men. The morning chapel services weren't attended by townspeople. On a Sunday night, the fifty male residents were free to invite their families to join us in worship and also any other townspeople were welcome to come. Many of the Saturday night services were attended by people from town as well. Stauffer truly had the gift of evangelism. He loved people and he wanted everyone to know the freedom in Christ that he knew.

Stauffer was distressed when he had to turn men away for lack of room. He was extremely concerned that the churches in other areas have the same availability to a local Christian rehabilitation home for the people in their area. Stauffer had a long-range vision that each state should have at least four Christian rehabilitation centers. He spoke of this burden whenever he had the opportunity and was always ready to assist in other cities when called upon.

From this vision, a rehabilitation center was started in LaGrange, GA. He had communicated his burden to the people there and eventually a Board was set up. My own sister, Ida, and her husband came from a place in New York where they had been working and assumed the directorship of the facility in LaGrange. This made me very happy because I now had other family members in the state of Georgia. We had a lot of men in residence that came over from Dothan, Alabama, and also from Mississippi. Rehabilitation facilities were to begin in these areas as a result of Stauffer's vision.

Our first assistant director was Jesse Hart. He and his wife, Martha, were a young couple that came to us with their little boy, Jesse, Jr. Jesse came as Stauffer's assistant and we had two happy years with them. Their two-year-old boy was the same age as Susan. They had another baby while they were with us. After their training, they went to Houston, Texas, where they have been running the rehabilitation center to the present day.

Our second assistant director was Rich Barth from our home church in Pennsylvania. Several people had come to us for rehabilitation from Jackson, Mississippi. They had gone back to their homes with a real conversion experience to live a sober life for Christ. A Board of Directors formed in Jackson. They asked Stauffer for a recommendation. After a couple trips, Stauffer recommended our assistant, and Rich took the position. He and his wife, Betty, were just the right people at the right time. They started a place known as Friends of Alcoholics which is still operating to the present day.

It seems like many of our out-of-state people came from Dothan, Alabama. Dothan was only perhaps ninety miles west of Albany, over the Alabama border. The pastor of the First Baptist Church of Dothan had a tremendous burden for the alcohol problem and he challenged some members of his congregation with this burden. As a result, many of the men who returned to Dothan went to his church. Stauffer then was asked to visit. The pastor and some of the men who had been at The Anchorage organized a meeting. They asked Stauffer who should be invited to this meeting. He suggested making the meeting known through the newspaper and having the news media, social workers, or anybody else, attend. He went to Dothan and spoke to this group.

After the meeting, Stauffer told a newspaper reporter that there was property somewhere in the Dothan area and that if he would give this vision a good write-up, someone would be led to donate this property. Stauffer was always looking for opportunities to help other sections of the state or other sections of other states to start rehabilitation homes for alcoholics. This meeting in Dothan was a prime example.

Several years after we went to Albany, Stauffer was named Man of the Year. It was a time of rejoicing for all of us because God was truly exalting this farm boy and honoring his faithfulness. He wasn't only preaching the gospel, but he was reaching out and finding solutions to the problems caused to the family unit because of alcohol. In 1959, I was named Woman of the Year in Albany for starting the Women's Division for the women victims of alcoholism in Albany.

Stauffer continued to be active in the International Union of Gospel Missions and attended meetings of the Southeastern District of the International Union of Gospel Missions. He and I went to these meetings almost every year. We hosted the District meeting in Albany many times during the years at The Anchorage. For several years, Stauffer was the president of the Southeastern District.

We had a radio broadcast every Sunday afternoon at one o'clock. Stauffer, the staff, and our family, all gathered in the chapel and broadcast directly from there. The service began with the men singing. Then, we had our three older girls sing trios. I usually read a letter or poem. The men gave their testimonies and Stauffer preached a short sermon. Larry, our only son, was taught to handle the controls for the broadcast. This was a time when we all as a family ministered together and had a good time in the process. The broadcast made Sunday a special day for all of us.

We received many letters from people who heard the broadcast and came to know Christ through the radio program. Interestingly enough, when I reflect on that now, we were doing the same thing on a small scale in Albany that we had experienced many years before with the service that we listened to out of Philadelphia. They had a vast audience compared to ours. In a small way, we had the same kind of witness in Albany. Though we didn't reach far out, it was a time of real ministry, even for the men. How they enjoyed taking part in that!

Although the First Methodist Church started The Anchorage, we were an interdenominational ministry. We asked for help from all the different churches. Stauffer was Judge Malone's substitute Sunday School teacher at the Methodist Church and also attended his Sunday School classes there when he wasn't teaching. However, we weren't just at the Methodist Church for very long.

One of the first church groups that requested to lead a monthly service at The Anchorage was a women's Bible class at First Baptist Church. Their teacher was a dear, Godly, elderly woman. She had a burden for the young women in her class to witness for Christ. To my knowledge, she had no alcoholism in her family. She just had a spiritually-born concern for the young men at The Anchorage and challenged the members of her class to pray for them. She came out to speak to the men once a month.

One Sunday, she asked if I would teach her Sunday School class at her church. Then, she had a lot of dental work done and asked whether I would come every Sunday for several months. This was just shortly after we arrived in Albany. Naturally, I took the children to where I taught and they got involved in the Baptist Sunday School class.

None of us could attend Sunday morning worship service. Stauffer taught Sunday School at the First Methodist Church. As soon as Sunday School was over, he picked the children and me up at the First Baptist Church and we went straight home. The cook had the Sunday dinner ready and the family, staff, and residents went immediately from that into the chapel to start the radio program. That was our Sunday schedule all the years we were in Albany.

From the very beginning, the demands on me were heavy. I made up the menu for all the resident's meals and assisted in any area where I was needed such as in the office or in food service where I spent a great deal of time. Increasingly, I was asked to speak to women's groups. There was the responsibility of the five children and keeping four girls in starched dresses. This was before the days of drip dry. Stauffer needed a fresh, clean, starched, white shirt every day. The large apartment had asphalt tile floors that needed polishing and scatter rugs that needed cleaning. It was my responsibility to keep the household running smoothly. Stauffer spoke to the Board about my need for help. Rather than put me on the pay roll, they said they would rather I hire a maid and let her help me. I would then be free to work wherever Stauffer needed me and also be free to be in the home.

This was during the days of segregation in the Deep South. Being from the North, our family had difficulty understanding the segregation mode when we arrived in the early 50's. Any help that I had needed with the children back home on the farm in Pennsylvania I was able to get from the family or from a local high school girl. For me to have a maid was something totally new. I cringed at the thought of having the children feel that they had a maid and that they could dump a lot of the work on her. I didn't even know where to start looking for one. We were in the country, on the edge of town. When I was given the go-ahead to hire someone, I got in the car and started driving the opposite way from the town. I saw a woman walking with her little boy who was about seven. It was still within the first year of our arrival in Georgia.

I stopped and said, "I'm a stranger in town. I have five children and I need help in my home. I'm going to stay home and I will work right with the person. Can you recommend someone?"

I told her who I was, where I lived, and I also gave her our telephone number. Then, I kept driving down the road to see if I could knock on any more doors for recommendations. There were none.

The next day, this very same woman knocked on my door and I recognized her. Her name was Georgia.

She said, "Mrs. Moses, I'd like to work for you."

I invited her in and she told me her story. She said that she was a school teacher with a college degree. Because Albany State Teacher's College for Colored was there in Albany, it was hard for her to get a job. So she was doing domestic work.

She said, "I already know you and your family and your ministry. I have tuned into your radio broadcast and I'd like to take the job myself."

Georgia started work the next day. She was a brilliant woman and just lots of fun. She loved the children dearly and they loved her. Truly, she was a gift from God to our family.

After school, the bus with the black students pulled up in front of our house and A.J., her son, got out. Then, the white school bus pulled up and my children got out. The children then played together until late afternoon when I drove A.J. and Georgia to their home.

I didn't allow the children to call her a maid because I didn't see her that way. She was simply considered to be part of the family. This wasn't very acceptable in those days. We accepted her as we had our aunts when they came into our home to help me back in Pennsylvania. She cleaned and she worked right with me to do this tremendously big load of laundry every Monday and Thursday. She was great at ironing. The work she did took a tremendous burden off of me and allowed me time to take care of the many duties in the ministry. More importantly, Georgia was a positive influence on the children. She was a devout Christian who really loved the Lord. I found a true friend in her through the ensuing years. Having her with us was a wonderful experience for all of us.

There was always a good cook who happened into our program and was willing to stay after his period of rehabilitation and work for his room and board and a small stipend. I worked with the cooks in planning the meals. In the dining area, there was a staff table for our family. Later, when we had an assistant and his family and a secretary, we had several staff tables. All of the years that we were there, we had our evening dinner in the main dining room of The Anchorage. This was a tremendous help. All the meals were well-balanced and nutritious with everything from vegetables and meat to dessert.

The commission that we have from the Lord is to make disciples, to give the gospel to men in bondage and see them come to freedom in Christ. Salvation was just the beginning of a new life for these men. To have a daily Bible study and to disciple them, it was important that we get a Bible into the hands of each man for his own personal study. For the first men, Stauffer purchased inexpensive Bibles out of our own budget. In consideration of the volume of Bibles that we would need, we saw the necessity of purchasing at a wholesale price. I acquired the address of Word Publishing Company, told them of our ministry, and requested wholesale prices for cases of Bibles. They agreed to send us the Bibles of our choice and also sent a catalog.

We selected an inexpensive Bible with a vinyl cover and a presentation page. Each week, Stauffer presented the new men with a Bible with his name and date of arrival. Inside the cover was noted "A gift from the Moses family." The Bible presentation became a vital part of the ministry throughout the years.

Because Albany had no Christian Book Store, we started ordering Bibles for family members that requested them. As a result of this need, I ordered commentaries and Bible study books requested by the men and members of their family. Little did we know that we were now embarking on another faith venture, that of starting the first and only Christian Book Store in the city. As our inventory grew, we moved from our study room in the house to an office in the main dorm and then to another building on the grounds which had originally been the PX when the British military was there. The inventory grew as we kept strict books and turned the profits into increased stock. This ministry became a family project. We involved the children in every aspect of this new venture. Later, my oldest daughter, Eileen, and her husband, moved a well-stocked Christian Supply Store into the main business district of Albany.

It was 1958, five years after we arrived in Albany, that Stauffer was diagnosed with diabetes. The choice was his whether to go on insulin or to take control of his health by checking his blood sugar level daily and maintaining a strict diet. After receiving this news, he spent the following three or four days fasting and in prayer. He concluded his fasting and prayer only after he could thank God for his illness. Stauffer had always been in excellent health and he believed firmly that God would either intervene with healing or give him the grace needed to discipline his life style that would now be greatly altered.

As his wife, I was grieved as I watched him make the necessary changes. However, his preaching and life became even more effective as he demonstrated the grace of God in his personal life. His preaching was more fervent than ever. He taught that there is victory in the Christian life available to men and women held in bondage by alcohol.

The children grew up at The Anchorage. Susan was eight weeks old when we arrived. She started school at a church kindergarten. She was our first child to attend kindergarten. All the others started school in the first grade. Larry was already in the sixth grade when she was in first grade. Eileen, Audrey, and Diane graduated from the Albany High School. Eileen and Audrey were both married by their daddy in the Anchorage chapel. They were married about a year apart. Both of them wanted to have the past and present residents see them get married because they were very much attached to them. Their invitations were announced from the chapel the Sunday before the ceremonies. The men and some of their families lined up around the walls in the back as they attended the wedding. Georgia, my dear friend, played a big part in assisting with the weddings. All told, we had ten very happy years in Albany.

In getting the churches involved in The Anchorage, we decided that I should develop a Women's Auxiliary. To start, I wrote to each church in Albany and requested they select a representative to meet with me to plan for the organization. During the years, the Auxiliary proved to be an effective asset as an organized group to represent The Anchorage in these churches. A group of women met monthly with portable sewing machines to mend the men's clothing. All the linens for both divisions were provided through the efforts of the Women's Auxiliary.

I don't know how many thousand men went through The Anchorage in those ten years, but with such great numbers it was reasonable to expect that some of the men would slip back into their old lifestyle and need to come back a second and sometimes a third time. Our telephone rang constantly, day and night. It was very draining and wore us down.

In the meantime, the folks in Dothan acquired a beautiful piece of land in a wonderful section west of town. Their board started planning the buildings and asked for our help in planning the kind of dorm and the kind of home that would be needed for their director. They wanted us to help find a director to run the place. Actually, they started hinting that they wanted Stauffer to take the director's position. Stauffer made several recommendations to them.

About this time, the housemother at the Women's Division called and asked me to come right up. She said that while Stauffer was speaking to the women, he became dizzy and she had to have him sit down. After he sat down, he fainted, but revived immediately. When I arrived, Stauffer assured me that he was fine. I became very concerned and convinced him to see his doctor. The doctor found nothing physically wrong and said the symptoms were those of complete exhaustion.

I didn't cope very well with this new development in Stauffer's health. After much prayer, I realized that the pressure of The Anchorage and all his other daily activities was finally taking its toll. The ministry at The Anchorage had grown tremendously large over the years. We were busy day and night, seven days a week. The only break we got was if we removed ourselves physically from the grounds.

Dothan Alabama

A director had not yet been found for Dothan. One day, I said to Stauffer, "If you want to start all over in a new ministry and want to go to Dothan, I want you to know that I am all for it."

He said, "Do you mean that?"

I said emphatically, "Yes!"

Of course, I came to that conclusion because I was concerned about his health and thought Dothan would be a less demanding ministry.

He said, "You know, I have been praying for months. I really have a longing to go to Dothan, but I knew that you wouldn't be in favor of it. I have been asking the Lord that if it was His will that He would give you a burden to go and would change your mind so that you would want to."

So, of course that was the answer to his prayer and we immediately started looking toward the west.

The decision to go to Dothan was confirmed in both our hearts. Stauffer and I looked forward to the move to our new ministry, The Haven, with great anticipation. However, informing our Board and making closure in Albany was difficult and quite painful. We also had to say good-bye to numerous other people and activities in Albany. In addition to our activities at The Anchorage, we had also started a Christian bookstore on The Anchorage grounds. Subsequently, it was moved downtown and managed by Eileen and her husband. They lived close by in a large home on the outskirts of Albany. By this time, we were grandparents to two baby boys. Diane was graduating from high school and was enrolled in Columbia Bible College.

The Board tried to persuade us to stay in Albany. However, we felt our direction from God to leave Albany was as clear as the direction we had received ten years previously to go there in the first place. It was now 1963. We gave the Board our recommendations for our replacements. They finally decided on Reverend William Wooley. Bill and his wife Madeleine had four children. Bill had been director of a small mission in Pensacola, FL. Before this, they had been home missionaries in Kentucky under the Christian Missionary Alliance. They had a real love for people and a zeal for mission work. We met him at a convention several years earlier and he and Stauffer seemed to have much in common. Stauffer recommended him because he felt that they would fit perfectly into the program that we had developed.

The atmosphere in Dothan was one of anticipation and excitement. A doctor's widow had donated the beautiful land that I described. The dorm for the men was built according to Stauffer's recommendations. The ranch-style home for our family was built along a magnificently tree-lined road.

God used the First Baptist Church of Dothan to inspire the ministry, largely because Dr. Sam Maddox, their pastor, had a heart for the alcoholics of the town. For some time, he had been meeting once a week with the alcoholic converts to disciple them in the Word of God. There were a good many men in Dothan who had been to The Anchorage. Their lives had been transformed there, and they were attending these meetings even if they weren't members of his church. Some families that were on the verge of breaking up were restored.

As a result, we started in Dothan with a large fellowship of converts from The Anchorage. The radio station donated a good bit of time during their public service announcements to the opening of The Haven. The public generally knew about The Anchorage. There were plans afoot in advance for Stauffer to speak to the Dothan congregations about the new ministry.

So, in July 1963, we moved into a lovely, new, ranch home. The contour of the land reminded us of the rolling hills of Maryland. Behind the house, fifty yards up a dirt lane on one of the rolling hills, was the brand new dormitory that would house the men. The kitchen had been planned as I had recommended, even before I knew we were going to move there.

We both felt an excitement and a relief that we no longer had all the responsibilities of The Anchorage, nor the telephone calls from the alumni that came any time of the day and night. I also didn't have the concerns of a Women's Division. We were going to start with far fewer men. I think the dorm held somewhere around twenty men. My desire, as well as Stauffer's, was to eat all of our meals at home, coming to the main dining room only to have Sunday dinner with the men. I believe he was as ready as I was for a higher-quality home life, especially since we were the young grandparents of two little boys, just ninety miles away. We wanted to be available to Larry, now fifteen, and Susan, now ten, as well as to our children living away from home. Our family life had been severely impacted by our previous ministry and we wanted to spend quality time with our children now.

We enjoyed starting all over again, hoping to avoid some of the pitfalls of our younger years. We anticipated that the Dothan ministry would grow as large as

The Anchorage in the years to come. The same program was put in place in Dothan that we'd used successfully in Albany. There was Bible study in the morning and the churches came out for evening services. Even before our arrival, Stauffer had many speaking engagements lined up because of all the publicity we had received prior to our coming.

There were now just four of us at home. Our two oldest girls were married and Diane was a college freshman in college in South Carolina. Larry was starting high school and Susan was in the fifth grade. Larry had a riding horse in Albany and Susan had a Shetland pony. When we moved to Dothan, of course, those animals had to go along with us. There were good dirt roads and acres of wonderful countryside on which to enjoy riding. Larry also raised homing pigeons. The children were as ecstatically happy as their mother and father.

Our first summer was busy settling into our new home, getting Diane off to college, and getting Larry and Susan enrolled in their new schools. The men's dorm was made ready for our first admissions. We knew by September we could settle into a routine. But this was short-lived. My mother was terminally ill with cancer and Stauffer urged me to spend a week or two with her in September after the children were in school. It was just a few weeks after Diane started Columbia Bible College that I decided to visit her. Stauffer said, "Since Diane is in school, I can manage things here with the two children. You just fly up and spend as much time with your mother as you need to."

She had sold her house after she became ill and was living on Iva and Ted's land in a trailer she had bought. As her condition deteriorated, they knew her days were numbered. When I arrived at her trailer, I found a nurse companion living with her and caring for her. During the first week, I had some nice conversations with mother. Then, she slipped into a coma. I asked the doctor what we could expect and he said she might pass away in a day or two or she might linger for a month.

After talking with my brothers and sisters, I decided to return home and await word. There was nothing I could do for her at that point. Stauffer's mother flew back with me to visit us in our new place until we had to drive back for the funeral. After being home only a few days, we learned that mother had gone to be with her Lord. We packed and drove from Dothan to Pennsylvania, taking Grandma Moses home and then going to be with my family for mother's funeral. We buried my mother in September.

At the funeral, I noticed that my sister, Nina, was in very poor health. I was deeply concerned about her and spoke to my sisters and brothers about my distress over her condition. On October 25, just five weeks after mother went home to be with the Lord, we got word that Nina had passed away at the age of 45. She left four children ranging in age from fifteen to twenty-three. Stauffer, Larry, Susan, and I packed up again to go and face Nina's children and husband. It was extremely painful for me to lose my mother and Nina within five weeks of each other. Of course, we had anticipated it, but it was the grief from the anguish that we saw her four children endure. Nina's two older girls were in college and her oldest son was in the Air Force. He had to fly home for the funeral.

After a week, we returned to Dothan to resume our life and our ministry there. I felt numb. I couldn't cry. I was far away from my siblings and we couldn't share our grief with each other. I prayed for tears but they wouldn't come. One day, Stauffer made arrangements for me to drive a woman to the Anchorage for admission. I was glad for the opportunity to visit the Anchorage and Eileen's family. On the ninety mile trip back to Dothan, the tears began. All the way home, I wept. God answered my prayer and the tears God gave me were a wonderful gift that became tears of healing.

It was early November before we could establish a routine and start the new life we had longed for. Stauffer was busy at The Haven where his office was located. He no longer had an assistant, but a former patient at the Anchorage volunteered to come and do his secretarial work. He was also an excellent pianist and we marveled at God's provision as we were establishing this new ministry. The alumni fellowship of local men volunteered their services in many ways so Stauffer enjoyed a support group of men who were living sober Christian lives since their days at the Anchorage. Now they were a vital part of establishing The Haven of Dothan, Alabama.

The community welcomed us warmly and I received invitations to join various social clubs. I chose a garden club, and looked forward to that diversion once a month. A board member's wife called me and said, "Mrs. Huck, please join our Book Club. It will give you an opportunity to meet many of the 'right people!'"

After talking it over with Stauffer, I felt it would be another activity that would be a noon meeting and I would be home in time to prepare dinner for my family. After I called her and accepted, she said, "Oh, by the way, it is a hat and glove affair!" This would indeed be a different life from the one I had experienced in Albany when our house was full of children!

Larry and Susan enjoyed riding horses together on the Haven grounds. Before long, Larry discovered that some of his classmates had horses and he requested permission to ride with them. He soon realized his horse was a mare that was not keen on racing. He convinced his dad that the mare was safer for Susan and that the Shetland pony could be sold or traded so he could negotiate for a faster horse.

Susan was happy that she now had a horse, and Larry started winning races with his hard-earned horse!

Larry also kept homing pigeons which provided him many hours of enjoyment. Saturday morning was a good day when father and son trained the pigeons by taking them a little further each time and then returning home to see them come back.

Since Larry was now fifteen, the age when boys get their learner's permit, he drove his dad whenever they had time together. Hunting season opened and this was the first year father and son went hunting together.

It was obvious that the move to Dothan was good. Larry had watched as his dad spent so much time with fifty men as well as the staff at the Anchorage. Now he was an important part of the new ministry as father and son bonded.

This same bonding took place with Susan and me. Her three sisters were gone and school was the only contact she had with other girls. She enjoyed learning to cook as we prepared the evening meals. She had been eating institutional food all of her life until now and she was finally experiencing a normal home life.

Eileen and Audrey and their husbands visited often. Eileen's two boys were a joy to us all. Diane came home for the Christmas holidays and between semesters, many times bringing college friends with her. She happened to be home on our twenty-fourth wedding anniversary. She wanted to plan a special celebration but Stauffer said, "No, next year will be our silver wedding anniversary. We can do something really big next year!" Instead, Stauffer and I went out to eat at a local restaurant so we could have some time alone. We agreed that evening that we were more in love with each other than we were the day we married.

Stauffer had many opportunities to present his ministry and to fill the pulpit for other pastors in their absence. Occasionally, he was asked to hold revival services. These services lasted from three to five days. Most of the local country churches had late summer revival services in preparation for the fall.

While our children were growing up, it was customary for us to send them to summer camp for at least a week. We were very concerned that they didn't have the normal church life of other young people. They always looked forward to a week or more at camp where they had fun and fellowship with young people their own age. We didn't require the children to come to any of the Haven's services except on Sunday night. In Albany, worship on Sunday morning had consisted of just going to Sunday School.

About an hour's drive from Dothan was a children's camp operated by the Children's Bible Memory Mission. We were initially made aware of this camp by a Dothan woman who visited us in Albany. Now that we lived nearby, she introduced us to the people at the camp. It was decided that Larry and Susan would go as campers. Nina's fifteen year-old daughter was spending the summer with us and also went as a camper. Diane went as a counselor. They asked me to come for one week as the "resident nurse" in case of an emergency. They thought that I could take care of the little "Band-Aid" emergencies and hand out aspirin where needed. Any other emergencies would be sent to the local doctor or hospital. Finally, my twenty-five year old dream of being a medical missionary was being realized!

It was a good summer. Before going to camp, we enjoyed a week at Panama City. We returned home to get ready for our week at the camp. It was the last week of July. While we were away at camp, Stauffer's week was filled with speaking engagements. Toward the end of that week, he drove over to the camp late one afternoon to have dinner with us in the dining room and to enjoy the evening service with us. Afterwards, when it was time for him to go back, I walked him to the car. In the moonlight, he gave me a hug and said "I could search the whole world over and I would still pick you to be my sweetheart and my wife."

One evening, at bedtime, I was checking the bunks and found that Mary Beth, my niece, was missing. No one had seen her since the evening service. In a panic, I ran down to the lake. I found her sitting on the ground, sobbing in despair. It was eight months since her mother died and she had been so brave. Now, as I took her in my arms, she let all her grief and anger spill out. I comforted her and shared with her that God was longing to comfort her and that we could tell him our feelings. After praying together, I tucked her in and thanked God that He brought her to us for the summer.

We came home from the camp at the end of that week on Saturday afternoon August 1, 1963. It was Stauffer's fiftieth birthday. During the week of camp, I was in touch with Eileen in Albany and also with the fellowship group at The Haven. They were planning a surprise party for him that Saturday after the regular evening service. We were excited while driving home from the camp. There was the added excitement of having Eileen and her husband and two babies come for the weekend. On our arrival home, we dropped all our dirty laundry in the laundry room, quickly changed clothes, and went straight to the service.

It was a large and caring group that gathered. After the service, we went to the dining room where Stauffer was most surprised to find a cake with fifty candles on it and a crowd of people that he hadn't expected to be there since they hadn't attended the service. Stauffer picked up his two and a half year-old grandson, and said "Billy, you are going to have to help me blow out these candles."

Sunday was a busy day. We all got up and went to Sunday School and we were able to go to church because we didn't have the radio broadcast. Stauffer was scheduled to conduct a four-day revival service at a little country Methodist Church, not too many miles from The Haven. He preached the first service there Sunday evening. I didn't accompany him, but some of the children may have. Upon his return, he said he felt most burdened to preach to the Christians there. He felt there were very few unbelievers taking part in this revival service. He seemed particularly burdened about what to say to the believers.

I usually conducted the Bible study first thing each Monday morning. When we awoke, he said "You have all the camp laundry to do. Why don't you let me take this morning and you take the morning that I usually take?"

He also said, "I'd like everybody to go to the Methodist church with me tonight."

That Monday was a busy, hot summer day in Dothan. The children all had their chores to do before preparing for the evening service. Diane was still home before returning to Bible school. Everyone looked forward to a week of fun right there at The Haven.

Meanwhile, Stauffer went to the doctor. The week before, he'd had some discomfort in his chest. Sunday evening it had returned. After running some tests, the doctor asked him to come back the following day for additional tests. He was told that he could preach Monday evening but that he should stop if he had any recurrence of symptoms.

Before Stauffer arrived for dinner, the girls and I practiced a trio number, "Only believe, only believe, all things are possible, only believe." That was one of Stauffer's favorite choruses.

When he came in from the office, he went into his room to have prayer in preparation for the service. He asked me if I would join him, and I said I would. When I came to the door, I heard he was already in prayer. I knew he was very burdened about the evening service so I didn't disturb his prayer time.

We all went to church that evening even though it was a Monday service, including Susan, Larry, Diane, and their cousin, Mary Beth. Stauffer asked me if I would lead the singing for the service and have Diane play the piano. He introduced all of us to the congregation and I started leading the singing by having folks request songs out of their hymn book. Then I asked the trio to sing "Only Believe." The look of surprise on his face was so evident! After several verses, I had the congregation join in the chorus.

Stauffer preached that night on the judgment seat of Christ. (2 Cor 5:10 NIV) "For we must all appear before the judgment seat of Christ, that each one may receive what is due him for the things done while in the body, whether good or bad."

He told them he believed the purpose of a revival service for them was to revive those who were lethargic in their faith and challenge them to go out into the entire world and witness for the Lord Jesus.

(Mark 16:15-16 NIV) 15 "He said to them, 'Go into all the world and preach the good news to all creation.' 16 Whoever believes and is baptized will be saved, but whoever does not believe will be condemned."

Stauffer also preached on the importance of keeping our hearts open and clean before God because at the judgment seat of Christ, we would answer to how we lived our Christian life. He made a statement during his message: "If I would go home to be with Christ tonight, I would not be ashamed."

While he spoke, my mind went back to the prayer meeting and how burdened he was and how he was searching his own heart for a message for these people. The service was peaceful and spirit-filled, and ministered to each of us in the family as well as to the congregation.

We hadn't had family worship that morning. When we got home that evening after the service, he got everybody together in the den and said, "Before you all go to bed, let's have family worship." Stauffer asked one of the children to open her Bible to Romans 8:35-39 (NIV).

> 35 Who shall separate us from the love of Christ? Shall trouble or hardship or persecution or famine or nakedness or danger or sword? 36 As it is written:
>
> *"For your sake we face death all day long; we are considered as sheep to be slaughtered."*
>
> 37 No, in all these things we are more than conquerors through him who loved us. 38 For I am convinced that neither death nor life, neither angels nor demons, neither the present nor the future, nor any powers, 39 neither height nor depth, nor anything else in all creation, will be able to separate us from the love of God that is in Christ Jesus our Lord.

We all went to bed and that was the end of a real good day.

That night, after we were asleep, he awakened me and asked me to call the doctor because he was having pain in his chest. The doctor told me to give him aspirin and said he'd see him in the morning. I relayed the message to Stauffer and he accepted the aspirin but told me to call the doctor back and tell him that he wanted to go to the hospital. The doctor seemed annoyed, but told me I could take him to the Emergency Room and he would call the nurse and let her know he was coming. Very calmly, Stauffer gave me instructions to awaken Diane and have her drive in with us. He wanted me to awaken Mary Beth and tell her where we were going in case Susan and Larry awoke, but not to awaken them at that point. He also gave Diane instructions to call a fellow by the name of Austin Buntin, who was one of the main Dothan men in our fellowship group. Austin had known us for several years since his rehabilitation at The Anchorage.

Stauffer sat in the back seat of the car on the way to the hospital and writhed in pain. He was in agony. While I drove, I repeated the 91st Psalm aloud.

When we got there, the nurse came out to the car. I asked if she didn't think he needed a wheelchair. She said "No, he can walk in by himself."

Stauffer walked into the emergency room looking very ill and got up on the examination table. The nurse examined him briefly and left the room to call the doctor at home. While I stood there, he suddenly seemed to be looking quietly off into the distance. Moments later, the doctor arrived and I left the room. By this time, Austin had arrived. Diane and Austin and I stood outside of the emergency room door and prayed together. First of all, I claimed the blood of Jesus Christ on this attack of Satan on Stauffer's life. As I prayed, I released Stauffer to the Lord and said, "Lord, I put him in your hands. He is Your child."

The doctor came out and said, "It's over." I realized that I had been with Stauffer at the moment of his death.

Stauffer could say, (KJV 2 Timothy 4:7) "I have fought a good fight, I have finished my course, I have kept the faith:"

He had poured himself out as a living sacrifice. (KJV Romans 12:1) "I beseech you therefore, brethren, by the mercies of God, that ye present your bodies a living sacrifice, holy, acceptable unto God, which is your reasonable service."

The children and I had to go on alone.

I already had a love for flowers by the age of 4. This was in 1924.

I am on the far right wearing bloomers, for those of you who don't know what they looked like. I was 8 years old. Two of the other girls are cousins and one is a friend.

Nina and I side by side provides an idea of our relative sizes even though I was 9 and she was 12.

Graduation from high school at the age of 16.

The little community chapel in Neiffer, PA, built in 1803. A disproportionate number of its members were called onto the mission field. Our congregation used this chapel until 1938 when they acquired a church in Limerick, three miles away. Rapid growth in membership caused this move. A small book *As God Did It* written by the pastor's wife, E. Grace Didden, tells the story of this remarkable group of people and how they were used by God to further the gospel.

I was baptized by the pastor, Clarence Didden, in Swamp Creek at the age of 17.

The Youth Group at the Neiffer Church became the center of my social life. This photo was taken at Ocean City. We went there and back by train one day. Dress was generally not as casual then as it is now. I am second from the right in the first row of girls standing.

My Sunday School class combined with that of another teacher. I am in the back row on the left side.

Part of the chapel family saying good-bye to a missionary, the fellow on the far right in the dark coat. Pastor Didden is the tall man just to the left. I am fourth from the right in the front row of standing adults.

When I began dating Stauffer Moses, he was working for his father in the dairy business. This was one of their new trucks in 1937.

Stauffer is on the truck on the left.

I am in the midst of a field of flowers with my sister-in-law, Emma Moses.

In 1939, Stauffer developed blood poisoning as a result of this wreck. After a near-death experience, he surrendered his life to the Lord completely.

Stauffer and I were married on April 6, 1940. We borrowed the money for the wedding so I could have a nice dress and Stauffer could buy a new suit. It was a simple event to have been attended only by our parents. Our siblings surprised us by showing up.

On our way to our honeymoon at the family cabin in the Pennsylvania mountains.

I am reflecting on life as a farmer's wife. We are now raising chickens in order to have enough money to purchase furniture for our house.

A light moment: Stauffer and my mother in 1946.

My parents, Ard and Elsie Barr, in 1954.

My family Thanksgiving 1946. Mom and Dad are seated. Standing from left are: Mildred, Linwood, Nina, Iva, Bud, Elsie, and Ida.

This is a photo of the Anchorage Men's Division after renovation was complete and the building was inhabited. You can get an idea of its relative size by the number of men standing across the front. Behind me is the highway.

An idea of the clean-up required before the buildings could be used. There were literally mountains of trash everywhere. Fortunately, we had lots of help.

This is the Men's Division from the left. It is about the length of a football field. Roughly half of the windows (several hundred) were broken and had to be repaired before anyone could move in.

The Men's Division is in the middle. Another identical building is present on the left but was never used. Our home was in the one-story building on the right.

Another huge building towards the back of the grounds was useful for our annual reunions, always well-attended.

Our family standing in front of our home on the grounds of The Anchorage in 1954 several months after our arrival.

In 1959, I was honored to be named Woman of the Year of Albany, GA. Stauffer was Man of the Year in 1958 for our work in rehabilitation of alcoholics.

Our family in the living room of the newly-opened women's division of The Anchorage. This was my first ministry.

The Haven in Dothan housed 20 men and was full to capacity quite quickly. There was no Women's Division. As you can tell, the entire facility is quite small compared with the Anchorage. We also had our very own house that was separate from the treatment center.

Our son, Larry, was very helpful as he operated the radio during our weekly Sunday broadcast from The Anchorage.

Stauffer always thought about the men and built The Little Chapel at The Haven as a quiet place for them to pray.

PRAY FOR US.....

YOUR HOME MISSIONARIES
The MOSES FAMILY

Elsie

Serving the Lord Since 1952 in Alcoholic Rehabilitation and caring for children from broken homes. Pray that God would bless us as we continue this Rescue Missionary Work, in whatever phase He leads us.

Diane

Will be assisting since graduating from Columbia Bible College, and also plans to do post graduate work.

Larry

Freshman at Columbia Bible College majoring in Biblical Education.

Susan

Freshman in High School.

Home address:
378 W. Ridge Pike
Limerick, Pa. 19468

"For we are labourers together with God..." I Cor. 3:9

Sowega Youth Home was next and an excellent training experience for what lay ahead.

From Sowega, we moved to Faith Cottage of Eliada Home, a ways from where this was taken. This also provided excellent training for Atlanta.

After Stauffer died, this went out to those who supported us. We then returned to The Anchorage for a period of time.

Thought to have been the first women's mission in the U.S. Originally built as a large private residence, it had been used more recently to provide housing for single women moving to Atlanta for education or employment.

Dr. William Huck as a younger man in England.

We took advantage of an opportunity to expand and moved into this abandoned school. All our projects were large and this was no exception.

I am settled in to my new office.

The front door to our new facility. It was only a few steps to the street with access to city bus transportation for the women.

Chapel service was part of daily life at the new Women's Mission.

My last major project in the home mission field was Village Atlanta for homeless women with children. We started in the old farmhouse on the left and were able to build a beautiful and functional facility (in back on the right) where a woman could have her own apartment and keep her children with her while she was being rehabilitated.

I was blessed by four overseas trips including to England, Germany and Switzerland, Korea, and Israel. This picture of me on a camel was taken just to show my grandchildren that I could do it. I didn't actually ride anywhere.

I am intently showing Jim and Ida Bell the plans for The Village before construction was actually underway. Ida was on my board.

Here I am volunteering for paint detail. This allowed me to leave a part of myself with the project.

I spoke at a Missions Conference at a large Methodist church in North Atlanta and they were inspired to raise money for us in this manner: a student from Georgia Tech designed a container to hold a million pennies. Heavy Plexiglas windows allowed progress to be monitored. The woman on the right is holding one of many signs encouraging people to "pitch in" and support the Village Atlanta building fund. Because of its weight, the container had to be placed in their basement where children as well as adults from the larger community including many other churches filled it. We collected $10,000. The story was picked up by the Atlanta Journal Constitution which undoubtedly aided the effort.

Group photo of me with my family in front of the newly completed Village. They were always tremendously supportive of me and my ministry.

I have been blessed with my third husband, Linwood Detweiler.

I have always been close to my grandchildren. Here I am with Eileen's three grown sons, Bill, John, and Robert on the occasion of the marriage of their sister, Renee, in 1993.

At another time, I enjoyed tea with three of my grown granddaughters: Laurie Streets and Heather and Tracy Stewart.

Lin and I celebrating my 80ᵗʰ birthday with my extended family.

Picking up the Pieces

We had been in Dothan only thirteen months. We moved there in July 1963 and it was now August 4, 1964. It was only ten months after losing my mother and my sister that Stauffer passed away. Nina was closest to me in age and in life's experiences as a single person. Now she, my mother, and my mate, had all gone home to be with the Lord within ten months of each other.

Just a week before Nina died, I was having symptoms of weakness and headaches. I had all kinds of ideas of what might be wrong with me and I went to my Internist back in Albany. As well as he knew me, he didn't know about my mother's death. I was worried that I had a brain tumor or something else terribly wrong with me. After a thorough history and physical examination, he said "I really can't figure out what is wrong with you, Mrs. Moses. You show all the symptoms of deep depression. Is there anything that you are depressed about?"

I said, "No, I don't think so. My mother passed away four weeks ago, but we expected that."

He said, "No one is ever ready to say goodbye to their mother. You should have started out by telling me this."

But he had diagnosed it properly. He asked, "How much do you cry."

I said, "I am not a weepy woman," and I said it with some pride.

He said, "But if you were, you wouldn't be sitting in front of me today. Right now you are fighting to keep from crying while talking about your mother."

A week later, I still hadn't cried. I was able to function with Nina's husband and her children. I stayed in their home while Stauffer stayed with his people. I helped go through her things and I was the brave one who was able to comfort them when they were all in grief.

Some weeks after I returned to Dothan, I drove over to Albany with a woman that needed treatment at the Women's Division of The Anchorage. On the way home, I just cried out to the Lord and asked for tears. I think I wept almost the entire ninety miles from Albany to Dothan.

I just wanted to mention that in spite of the grief of our great losses, the Lord intervened and gave us comfort. We were provided with the courage to go on with the ministry at The Haven and the next year was a good year.

It was because of Nina's death that Mary Beth was with us for most of the next summer, and came to be involved with the summer camp experience before her favorite uncle went home to be with the Lord. In God's providence, I remember at the camp, being the acting school nurse, I saw her down at the lake at dusk all by herself and I went down to her. She was a fifteen-year-old girl. She was sobbing, but was able to lash out with her bitterness and her anger over her mother's passing. In dealing with her on the loss of my sister, her mother, it was ironic that just a few days later she would be comforting my son, her same-age cousin.

When Diane and I returned home from the hospital after Stauffer's death, Mary Beth was waiting for us. I said "Mary Beth, I would give anything for you not to be here."

She replied, "I believe God brought me here for this very reason."

I am sure that for the next week, her presence brought great comfort. She was such a happy, sweet girl, and she grieved with all of us.

At this time, we had only been in Dothan for thirteen months. The president of The Haven board was informed, as was Roy Blanton, the founding father of The Anchorage board. Within hours, Roy was by my side, making contacts, and helping the children with all that we had to think about. My home pastor from Pennsylvania called almost immediately. He knew that we would not want to have Stauffer buried in Dothan since we had been there such a short time and probably wouldn't have stayed there indefinitely. He advised me to bring his body back to our home church and have him buried in a cemetery near the farm and near the church. We decided to have a memorial service in the First Baptist Church of Dothan and to have an open casket one hour before the chapel service so people coming from out of town, especially from Albany, could view his body. There were so many men who requested to stand honor guard at the head and foot of his casket, both from Dothan and Albany, that they had to change every ten minutes during the several hours before the memorial service when the casket was closed. I was numb from my loss and unaware of what was being planned. I am sure the plans were made by Roy, the two boards, and our older children and their husbands. When I walked into that big sanctuary, it was full. Men came from Albany and from far and wide. It was decided to send his body to Pennsylvania by train and that was also taken care of by both boards.

We started the long trip from Dothan to Pennsylvania by car, staying one night in a motel. Mary Beth and Diane spent the night trying to comfort Larry and Susan. Eileen's husband drove for this trip. She had someone in her home taking care of her two little fellows.

Grandma Moses was grief-stricken from the loss of her adult son. Grandpa Moses had died some years before. Through the years, she had been an inspiration to us in our ministry and had provided prayer support. Upon our arrival back home, she was a great comfort to the children and to me, as I am sure we were to her.

The memorial service was held in our home church Sunday afternoon. It was decided that he would again lie in state in the church so those that wanted to view his body could do so. It was almost a repeat of what it was like in Dothan. Instead of all those men standing honor guard, it was my two young daughters' husbands who spent an hour at the head and foot of his casket while all the home folks and relatives from that area passed by. I don't remember much about any of this except that when the burial at the grave site was over, I felt like I couldn't move. I requested the minister have everybody sing Amazing Grace, the first and last verses. The last verse goes, "When we've been there, ten thousand years, bright shining as the sun, we've no less days, to sing God's praise, than when we'd first begun." I guess the reason I spontaneously made that request was because Stauffer loved the hymn above all others. He always enjoyed the conviction and the intensity with which the Southern people sang it.

Stauffer and I were married twenty-four years, twelve years in the business world, living in the country, and twelve years in Christian work. Clearly, in the last twelve years, thousands of souls were saved through his ministry. During the first twelve years, many times in our prayers together, Stauffer prayed, "Lord, send us where you want us to be. Time is going by and it seems like we are getting so much older." Then, when we finally went into Christian work, he prayed "Lord, restore to us the years the cankerworm has eaten."

The scriptural reference is to Joel 1:4. "What the locust swarm has left the great locusts have eaten; what the great locusts have left the young locusts have eaten; what the young locusts have left other locusts have eaten."

The pastor asked me when we were returning to the South. I told him it would be the next day, which was Monday. He asked me to stop by his office before we left. As he requested, I stopped by his office the next day and he asked me if I wanted to return to Limerick, saying that they had an opening on the church staff to work in the department of ministry to children. In particular, they wanted someone to work with the Bible Club movement, and to conduct Bible clubs in the area. Children's ministries were a major concern of the church.

He said, "While I know that we advise people who have lost a mate to not make any crucial decisions for a year, I know that you are faced with making some major decisions immediately."

It was August. They were going to start the Bible clubs in September. He gave me the date by which he would have to hear from me. Otherwise, he would have to hire someone else to fill the position.

We started the long journey back to Dothan, still in a state of shock and disbelief. I was now without my mate. The children were without their father. Alternatively, we cried and tried to comfort each other. It didn't seem that this could really be happening.

We finally reached Albany, Georgia, to refresh ourselves in Eileen's home before going the last ninety miles to Dothan. Her telephone was ringing. It was Bill Wooley, the director of The Anchorage. He told me he had been calling every half-hour during the day, knowing I was going to be passing through Albany. He said he wanted me to come back and be on the staff of The Anchorage and be director of the Women's Division. I told him that it might not be the wise thing to do since I had helped Stauffer start The Anchorage eleven years before, and asked him how his board felt about it. He said he had called an emergency board meeting and they were unanimous in wanting me to come. I responded that I thought the Dothan board might want me to run The Haven until a replacement could be found for Stauffer. This meant there were three opportunities open to me as I left Albany.

That night, Larry, Susan, Diane and I pulled the two twin beds together in Eileen's guest room. We needed the comfort of our closeness to each other before completing the last ninety miles of our journey to Dothan and the house that awaited us—without Stauffer.

Little did I know what would face me in Dothan on our return.

Return to Dothan

We arrived back in Dothan less than a week after we'd left. Things had already changed. I was notified that a new "temporary" director was already in place. He was one of the men who was actually in the rehabilitation program at the time. He had been in rehabilitation centers all over the country because of his seeming inability to achieve sobriety. Because he had been drinking again, he was with us when Stauffer passed away. The board put him in charge because he at least had some exposure to sobriety. A committee of board members was assigned to work closely with him until a permanent director could be secured. Adding insult to injury, the board requested that I write a memorial letter for Stauffer's passing that they could use for fund raising. We were on the budgets of forty-two Dothan area churches, but they wanted more. Finally, they told us to find new housing for ourselves because they needed our house within two weeks.

I was in shock but I kept busy. I wrote the memorial letter for them. When the president of the board read it, he said it was a beautiful letter, but it wouldn't do for their fund-raising purposes. I told him I had agonized over the letter and had gotten it together as best I could. The truth of the matter was that I was simply not going to help them exploit Stauffer's passing.

Now I didn't know what to do or where to go. I was under pressure to vacate my home. At that point, the children and I would be, for all practical purposes, homeless.

At least, while I was packing up, other business opportunities were being presented to me. A veterinarian who had come to know Christ through Stauffer's witness offered to purchase a gift store and set me up in business on the perimeter circling Dothan. He knew of my prior experience with the bookstore in Albany which Eileen and Bill were now operating. Eileen and Bill asked me if I would come back in partnership with them. Not knowing what to do, the children and I packed up the furniture and put it in storage until we could decide what our next step would be.

A week after our return to Dothan, I took a trip with Susan, Diane, and Larry to spend a weekend in LaGrange visiting my sister and her husband. While there,

I got a telephone call from the director of the big rescue mission in Washington, D.C.

He said, "I am so shocked by Stauffer's death. He was one of the younger men in the International Union of Gospel Missions, and he certainly worked himself to death. I'd like you to come here and take over our children's ministry so that my wife and I can take it easy."

When I hung up after talking with him, I was facing for the first time people's responses to Stauffer's "untimely death." With bitterness, I said, "So he thinks Stauffer worked himself to death and now he wants me to work myself to death for him and then my children will be orphans and he will still have his children, who are older and already married."

Eileen and her husband graciously invited us to stay in their guest room. Eileen was eight months' pregnant with her third child. Her two little boys were then one and a half and two and a half years old. We settled down in her guest room, again pushing the twin beds together. Susan and I slept in the middle with Diane on the other side of Susan and Larry on the other side of me. We generally talked ourselves to sleep at night.

When school started at the end of the month, I enrolled Larry and Susan back in the Albany schools, which they had left just a year before. Diane started back to her second year of Bible College in Columbia, SC. She wandered around the campus for a few days and then called me and said I should come and get her. She wanted to come home. The Lord gave me the grace to say to her, "Dad and I were able to save enough money for your first quarter and you must at least stay for that long. I'm doing fine, so you just stay there."

The day came that I was supposed to call the pastor of our home church to give him an answer about the position open to me there. When I picked up the telephone, I had no idea what my answer would be. I planned to tell him that I hadn't reached a decision and that is exactly what I told him when I got him on the telephone. Then, I said, "I suppose if I don't take the position in Limerick, there are other women waiting in line to fill that need."

He said, "Well as a matter of fact, there are others that really want the position."

I would have really welcomed a response like, "No, Elsie, there is no one to fill the need and we really need you and want you up here and we feel that you need to be back here with your children and your families and your church."

When I knew that there were others waiting in line for the job, my words spilled out in anger and I said "Everyone cares about children. I care about children too, but no one cares about women. I don't know anyone at all that cares about women." I must have felt pretty strongly that no one cared about me very much right then either.

A surge of compassion filled my heart once again for women who were in crisis and were in such deep pain that no one seemed to understand. Now I was in that situation myself. My children and I had no one to support us and nowhere to live. I had to finish raising the children alone.

Very lovingly, my pastor answered, "That's true, Elsie, but you care. Could the Lord be affirming in your own heart and in your own call that He wants you to minister to needy women?"

It all became clear to me exactly at that moment. I blurted out my decision: "Yes, and I am staying in Albany. This is the only place open to me for that sort of ministry. It is the place that I love and I will stay here."

So, while I started the telephone call not knowing what I was going to do next, I hung up with the full assurance and peace that God was indeed directing my path.

I called Reverend Wooley and told him my decision. Immediately, we started making plans for me to return to The Anchorage. Of course, by now, the Wooleys had settled into the large apartment area which had been our home for ten years. Our old quarters were taken. On the other end of the building was the private entrance to Mary Rex's old apartment. Behind that was an apartment where our assistants had always lived. In the present situation, one-third of the building was now vacant because Reverend Wooley's wife, Madeline, was his secretary and he didn't have a live-in assistant at the time. I was able to move my family into the other end of the building and we occupied the two smaller apartments. We each had our own private bedroom once again. Every day, I went up to the Women's Division. For the first time in the history of The Anchorage, there was a director for the Women's Division, me. Our housemother was still there, too, to be in charge at night.

During the year that we were at The Haven, Bill Wooley had called Stauffer several times a week to ask him questions about the problems that confronted him. We spent time with Bill and Madeleine in Albany and they spent time with us in Dothan. There was probably no one that sensed more keenly than Bill the loss of a friend in ministry. Where could he now turn for help? There were so few in rehabilitation, and he had only just entered that field of service himself. It soon became part of the routine that I went up to their apartment every evening. We sat and talked about the problems of the day. He asked how Stauffer would have handled each issue. Bill told me that he still wasn't well-acquainted with the people or the churches of Albany. He needed me desperately to continue speaking to keep the ministry in the public eye. This was an area he didn't enjoy and I did. His strong suit was the actual running of The Anchorage.

Although the children and I were going through a period of deep grief and loss, there were light-hearted times as well. Bill drew Larry in to a relationship with him, and Susan played with Bill's daughters.

Dr. Hatch, one of Diane's professors at Columbia Bible College, wrote me that September. It was the first month of the school year. He said, "I want to give you a portion of scripture that I am claiming for you." It was Philippians 1:12 and 19 (NIV).

> 12"Now I want you to know, brothers, that what has happened to me has really served to advance the gospel." 19 "for I know that through your prayers and the help given by the Spirit of Jesus Christ, what has happened to me will turn out for my deliverance."

I read it again and again and wondered how Stauffer's death could result in a furtherance of the Gospel through me. He was the evangelist and the pioneer. He was the one who was starting rehabilitation centers and who had a burden for centers to be started in every state in the South.

In his letter, Dr. Hatch reminded me that Reverend Moses had a speaking engagement to the student body in the assembly in October. He wondered whether I would accept his invitation to come in Stauffer's place. I told him I would be happy to, knowing in my heart it was an assignment Stauffer would want me to take.

Needless to say, I felt so inadequate and uncertain that I just cried out to the Lord for an affirmation that I had done the right thing by taking this speaking engagement. I wanted confirmation that this was the course I should take. Doubt flooded through my being. One morning after the children had gone to school, and while I was having my devotions, I asked the Lord to give me the assurance that I was, indeed, exactly where He wanted me to be. I was reading the 41st chapter of Isaiah and I came to these words in the 9th verse: (NIV) "I took you from the ends of the earth, from its farthest corners I called you. I said, 'You are my servant'; I have chosen you and have not rejected you."

God met me in a wonderful way at that moment. The very words of scripture described my innermost feelings of being a castaway and God assured me through His word that I was not a castaway.

I had been happy to be the helpmate of a servant of God. In that role, I felt that I had been a faithful helpmate to my husband. Now I knew that God was showing me His grace by assuring me I was still His servant and that He indeed had chosen me. Overwhelmed with His presence, I read the next verse, Isaiah 41:10(NIV) "So do not fear, for I am with you; do not be dismayed, for I am your God. I will strengthen you and help you; I will uphold you with my righteous right hand."

It was one of those times that I felt that I was on Holy ground, wrapped in the presence of a loving, caring, Father. He indeed affirmed the path I had taken. I needed only to trust Him because He was upholding me with His righteous hand.

I accepted the invitation to speak to the student body of Columbia Bible College and I spent a great deal of time in prayer and preparation, writing down every word that I intended to say. In preparation, I thought of everything Stauffer would have said had he been there for that assignment.

As I sat on the platform with Dr. Hatch and other members of the faculty and looked over the large student body all gathered together, I prayed, "Lord, you are going to have to speak through me. I don't know how I'm going to get through this."

The student body arose to sing the song "To God be the glory, great things he hath done" and then the chorus, "Praise the Lord." I don't think there was one person in the audience who was not singing with all the fervor and enthusiasm that only young students can who are preparing to take the Gospel to the uttermost parts of the earth. I felt lifted up and energized. After I was introduced, I stood before them and said simply, "I'm here in my husband's place because he is home with Jesus."

I looked into the youthful, expectant eyes of the hundreds of students before me. My heart leaped with joy for this opportunity and I began to speak. I challenged them to really care about the people, perhaps in their neighborhood, in their churches, all around them, who were struggling with addictions. I explained that people with an active addiction problem are less likely to be sitting in church with them. However, perhaps the family and friends were more likely.

The treatment of addictions was a new mission field, a mission field that was virtually untouched, especially when it came to addressing the needs of women. Then, God just burdened my heart to depict for them the destitute women who were too embarrassed to let their friends and neighbors know about their problem, and who were struggling alone and totally defeated. Christ was the answer! It was a mission field that I trusted some of them would see fit to enter.

I returned to Albany, and the next day I went to the Women's Division with a new vision and a new burden. The words that God gave the students through me were meant for me as well. In fact, I had spoken more to myself than to the student body. While I had always had sympathy and compassion for the women who came to us during our last five years at The Anchorage when I was the Bible teacher and assistant house mother, that all changed now. I was still going through my own grief, dealing with the numbness and the hurt and my own struggles, but I was discovering something new. The women coming in intoxicated and in need of help and love were at a crucial time in their lives. Sometimes their husbands had threatened divorce. In many instances, they were already divorced and were wearing out their welcome with their children or with whichever relative was currently putting up with them. I saw them come in with this deep grief and numbness and now I could truly empathize with them. I knew that their grief was imposed by the excesses of their own life style, but their grief was just as real as mine. With a new fervor and a new sense of determination, I spoke to these women about the love of Jesus.

At the same time, my visits with the Wooleys over a cup of coffee were even more precious. There was much healing for me in being able to talk with them. It often seemed that those close to me didn't want me to talk about my losses and my grief, thinking it would be more helpful if I would turn my mind away from it. That made it even more difficult. The Wooleys had a need to hear more and to talk more, which met my needs, so it was very comforting.

Much of my grief was for my five children. I knew that each of them would have to find his or her own way through the healing process, just as I had. Eileen was now the busy mother of three children. Her first little girl arrived October 26, just a couple months after Stauffer passed away. Audrey was working while her husband was a student at Columbia Bible College. She found it extremely hard and wrote me several letters a week which were very comforting, both to her and to me as we searched scriptures in order to find consolation. Diane, also at college, wrote frequently and came home as often as she could. Her letters could make up a devotional book because of the comfort she found in the scriptures that she shared with me. Larry, being the only boy, had a very deep grief. I often found him apart from everyone else, crying. Even while we were still staying at Eileen's house, before we moved back to The Anchorage, I frequently found him in tears. One evening, after dark, I couldn't find him anywhere. He was nowhere around. I called him and he didn't answer. Fear gripped my heart because I didn't know whether he would simply run away in his despair and grief. I finally said, "Larry, if you hear me, please answer."

Eileen's house was a one-story ranch-style, and he was sitting on the roof under the big tree over the house, hidden by Spanish moss. He was reading a book, *The Return of Jesus Christ*, and weeping. He was taking comfort in the promise of Christ's return. He felt alone, being now the only male member of the family.

Susan was now eleven years old and she didn't want to talk about her grief. She simply walked away whenever the subject came up. I found out later that she pretended in school that her daddy was still living, since she was back on the grounds in the same place where she had grown up. She always played with the Wooley children until I came home from the Women's Division and called her for the evening meal. She often spent time in her old bedroom with the Wooley daughter, who was her age.

One evening, Susan came into the house sobbing. I hadn't heard her cry like that before. I asked her what was wrong and she said that Reverend Wooley had come in the back door and had walked through the hall and she had jumped on his back like she used to do to her dad. For a moment, she thought it was her dad. Then, she had the sudden realization she would never jump on her own dad's back again. This broke her and she cried uncontrollably for the first time.

After she quieted down and I got her talking, I learned that something else happened in school that day. One of her little friends said, "Your name is Moses. We used to listen to a Moses preacher on the radio, but he is dead now."

She said, "That was my dad."

He said "Oh, you're lying, that wasn't your dad."

She replied, "Yes, that was my dad and he is dead."

This was the first time that she verbalized Stauffer's death. She faced the reality of his death. Up to that time, she pretended that her father was still living and she avoided talking about her family. Being back at The Anchorage provided healing for all of us.

In November, as was customary, we had the annual reunion. The towns' people and the former residents of The Anchorage came out and had a morning celebration. Following this, there was dinner on the grounds and then a rally in the afternoon at which time the towns' people would come out for more celebration. This was the twelfth anniversary since The Anchorage had been formed. During the service, Judge Malone brought a eulogy in memory of Stauffer. In the eulogy, he said, "For ten years, I listened to Reverend Moses preach when I wanted to be inspired. I attended services at The Anchorage on Sunday nights and it was like going to Methodist camp meeting service with my mother when I was a little boy. One night, when Brother Moses gave the invitation for those to receive Christ, I saw sixteen men kneel at the altar."

Sowega Youth Home

I need to digress here for a moment. During the ten years that Stauffer and I were at The Anchorage, there were many times when I visited among the alcoholic women of Albany. I knew there were mothers who couldn't come and take advantage of the services at The Anchorage or who couldn't come for the eight-week period because of their young children. There were occasions when I told Judge Malone we needed some more of his buildings on the grounds so we could have an emergency temporary home with a housemother to take care of children while the mother received help at The Anchorage Women's Division. He thought it was a good idea and challenged the men of the Rotary Club to consider it as a project. Several men agreed there was a need but wanted the buildings to be off The Anchorage grounds.

As a result, interest was aroused among the people of the town and a temporary home was started for the children of alcoholic mothers. They occupied a vacant motel in Albany near Radium Springs, on the other side of the Flint River. Because it was my idea and the city picked up on it, Stauffer was given the privilege of being on the advisory board. In retrospect, I wonder why I wasn't given that privilege.... He was able to recommend a fine young Christian couple to be the first house parents of this new ministry called Southwest George Youth Home or "Sowega" Youth Home. Judge Malone was very pleased about this. One reason he quickly took up this project was because he saw children being removed from their families daily as a direct result of their mother's drinking problem.

Two years after my return to The Anchorage, I was approached by the president of the board of the Sowega Youth Home. They were losing their director and wondered if I would come and take his position. My first response was that it would be unethical. Albany was not a very large city. For twelve years I had been doing public relations for The Anchorage in soliciting contributions from the groups I spoke to. Now, to solicit funds for another para-church organization didn't seem ethical to me. I talked with Reverend Wooley about it and told him how I'd replied to the board. While he appreciated my response, he said that he supposed their contributors would probably be totally different from those who donated to The Anchorage. The latter were mostly people who either had an addiction problem in their family, had been helped themselves, or were people who were sensitive to the problem of addiction in adults. He believed this would be a totally different group from those who would contribute to a children's home such as Sowega Youth Home. He told me if there was no other reason for me not to take the position, he would stand behind me and be supportive of me in that endeavor. After much prayer with the Wooleys and with my own children, I decided by faith to take that next step.

The old motel where the Sowega Youth Home was located consisted of an office in one building with a dining room and a large recreation room. There was a wing on either side of this building, each with individual motel rooms. One wing was used for the girls and the other wing for the boys. In each of these tiny rooms, there was a bunk bed. There were two children in each room. It really wasn't a very satisfactory place to have a children's home. The buildings were old and we discovered that we were having problems with rat infestation. We started making plans to find other facilities into which to move the children. Nearby, there was a government Nike missile base that hadn't been in use for several years. The buildings were nice, typical of government construction, and there were two dorms as well as a dining room with adjacent kitchen facilities. Adding to the interesting landscaping was the missile silo, which was fenced around for safety. We, the board of directors, negotiated with the city and agreed on a price. I had live-in house parents and adequate staff to keep the ministry running smoothly. Fund-raising efforts to pay for the new facilities and to move the children were started immediately. I also had to do public relations work among the churches in order to furnish the building properly. Before long, enough contributions came in to buy the property and to move our children into the new facilities.

After we moved into the new facility, a very wealthy man in the city, who was not sympathetic with the work at The Anchorage but who liked what he saw going on at the Sowega Youth Home, came onto the board. He was immediately made president, contrary to my wishes. I feared from his reputation that his primary interest and concern was other than the children's welfare.

One day he came to see me and said, "Mrs. Moses, I really like your public image in Albany and how you present Sowega Youth Home as a missionary work. I have time to spend out here. I'm going to run the program while you do all the speaking and present it as a missionary effort."

I replied, "You are not going to exploit my public image. Whatever image I have, I have by the grace of God and through the many years of work at The

Anchorage. The board is paying _me_ to run the program and that is exactly what I am here to do."

The next morning, he appeared in my office and asked to see the file on each child. The Court had placed a boy with me who was abused by his alcoholic father and stepmother. Upon learning that the father was working, he told me he wanted me to take legal steps to have the father's salary garnisheed so we could claim board and room. Another day, he had all the little boys scrub their whole dorm. When they were finished, he told them to scrub everything again. He told the housemother the work was good for them.

I knew the power of this man in Albany, and also the power he exerted over the board. I called my home pastor in Pennsylvania and poured out my heart to him.

He said, "Elsie, you have been on your own for some time now since Stauffer's death. If you want to resign that position, come home, live in one of our missionary cottages, and just wait on the Lord until you have a new direction."

After praying and talking with the children, I sat down and I wrote a letter of resignation to the board of directors, sending a copy to everyone. One of the fine Christian men on the board came out to see me as soon as he received the letter. He sat in my office and said, "Mrs. Moses, I'm shocked, and I regret your decision. Did you think by sending each of us a letter that we would ask this gentleman to resign?"

I responded, "No, I didn't think that at all. You go over to my apartment and you'll see that I am almost packed and ready to move. This gentleman has been in Albany fourteen generations and I have been here only fourteen years."

He asked, "Do you have another place to go?"

I said, "No, I don't."

He continued his interrogation by asking, "How are you going to live?"

I asked him, "Sir, do you believe that when you die you are going to go to heaven?"

He said, "I certainly do."

And I said, "It takes more faith for me to believe that I am certain of heaven than for me to believe that God will take care of me and feed me and my children and provide for our daily needs."

He pulled out his checkbook and handed me a check for two hundred dollars. With tears rolling down his cheeks, he said, "God bless you, Mrs. Moses." As he left the office, I felt a load had been lifted from my heart. I knew once more that God was moving us on by faith. At this time, Diane was a senior in college, Larry was a college freshman, and Susan was in Junior High School.

Susan and I packed our suitcases and headed for Pennsylvania. My home church provided us with a lovely furnished two-bedroom house trailer that was near the church and just a mile from the dairy farm. Once again, as we'd done in Baltimore, I stored my furniture.

We had only been settled into our temporary quarters for several months when I received a letter from Eleida Homes in Asheville, NC, an orphanage. It was an invitation to come to Asheville to direct their maternity home, Faith Cottage.

Faith Cottage

After much prayer, I accepted their invitation. Susan and I moved to Asheville, to an altogether new ministry where God gave me another opportunity to work with women in crisis. These young women were mostly college age although some were in high school. They came from homes where the parents sought anonymity for their daughters during their confinement. Upon discovering they were pregnant, the girls would drop out of school and come to us while they were in the first trimester of their pregnancy. They remained till the babies were born, and then adopted them out before returning to school. The parents always brought the girls to us. A social worker was assigned to each woman and proper plans were made for their baby's adoption.

Most of these girls were from good homes and had been raised in church. For the most part, they had "gone steady" too long. Nevertheless, they were in crisis, and had brought shame to themselves and their families. They were very open to receiving the certain knowledge that God was a loving, forgiving, and compassionate God and that there was a future for them. It was a very fruitful ministry and very satisfying.

Diane completed college and joined us, taking a job as a teacher in the city school system. Susan was a freshman in a high school right near Faith Cottage. Larry attended technical college in Asheville. We lived in a very comfortable apartment in downtown Asheville.

Faith Cottage had a capacity for sixteen women. They went to a nearby hospital for the delivery and came back by ambulance several hours later to a building on the grounds where a registered nurse cared for them. As soon as they had convalesced and had signed the adoption papers, they returned to their own homes.

Faith Cottage was a beautiful Victorian house within walking distance of the famous Biltmore House. There were servant's quarters on the grounds where the nurse lived who cared for the girls when they came home from the hospital. In the main house, we had a woman who cooked all the meals and also stood in as housemother when needed. We had an examination room down in the nurse's quarters and a doctor who came in weekly to check on the girls.

One of my responsibilities as administrator was to plan the menu. Back then it was considered extremely important for them not to gain any weight and it was my responsibility to make sure that the cook had a menu made out by me that allowed the girls only 1,000 calories a day. The doctor came every Thursday. If a girl had gained no more than allowed that week, and if the doctor OK'd it, her reward was a special meal from Shoney's that evening. An incentive for them to be very careful about their diet was that most of them would soon return to their own communities and schools.

During this time, we had an opportunity to buy a house in West Asheville for just $1,800 down. We decided to do it since Larry was working part time and Diane was working full time. For the first time, we felt that we could put our roots down. Verses from scripture comforted me. One was Psalms 146:9 (NIV): "The LORD watches over the alien and sustains the fatherless and the widow..." A second was Isaiah 54:4-5(NIV):

> Do not be afraid; you will not suffer shame. Do not fear disgrace; you will not be humiliated. You will forget the shame of your youth and remember no more the reproach of your widowhood.
> For your Maker is your husband the LORD Almighty is his name the Holy One of Israel is your Redeemer; he is called the God of all the earth.

Yet another was Psalms 68:5(NIV) "A father to the fatherless, a defender of widows, is God in his holy dwelling."

Many times I claimed the promise that God was the father of my children and many times I saw him honor that promise.

A young widow once told me that God wanted to be my husband and showed me the verse where that is found in scripture. I remember at the time thinking that what I really wanted was a husband that could scratch my back. I just couldn't see where that promise was for me. However, during the time that we moved into our new home I had the feeling that everything was going to be all right. I loved Asheville and the surrounding mountains. Three of my children were at home with me and everything seemed to be fine, for just a little while.

Eleida Homes was a well-respected children's home begun many years ago as an orphanage. The budget was tremendous and the staff large. Many of the children came as infants and grew up there. The director had the responsibility for raising funds. Medical expenses were a big item in their budget.

Faith Cottage, a division of Eleida Homes, was also started in the early 1900's. That division was supposed to be self-supporting. The girls' families paid all their medical expenses.

Somehow the corporation faced a financial crisis; the girls' bills were not always credited to their personal accounts as they were supposed to be. As a result, our bills sometimes were not paid. We feared that our ministry would not be able to continue.

Another concern, shared by the doctor, was that the girls' anonymity was not always honored. Several of the girls were so concerned about this that the doctor asked me to take them into my own home. We fixed a few rooms up just for that purpose. The daylight basement made a nice area for these girls.

Diane was dating a young man who was in the Air Force and they talked about getting married. Larry had completed a year at Columbia Bible College and now he was going to the Tech School in Asheville. He had met a young lady and they were also talking about getting married. Because I believed that God would supply all my needs, and because I had no authority to insist that they consider me in their plans, I did nothing to discourage either of my children from making their wedding plans.

Diane was still teaching school and yet she was very sensitive about the needs of the family and very protective of her younger brother and sister. Our combined income was not much and that made her feel accountable for the home. I was increasingly concerned about how I was going to make it without her pay check, but my immediate concern at this time was how she could afford the small wedding she was planning at the church if she couldn't keep her check.

I remember falling on my knees by my bed one evening and crying out to the Lord on Diane's behalf saying, "Lord, you promised to supply our needs. Diane is taking the place of my husband here and supplying those needs and it's not fair to her."

As I cried out to the Lord, He very gently reminded me of the promise in Isaiah and that I was refusing to look to Him as my husband, provider, and protector, and that I expected this from Diane instead. Before I got up from my knees, I said "Lord, I'm going to trust you for my needs and I pray that she can keep her entire next months' paycheck and provide for her wedding."

Shortly after that night, I received a letter from the board of directors of the Atlanta Union Mission. I had received a letter from them a year earlier asking me to consider coming to Atlanta to start a Women's Mission. At that time, I turned it down because I couldn't see doing rescue mission work, especially for women, when we were so convinced that rehabilitation was the answer for the alcoholic. This letter stated that they had now purchased the property for the Women's Mission. It was a building that had been used previously for business and professional women and was now vacated. The board was definitely going to start something for women and wanted me to come to Atlanta to talk with them about it.

I took a trip to Atlanta and talked with the board. I told them my concerns about the need for rehabilitation instead of providing a revolving door type of experience for transients who only remained two or three days and were then back out on the street. The only way I would ever consider doing rescue mission work was if I could also keep women that indicated they wanted a time of rehabilitation. I went home from that interview really concerned again about definitely knowing God's will for our lives.

It occurred to me why I had purchased a home just one year before. Maybe this was the way God would block me from taking the wrong step. If I had been paying rent, it would have been a simple matter. Now, it was going to be quite complex. The children and I prayed about it. We had put some money into the house by making two extra bedrooms in the daylight basement and by purchasing a new refrigerator and other appliances.

I contacted the real estate man who sold the house to me. He looked through the house and said, "Well, Mrs. Moses, you have put a bathroom and two bedrooms on the ground floor. What you have here is a five-bedroom house with two and a half baths in an area of three-bedroom houses. If people want that large a house, they'll go to another section of town. No one would pay the amount you have to get out of this house. And you'd have to ask even more to cover my commission."

He was very pessimistic that I'd be able to sell the house. I thanked him and then called the local newspaper to place an ad that cost me $1.90. I advertised the location of the house and its size. A young woman came to see the house. I told her how much cash I'd need to cover the down payment and the cost of doubling the living space. She saw there was no room for negotiating since I couldn't move out unless I was debt-free. The house suited her needs perfectly. I also offered that she could assume the mortgage payments. She had received word several months earlier that her husband had been killed in action in Viet Nam. With her G.I. insurance money, she had exactly the amount she needed. This was precisely where she wanted to be, and she also wanted an area away from the main living area that she could rent out. She sat down right then and there and wrote me a check for the necessary amount. I was free to accept the call to Atlanta.

William Huck

William Huck was born in Appleby, England about 1890 and was raised in a mostly typical English family. Although they lived in town, they had a small farm with some acreage on the fringe of the small community. During the school year, Bill's job was to go over to the farm, milk their one cow, and then deliver the milk to various houses on his route back home. He probably carried the milk in a large bucket which he pulled in a wagon and measured out to the customers at their homes. This was his family responsibility every morning before going to school and again in the evening. He spent his summers as a shepherd boy north of Keswick near the border of Scotland in the beautiful Lake District of England.

The Anglican Church was the national Church of England, but was not where the Huck family worshiped. They were devout Methodists, and as such they were considered to be nonconformists. The young people in the Methodist churches were very zealous and weren't afraid to witness to their own faith in Christ. Bill made a confession of faith as a young teenager. He and a brigade of young people traveled from town to town by bicycle where they had outdoor evangelistic services on the village greens.

Bill entered the University of Manchester as a law student. His aspiration was to become a solicitor. By the time he graduated, he knew that God was calling him into the ministry. He changed his course of study and entered the seminary in Manchester. After his seminary training, he became pastor of several small Methodist churches in different parts of England. During this time, he began to correspond with a Congregational Church in Canada. Finally, he left for Canada by boat. En route, he met an Irish woman who became his first wife. They had two children. After several years in that cold climate, she expressed a dislike for the frigid temperatures and he started writing to the Presbytery in Atlanta, Georgia. Subsequently, he became the pastor of Atlanta's Rock Spring Presbyterian Church.

At that time in the history of Atlanta, the church was still on Rock Spring Road out in the country with dairy farms all around it. After Bill's arrival, the congregation soon outgrew their church building. His burden was to build a new church building in the Old English style with the help of the congregation. Construction only took place as funds came in so no debt was incurred.

Today, the church is no longer in the suburbs of Atlanta. With the tremendous growth of the city, it is now actually located in midtown. People from all over the area like to have their weddings in that chapel because of the quaint, beautiful, Anglican lines of the church. In 1990, my granddaughter, Laurie, was married there. The church is also a national historic landmark since it was built around 1918 in true Anglican style.

By the time the first sermon was preached there, the church had been paid for. However, it was not William Huck who preached that first sermon. He was no longer their pastor. Instead, he had been selected by the Presbytery to be their executive secretary. Among his responsibilities was placing young pastors in churches throughout the twenty-two surrounding counties. In many of these counties, there were not yet any existing Presbyterian churches.

Columbia Seminary, the Presbyterian college and seminary, is in Decatur, now a part of metropolitan Atlanta. During this time, Peter Marshall came from Scotland to be a student there. During his seminary days, Marshall spent his summers helping Bill conduct a camp for the youth of the area. The camp was open not only to Presbyterian youth, but to any young person who wanted to spend a week at camp. Peter Marshall had a talent for working with young people, and had a good voice for teaching them songs. Bill and Peter had some happy summers working together. Bill recognized Peter's potential as a gifted orator.

Before Marshall's graduation, Bill assigned him to two small churches in the rural area. Upon his graduation, Bill assigned Marshall to a large downtown church that was in need of a pastor.

One of his colleagues said, "Bill, of all the students, you assigned somebody that was born in Great Britain to that church. Don't you think you are showing partiality?"

Bill replied, "That's what America is all about. Young people are to be rewarded for their ability and not according to their social standing."

People swarmed to Peter Marshall's church. In the summer time, they even stood outside the windows to hear him preach. It was from this church in Atlanta that Marshall was selected by the Search Committee of the great Presbyterian church in Washington, D.C. From there, he was quickly assigned to the position of Chaplain of the United States Senate.

Bill was educated in England where social work was part of his college curriculum. He received training not only in the ministry, but also in all the social programs of the day. As a result, he was very sensitive to the social needs of Atlanta and the surrounding counties.

In 1937, President Franklin Roosevelt selected people to start welfare departments in various cities. Bill was selected as the person to begin and head the welfare department of Atlanta because of his knowledge and past experience in England with social programs there. He resigned from the Presbytery and became the first director of the Department of Family and Children's Services. There was no one that he could hire who had a degree in social work. He said that any qualified young person with a bachelor's degree in any field would be eligible to be considered for the position of social worker. Of course, Bill then had the task of providing them with any training they needed for the position. Bill also had responsibility for setting up the guidelines to determine which families qualified for assistance by the welfare department.

The welfare department was devised to meet the needs of children and their families. There were many men on the street who didn't qualify for assistance. Bill felt strongly that providing this assistance was not the responsibility of the government but of the churches. He believed the church should reach out to care for people who had lost their way because of addiction. He believed the greatest need of these people was to know Christ and to receive His life-changing power.

During his college days, Bill visited the great Rescue Mission in London, England. There, he had seen the churches at work, reaching out to the destitute, to the "winos" of the city. He visualized a similar undertaking for the city of Atlanta, and started talking to the pastors of the various churches about the need for a Rescue Mission. Ultimately, he resigned from the Department of Family and Children's Services and, in earnest, sought a place to start a Rescue Mission for homeless men. After organizing an interdenominational board of directors made up of pastors and business men, the Atlanta Union Rescue Mission was opened in 1942. The newly formed Board of Directors found an appropriate building. For the previous four years, it had been used as a hostel for men who were working in the city. They were challenged by faith to negotiate for its purchase from the widow who had operated it.

Bill was a gifted preacher and a man of faith. He assured his newly-formed Board that he would trust God for his salary as the first director of the Mission. He turned to the churches of Atlanta to support the Mission and lived on his savings. He sometimes paid the Mission's utility bills out of his own pocket. God wonderfully blessed his efforts. Before long, "Atlanta Union Mission" became a household word.

From the time we arrived in South Georgia in 1953, Stauffer and Bill became close friends. Stauffer called him often for his wisdom and to talk with him about problems in Albany. Bill and his wife later visited the Anchorage in Albany and saw the value of working with men on a rehabilitation basis. Bill, his wife, Stauffer, and I, attended national conventions of the International Union of Gospel Missions (IUGM) in different parts of the United States. There were other times that we were with them at District meetings because the Southeast District included the state of Georgia. When Stauffer and I moved into the Albany area, Bill was president of the Southeast District. During our ten years in Albany, Stauffer replaced him as president of the District. Stauffer held that position for several years.

I remember Stauffer saying one time, "It's been said that a man has five true friends in his lifetime. I count Bill as one of mine." In 1964, when Stauffer passed away in Dothan, Alabama, Bill and his wife were there for the funeral. Bill had a part in the funeral service.

In 1967, Gerry, Bill's wife, passed away. I went to Atlanta to attend her funeral.

Bill had already retired from the active work of Executive Director of the Atlanta Union Mission in 1962. However, he was on the executive committee of the board of directors. The current executive director, Reverend Strange, was chosen by the board of directors to succeed Bill. Bill's assistant, Harold Kelly, continued as Reverend Strange's assistant. Reverend Kelly and his wife had attended many of the conventions and knew Stauffer and me very well. Reverend Strange and his wife became our friends between 1962 and 1964 as well.

The Women's Mission

It was Kelly and Strange who recommended to the board of directors in 1969 that I be contacted about coming to Atlanta to start the Women's Mission. When the board told Bill about their recommendation, he said, "Well, I don't think she'll come to Atlanta. She seems settled in what she's doing in Asheville, and I really doubt think she'll come; but, you could contact her."

I want to establish that although Bill and I had a great respect and friendship for one another, he was not the one who initiated the call to me because he was no longer executive director of the Mission. However, he did say that he didn't know anyone that would be more qualified to start the Women's Mission than I would be.

At that time, the only qualification I had to start a Women's Mission was a lot of practical experience. I'd had no formal education whatsoever in this field. However, in those days, there wasn't much of this sort of formal education available anyway. No one, to their knowledge, had the experience that I'd had. The board of directors told me that if I knew of any Women's Missions anywhere in the United States, they'd send me there to help me develop guidelines for the newly-organized Women's Mission in Atlanta. Despite all the conventions I'd attended, I'd never heard of any other Women's Missions. I called the National Headquarters and they informed me there were no Women's Missions in the IUGM. Once again, I was at the point of launching out and pioneering, just as Stauffer and I had done with the rehabilitation centers in Albany and Dothan and as I had done with the Sowega Youth Home. Once again, I faced the challenge of just trusting the Lord and finding out what He wanted me to do to meet the needs of the destitute women in Atlanta.

I was at a place in my life where I really didn't want to live in the Mission itself. Stauffer and I had raised our family on the Anchorage grounds. I had lived on the grounds of every place where I had worked except for the brief time in Asheville. Thus, before I accepted the position in Atlanta, I requested that I be allowed to live off the grounds. I had done so in Asheville, and it seemed so much more effective.

The board, however, requested that I move into one area of the Mission for a year to get the project off the ground. After that, I could find a place away from the Mission and move out on my own.

The building had about thirty rooms. I was given the opportunity to select any area I wanted to place my furniture and set up a functional apartment. Susan and I chose space on the second floor where we had a pleasant living room, a dining room, a kitchen, two bedrooms, and a bath. Our living room was in the front of the building and had a nice porch outside that overlooked the city.

During the busy days of packing and moving to Atlanta, the board informed me that we couldn't open the Mission right away. The city's building inspectors had been in and had decided that new fire escapes were needed and several other changes were required. It might be several months until we could open. This gave Susan and me an opportunity to take a trip. We visited Diane, who was then living in Mississippi, and Audrey, who was living in Texas.

Upon returning to Atlanta, we unpacked and got settled in our apartment. We watched the renovations with great anticipation. The workers labored in different parts of the building making the necessary upgrades so we could open as a Rescue Mission for women.

I remember sitting on the front porch on the second floor outside my living room and looking over the city with all its lights. The excitement of being a missionary in the big city welled up inside me. I just sat and wondered how great the need of the city might be. I knew that I would have beds for thirty-five women but I wondered if the need was that great. Would we really need that many beds?

During the time before we opened, Reverend Kelly and I visited the social service departments of the hospitals and of the different agencies. I remember how warmly they welcomed him because of the outstanding work the Men's Mission had done all those years. They were all glad to learn there would finally be a place where they could refer homeless women.

The longer I waited to open the Women's Mission, the more excited I became. I saw the great work that had been done in Atlanta by The Atlanta Union Mission, not only for Christ in a spiritual way, but also in a physical and emotional way in meeting the social needs of the men. In those days, it was rare for the founders of the Rescue Missions around the country to have rapport with the social agencies. The cooperative spirit I observed here was just very heartwarming to me. It was undoubtedly a result of the foundation laid by Bill years before with Social Services. I felt proud to have been given the privilege of starting a Women's Mission in a city with that kind of background. My married children were a little apprehensive about Susan and me moving alone into the big city. I remember them saying, "Well, there is one thing that we are glad of. We are glad that you will be in the same city with the Kelly's and with the Strange's and especially with Bill Huck. Since you already know them so well, we feel like you already have friends as you start out."

Whenever my children came to town for a weekend and we wanted to go to a park or do anything as a family, they always wanted to invite Bill. His son lived in Florida and his daughter in California so he had no family locally. He quickly adopted our family as his own.

Bill offered to help me in any way he could in setting up the office once we opened the Mission. He was a great Atlanta Braves fan and sometimes got tickets to the Braves' games and invited Susan and me to go with him. Susan turned sixteen that summer, right before the grand opening of the Women's Mission. So far we were pretty much alone in the city and Bill took Susan and me out for her birthday supper.

Susan and I spent our Sunday afternoons on the quiet streets of downtown Atlanta where I taught her to drive. That's about the only time those streets were quiet. Once she turned sixteen, she was anxious to get her license. As a result, we became well acquainted with the streets in the area around the Mission. In September, she started her junior year at Grady High School.

It was in the early fall of 1969 that we finally announced the opening of the Women's Mission. Before we officially took people in, the Board planned an open house. The news media showed up with their television cameras. This was big news for the city of Atlanta. In 1969 there was literally nothing being done anywhere for homeless women who required a place designed specifically to meet their special needs. I want to qualify that by saying that although there were Christian organizations scattered throughout the country for unwed mothers and for women with addiction problems, to my knowledge there were no Rescue Missions like the one we were setting up. There were several hundred men's Rescue Missions in the U.S., but no place where a woman could come in off the street or where a police officer could bring her, or where she could just wander in, and she'd be accepted and questions asked only after she was already admitted.

The Women at The Mission

I had no idea what the problems of the homeless women of Atlanta would be and it was a certainty that the church people who were asked to support us and get behind our efforts wouldn't know either. This would prove to be a learning experience for me. Then, it would be up to me to educate the church people about the kind of women who were in need of our services and to encourage them to be sympathetic and supportive. The general feeling seemed to be that any woman who was a good woman couldn't possibly be destitute. "Destitute" was considered to be synonymous with "delinquent." We found out quickly that this was not the case.

Initially, I believed that we could meet the needs of all destitute women. However, upon opening, I had a visitor from the city social service department.

She asked, "Mrs. Moses, what kind of women are you going to take?"

I replied, "Well, any woman that is destitute is welcome here."

She asked, "What about women with children?"

I responded, "Especially women with children."

She requested to see the building and I proudly showed it to her. She said, "I'm sorry to tell you this, but you are just not equipped to have women with children. You're going to have to take only women without children."

After she left, I sat stunned and disappointed. Surely, I thought, we would never fill all thirty-five beds with destitute women. I wondered what I was even doing in Atlanta if I couldn't take women with children. Would I have accepted the challenge to come if I'd known we'd turn women with children away?

However, within just a short time, all thirty-five beds were filled with women in need of our services. Very few of them had an addiction problem. Those that did were generally sent to us from the local jail where they had just served fifteen to thirty days. Instead of being returned to the street, they were referred to us by the warden, who I learned was a Christian. She had become acquainted with us during our opening days and said it was good to have a place to send women that she knew wanted to change their lives. She sent them directly to me.

However, these women didn't make up most of our population. I remember that at one time we had nine young women who were pregnant. I was really excited about this aspect of our ministry because I had left the home in Asheville where parents had lovingly brought their pregnant daughters to us and had then seen them through a difficult time in their lives. I now faced young women who really were throwaways. They were thrown out of their homes because they found themselves pregnant. Their family didn't stand by them. As a result, they were literally out on the street. The social workers were delighted to have a place that would receive these women. We quickly learned how valuable the welfare department was to us and how valuable we were to them. They brought the women to us. They also made plans that if the young women wanted to keep their babies they were given priority in the housing projects after the babies were born in the local city hospital.

We started having women sent to us by the Social Service department of Grady Hospital, the city hospital. These women had been ill and in the hospital for so long that they had lost their jobs and so couldn't go back to work; as a result, they were now homeless and had to go on welfare. These women didn't know which way to turn and were destitute through no fault of their own. We could keep them until they found something more substantial.

I quickly found out that Grady Hospital was a tremendous asset to the Women's Mission, as it had been to the Men's Mission for all those years. Grady Hospital is huge and has many clinics in it. Each clinic has its own Social Service department. They were not only sympathetic to the Mission and its function; they also needed the Mission desperately for women that didn't have homes to go back to. The social workers in many of the departments used the Mission. We probably got more women from the hospital than from any other agency. These weren't women who were convalescing and in need of medical care. They were homeless and yet were ready to get back into the main stream of life.

We also had women who were abandoned or battered. We had women who were vulnerable out there in the street. I quickly learned that there were many women who feared being on the streets so much that they would move in with anyone who offered them a home. This was especially true of the women with an alcohol problem. Alcohol was their problem and not prostitution. They would accept the offer of being a housemate to one man rather than be vulnerable to many men on the street.

When an Atlanta woman had an alcohol problem, there was no place for her to go to sober up. The Atlanta Union Mission had a detox area where a man could be cared for. A woman had no place to detox other than the city jail and that was without proper medical supervision. In those days, drinking in public was a misdemeanor. Those arrested were put in the city jail to await "drunk court" the next morning. Because of the strict laws, the weekend arrests resulted in several hundred appearing before judges on a Monday morning. The jail was always over-crowded and it was often an explosive environment. The sentences handed down were usually for fifteen to thirty days or more to be served at the Prison Farm on the edge of the city. At the Farm, the women prepared the food that was raised there by the men. The long days in the kitchen and on other work details provided a period of time where the women felt safe from the streets of Atlanta.

Many women told me that upon release from the Farm they would take a drink so there was alcohol on their breath and then deliberately stagger while walking down the street in order to be sentenced back to the Farm. There, they were assured of a bed, food, and safety from the streets. As a result, many of the women counted the wardens and the people in jail as their friends. It was a really strange situation. It was a setting that was very ripe for a place like the Women's Mission, where women could feel the safety of being out in freedom and yet feel safe and not vulnerable to perpetrators.

There was so much to learn about women in crisis. I was used to seeing men in a homeless situation. They sought out a Mission or something similar designed for men. In every city, large or small, there were places like the Salvation Army or Rescue Missions for men. Women, when they became destitute, could only go to a church, a hospital, or a social agency for help. While men simply wandered into Men's Missions, invariably our women came to us through either a church or a social agency, simply because they didn't know that there was a place available like the Mission. Often, that is still the case. Women tend to reach out for help to other people, to agencies, to churches, rather than wander blindly into a Mission.

Naturally, the destitute women, or the women in crisis who were candidates for a Rescue Mission, had used up their families. Either they had no relatives, or the relatives weren't sympathetic with their plight. These women were just like the young women who were ordered out of their homes because they were pregnant. These were the days before "the pill" and before legal abortions. This was in the days before young women felt it was not a dishonor to have a child out of wedlock. So, with great shame, they would try to find help somewhere, and be sent to us.

Within months, I had many speaking engagements in Atlanta. This was 1969. The Men's Mission was started in 1942 and already had twenty-seven years of credibility and a good standing in the city. We were a new ministry to a population usually looked down upon. The first Christmas I was director, the Mission had only been in operation for a few months. I was asked to be the guest speaker at a large women's club in Decatur before several hundred guests at their Christmas banquet. Not only did they ask me to be a guest speaker, they also invited Bill. He was sitting at another table and was introduced in the opening remarks as the founder of the Rescue Mission. I had prepared what I wanted to say to them and my main remarks concerned the plight of destitute women. When I began speaking, I was really intimidated by his presence. He was quite a great orator and I didn't know how I was going to get through this with him in the audience. I usually did really well when I was just speaking to a large group of church women. However, having a mixed audience at a Christmas function, and especially having Bill there, I was quite unsettled and nervous. I was so caught up with the new ministry and with the sad stories of the thirty-five women who occupied the thirty-five beds, that I quickly put aside my written remarks about the plight of the destitute women in favor of describing some of the human interest stories and the desperate need of these women for the Mission that was already functioning at full capacity. I got so caught up in what I was saying that I turned to Bill and asked, "Why in the world didn't you start a Women's Mission first?" Everybody broke out in laughter and Bill laughed harder than anyone. After that, speaking to groups was much easier because I saw how eager the Atlanta people were to get behind anything that Bill felt was needed.

Yet, I sensed their confusion about the need, and the kind of women that we would be reaching. Whenever I opened my talk up to questions in a mixed group, invariably, there would be a gentleman in the audience that would inquire rather cynically "How many prostitutes do you have in the Mission?"

Of course, I quickly learned to reply that prostitutes didn't need a Mission. They already had plenty of places to sleep in the city. It was the people who were victims of addiction or other hardships that needed a place to stay.

While I meant that women who were prostitutes didn't need a bed with us, I also recognized that homeless and helpless women did prostitute themselves by moving in with one man rather than being vulnerable on the street. This is the plight of women who come to the end of their road and have nowhere to go. Eventually, without options like a Christian rehabilitation center or an emergency shelter, their situation becomes hopeless. The driving conviction that God placed in my heart was their need for hope in Him. First, though, we had to meet their basic needs for survival.

Because I was pioneering, I didn't have many rules, except ones that were obviously needed for women to be able to live together. Of course, rules were made as we saw a need for them.

The board agreed that women who were eager for rehabilitation could stay as long as necessary. I didn't have to limit a woman's stay to just two or three days as typical men's Rescue Mission would. It was natural, too, that there were many women who would want to stay indefinitely. There were always enough women leaving that I had room for the transient women who were only there a day or two.

Susan and I lived in the first apartment on the second floor at the top of the stairway. The women who lived in the other areas of the second floor had to pass our door. This arrangement was not new to me. Back in Savannah, sixteen years before, we'd had the same set-up.

I was facing this alone with my one daughter, trying to make my way as a single mother raising a daughter right in the Mission. When Susan came home from school, she rolled up her sleeves and did whatever there was to do, just as she had at the Sowega Youth Home and at Faith Cottage.

Bill came in several mornings a week to help with the office work. I used residents who were qualified to help with cooking or in any other area of need. I had to figure out what kind of staff I needed. Naturally, I had to depend on church volunteers at the start. As time went on, those residents who were able were glad to help in any way that they could. The church women brought in clothes that were sorted and then given out to those in need. We used volunteers and residents for that as well.

When Susan and I moved to Atlanta, we decided to visit several churches to find a new church home for ourselves. One of the first churches we attended was North Avenue Presbyterian Church. The Adult Sunday School class was taught by Roy Revere, who was teaching the Book of John verse by verse. Susan enjoyed the young people so we settled there and joined that church.

In November, when the Mission had been open just a little while, I got a telephone call from the assistant pastor of North Avenue Church. He said, "I have a young runaway girl sitting in my office." He told me her name and he said, "But she also admitted to me upon further inquiry that's not her real name and that she's not yet eighteen. She refuses to give me any more information. If you have room for her, I'll send her over in a taxi."

When I opened the front door to greet her, I saw a beautiful, tall, slender, young woman wearing granny glasses. I invited her into my office where she sat across the desk from me. I asked her name, but because I didn't want her to be untruthful to me, I handed her the registration card and asked her to fill it out. She wrote her name down and I saw she was painstakingly writing backhand in order to conceal her handwriting. She put her age as eighteen. Under marital status, she put "none."

I looked at the card and asked, "Is that all the information you want to give me?"

She replied, "Yes."

I said, "I'll let you stay on the condition that you call your parents and tell them you're safe. My son and his wife will take you to his place of business where there's a WATTS line."

She said she would. Larry and Sheila took her and witnessed that she obeyed my request. She moved into the Mission and Susan became her friend. I saw that she must come from a fine family. I recognized also that she was used to home life and I allowed Susan to bring her into our apartment so that we could be closer to her.

Our first Christmas was approaching and the church people brought in many wrapped Christmas gifts. Because of earlier experiences, I recognized the need to unwrap them to see what they were. This was to make sure that the gifts weren't used clothing or something else that we would not want to give as a Christian present. It was then necessary to re-wrap them and put the recipient's names on them. The three of us, this young lady, Susan, and I, sat in the middle of the living room floor with gifts and wrapping paper all around us. They were laughing and talking as teenagers will. I was half concentrating on the work I was doing, but also half listening to their conversation.

I heard Susan say, "Well, I'm a PK and that doesn't mean privileged character either. That means I'm a preacher's kid."

Her new friend said, "Well, I'm a preacher's kid, too."

Susan jumped to her feet with her hands on her hips saying, "I don't believe you, that you're a preacher's kid. You have your father worried sick about you. I wish I had a father. I wouldn't run away from him."

To this, the other young woman jumped to her full height, placed her hands on her hips, and said, "Don't get so uptight, Susan. I don't think my father's congregation blames me one bit for running away."

Now I had a clue from what part of the country she probably came. The only information I could glean from her was that her father drove a large tractor trailer truck. By her accent, I recognized that she probably came from Pennsylvania, from the state that we came from. Therefore, I decided that this young woman must be Mennonite.

I said to Susan later, "I believe she comes from somewhere between Philadelphia and Harrisburg."

When Susan told her that, she replied, "Your mother scares me."

These were the days that the hippies had a strong presence in the city. The area between 10th and 14th streets was crowded with hippies spaced out on drugs; many were on LSD. I recognized that this young woman could have easily walked on down the street rather than going into North Avenue Church for help when she got off the train. Instead of going into the church, if she had just walked down the street for several more minutes, she would have been right in the midst of the hippie area.

We didn't have many hippies coming to the Mission. While we were starting the Women's Mission, the Salvation Army was starting the Girl's Lodge. The Girl's Lodge was designed to reach out to runaway girls. We quickly learned to work together. In the providence of God, two Christian ministries were started for women in Atlanta, the Salvation Army Girl's Lodge for runaway girls, and the Women's Mission for the homeless women. Both kinds of needs were being met simultaneously.

A traditional Men's Mission has chapel services every night of the week. The men who come in are required to attend the chapel service, after which they are assigned their beds. I only had the traditional Rescue Missions for men as a guideline for a Women's Mission. Yet, I knew that the needs were quite different.

In a traditional Men's Mission, in the morning after breakfast, the men are required to leave and look for work and just clear out of the building. They return at night if they still need to come back for a bed. They attend a chapel service and get their bed assignment. The same cycle is repeated day after day.

It was much different in our Women's Mission. There was no way I could ask these women, especially those who were pregnant, to leave every morning. I just couldn't say "Get out of the building at 7:00, or 7:30, or after breakfast, or whenever, and come back tonight if you need to."

It was also difficult to invite church groups in every night for services. At that time, we didn't even have a designated space for a chapel. Instead, folding chairs were set up in a larger room behind the kitchen on the first floor. All that we had in this room were the folding chairs and a little lectern.

However, every morning after breakfast, I gathered the women in that room for a chapel service. Once a week, Bill came in and gave the chapel service. Otherwise, any morning that we didn't have a guest speaker, it was up to me. Many weeks, I had the chapel service five and six times. This included the Sunday School hour. Chapel attendance was not required in the evenings unless there was a special group coming in. If a group volunteered to come, we made it a special occasion for evening chapel.

About a month before Christmas, I gave each woman a Bible and asked them to follow along while I read the Christmas story starting with the first chapter of Luke. Instead of me reading to them, I had them all read the Christmas story with me. By the time Christmas day rolled around, we were reading every morning for about twenty minutes and then singing for another ten minutes. I taught them many choruses from some old, used hymnals that were donated to us. We worshiped every morning for half an hour and saw increasing enthusiasm on the part of the participants.

After Christmas, whenever we didn't have a guest speaker, we continued reading through the New Testament. We started with Matthew and then went on to Mark. Because we had already read Luke, we went right on to John and then all the rest of the way through the entire New Testament. At the end of the New Testament, we started reading the Psalms and then Proverbs. After that we read the Book of Ruth and then the Book of Esther.

One day, I said to Bill, "I hesitate to read Genesis, Exodus, and Leviticus."

He asked, "Why?"

I replied, "Well, because...like Noah getting drunk and all the weaknesses of the men of faith, they might not understand it."

He said, "It is all the word of God."

So, we started with Genesis. If my memory serves me right, I think we read through the remainder of the Bible at that point. Bill came in every Thursday morning and had a time of devotions and Bible study with them. They were always glad to see him. When he came, they didn't have to sit in the chapel and read and sing. He was an orator. He made the Bible come alive and made it something very applicable to them. They really learned to love him.

Surgery and Cancer Scare

During our first year in Atlanta, Bill increasingly became a part of our family. When the married children came into town, he was usually involved with the family activities. I remember at one point, Diane asked, "Mother, if Bill ever asked you to marry him, would you do it?"

I said, "What makes you ask me that?"

She said, "Well, I catch him looking at you sometimes like I remember dad looking at you."

I didn't admit to her that Bill had already made the suggestion to me. I knew he would not mention it again because he didn't want it to affect our friendship and was afraid I would push him away. During this time, perhaps Susan noticed the same thing, because I saw her becoming more distant and cool to him.

Starting with the last year in Asheville, I had increasing physical problems surrounding menopause. Here in Atlanta, I was now in my late forties. My doctor decided I should have a D&C. This was just supposed to have been a simple procedure. Diane came from Mississippi the weekend that I went into the hospital.

After the procedure, the doctor came into my room and told me, "Mrs. Moses, I must tell you that you have cancer of the uterus."

I asked him if it could be terminal. He acknowledged that it could be, and said that we would discuss it when he knew more and could select an appropriate course of treatment.

The next day, I was ready for discharge. Not only did Diane come for me, but Larry and Susan as well. They were going to take me out for breakfast on our way home. Since it had not been a major surgery, I was a little perplexed about their attentiveness. They acted very upbeat and very attentive to me and they carried on a good bit. I thought to myself, "This is going to be terrible when they find out, because this has been a fear of theirs. They lost their father and they have a real fear of losing me."

Two days later, I was to call the doctor right after lunch. I'd been working in the office all morning, although I should have taken a few days off. Bill came in and was helping in the office. About one o'clock, he said, "I think you have a telephone call to make."

I wondered how he knew, but I went into the next office and I made the call. The doctor said, "I have good news for you; you don't have cancer after all."

When I told Bill what I had gone through and what the doctor said, he told me to go right back into the office and call Diane. The doctor had told the children that I had cancer. Before she left for Mississippi, Diane had gone to see Bill. She was brokenhearted and didn't want to leave. Bill told her that he would have me call her immediately when I learned something.

Marriage to Bill Huck—and The Mission

Susan's whole attitude toward Bill changed. One day she said, "Mother, Dr. Huck is so good to us and he treats us like dad would if he were here."

With Susan's attitude being one of acceptance of him, I started feeling that I had refused to have any serious relationship with him because of the difference in our ages; yet, he could live another ten or fifteen years. For a while, I'd feared I only had six more months to live, if I'd actually had cancer. I began to have an open mind to thinking that if it was God's will for us to establish a home together, for however long, that I would be open to prayerfully consider it.

In May of that same year, we were married in the beautiful chapel at Callaway Gardens. It was a morning service and all my children and grandchildren were there. It was followed by a big breakfast in the hotel dining room. Then we left for Panama City for a few days' honeymoon.

Only a year had gone by since I had moved to Atlanta. Instead of moving out of the Mission to find a home as a single mother with Susan, we moved into Bill's home. He had made the upstairs into an apartment for college students some years earlier. Susan and Romaine, her friend from the Mission, both now in college, moved into that upstairs apartment. The house was located across the street from a lovely park. This home was to be a happy setting for the next five years. The children once again had a home place, a father to come home to, and a place where the married children could come and visit. They could take their babies across the park to the swings and we could sit on the front porch and watch them. Bill loved the children. As the grandchildren came along, the little ones often passed me as they ran into his arms. He loved to sit on the front porch and rock the babies. During the next few years, all four married children each had a baby. We were a busy household. Because Bill so wholeheartedly accepted my children as his, and loved the grandchildren, I would have been content at this time to be a homemaker and mother.

However, knowing the importance of the women's ministry, and being married to the founder of the Rescue Mission, we both acknowledged the wisdom of me remaining active in the Women's Mission. I teased him that he was vicariously back into mission work himself by me continuing as the director of the Women's Mission.

I discussed most Mission matters with him but he was careful not to make any decisions for me. I'd reach a decision but not tell him what it was. Then, I'd ask him how he felt about the different possibilities and he would arrive at the same conclusion. It was truly interesting how often we arrived at the same decision. I suppose I reached my conclusions through my emotions and my gut feelings as a woman working with other women. He had a compassionate heart, but reached his decisions through logic.

It was exciting to again have a husband that prayed with me and that I looked up to and that had the same heart for mission work that I did. Bill was in good health when I married him and he enjoyed traveling. Despite being older, he still drove his own car and he continued to come and speak to the women once a week. He also went to the Men's Mission to preach. Every Christmas and Thanksgiving, he conducted services at the Men's Mission from morning until late in the afternoon, one service after another. The men filed into the chapel for a celebration service, and then were served a big holiday meal.

We looked forward to traveling together. Immediately after our marriage, he started making arrangements to go to England by boat so I could meet his family. We planned to sail the following June, 1971 on the Queen Elizabeth II and enjoy a month's vacation in England.

It was two months before we were to sail that it had become necessary for me to go into the hospital for a total hysterectomy. I told the surgeon about our plans to sail to England. He noted that we were to leave exactly six weeks from the day of the surgery. If it had been any less, he wouldn't have let me go.

I really looked forward to that time with Bill. The first week was to be on board the Queen Elizabeth, followed by the leisure, pleasure, and excitement of a month in England. Our itinerary called for the ship to dock at the end of the fifth day at a French port where passengers traveling to France were to disembark. Then, that night, the ship was to sail across the English Channel and put into port in England. We were to be in Southampton, England, the next morning. From there we'd spend time with his three sisters and with his nieces and nephews, then spend a week at Keswick in the Lake District, and from there go to Appleby where he was born.

The day that we were to arrive in France, we were on the deck sunning when Bill became quite ill. I helped him to our stateroom and called the doctor. Although the doctor said it was only indigestion, deep inside me I knew that he'd had a heart attack. When we got off the ship, his sister, Maud, was there to greet us. We were to go by train to London where she had the evening and the following day planned for us to go to theater, dinners, and many other places. I told her my fears. Although it was the first time I had met her, she said I was being foolish, that the doctor would certainly know what he was talking about. However, by the time our train arrived in London, Bill was so ill he just had to go to bed. We forfeited our tickets to the theater and his sister and I walked through a lovely park, seeing the beautiful roses. All the time, I didn't know if my husband would be alive when I got back to the hotel.

The next day, we again boarded the train and traveled all the way to Doncaster in central England. When we got off the train, his nephew was there to greet us. We were to stay with him for a week. The elevator that would take us up to the street level was out of order and Bill had to go up a long flight of stairs. By the time we got to the nephew's house, his wife had afternoon tea ready. I shared my concerns with them. It was evident that Bill was very ill. He sat there and tried to eat, but couldn't. He kept repeating himself. His nephew quickly called the doctor who diagnosed that Bill had indeed suffered a heart attack. He was immediately put to bed. Because of England's system of socialized medicine, the doctor wanted Bill to stay quietly in bed at home and not see any members of the family for two weeks. The Chief of Cardiology of the Royal Hospital in Doncaster came to the house with all his equipment and did an EKG and other tests and found out there was indeed damage to the heart. He wouldn't allow us to travel for six weeks. As a result, we couldn't follow our itinerary. I was in contact with my family and with his son and settled down for a six-week stay in England, learning much about the country and about the family into which I had married. My taking care of him at the house during the early part of his illness was frightening to the doctor. He said that any woman who had a hysterectomy in England had to be quite immobile for three months instead of six weeks. I found that the doctors were as much concerned about me as they were about him.

During our stay in England, against our wishes and disobedient to what we wanted, Romaine, our "adopted daughter," took Bill's car and totaled it in an accident. She wasn't injured. However, he was brokenhearted because he was proud of his car and had wanted to continue driving, believing that he was still a good driver.

At the end of the six weeks, at the doctor's orders, we changed our flight from tourist to first class and returned home. At the airport to greet us when we returned to Atlanta were my children to take me to my doctor, and his son to take him to his doctor. We were both fine, and we settled down to life once again.

Bill's son felt that it might be a good time for his dad to quit driving. He was concerned about his father driving in the busy traffic of Atlanta. Therefore, I, or one of my children, drove him wherever he wanted to go. This meant that wherever he went, whether it was to visit his friends, get a hair cut, or whatever he wanted to do, he was now limited. Having Diane at home, and with her being so attentive to his needs, there were many times that they and Laurie would go on his errands late in the morning and have lunch before they returned home.

Bill lived almost five years from the time of our marriage in May 1970; he went home to be with the Lord in January 1975. During that time, our Christmases were family events. Family members came home and we had a big Christmas tree in the living room and enjoyed large family dinners. Any families that were in town came over for Sunday dinner. The time after church was always a happy time, gathering the families together and seeing the children and the young mothers play in the park. Diane and her husband and Laurie were still living in Mississippi and came home frequently during that time. Audrey was living in Texas and had two little ones, Audra and Tommy. Eileen was living in Florida and by this time she had four children, the youngest one born just two weeks before Bill and I were married. She was at our wedding with a two-week old baby. Larry lived in Atlanta and had one little fellow, Michael. Susan had completed a year of junior college and had started at Taylor College in Indiana. Bill's grandchildren frequently came for several days, as did his son from Florida and his daughter from California. On one or two occasions, we went to Florida to visit his son. Sometimes we took a vacation in Panama City while his son came up from Tampa to visit us.

Every May, we went to the International Convention for Rescue Missions in whatever city it was held. As a result, we did a good bit of traveling. He saw many of his dreams realized that he couldn't have fulfilled before we were married.

Two years after we were married, in 1972, he was diagnosed with lymphoma. The doctor told us that it was going to be an illness that would develop slowly because of his advanced age. He said that he would watch it closely and only put him on medication should it become indicated. After this news, we went to a convention in Pennsylvania by car and spent a week there. He had the Sunday morning service at the First Presbyterian Church of Lebanon, PA. After that, we went to the area where my family lived to visit them. My mother-in-law, Grandma Moses, graciously invited us to stay with them for a few days, which we did.

While we were there, Bill took violently ill. We were taken to the airport the next morning to fly him to Atlanta for hospitalization at Piedmont Hospital. Larry flew up to Pennsylvania, picked our car up at the airport, and drove it back to Atlanta. His illness was a mystery. We sent for his son because the doctors gave him little hope. I stayed in his room day and night sitting by his bed. His son came up and kept vigil when I couldn't. I remember Bill saying once, "I guess it's my time because I'm an old man."

This made me angry and I said, "I know men that are ten years older than you that are still healthy and alive."

He said, "You're right," and from this point, I could actually see him start to fight. The doctors finally figured out he was suffering from toxicity to his medications. They discontinued the things that were poisoning him. He began improving and we had three more good years together.

At this time, Diane's husband was given an early discharge from the Air Force. They moved their furniture from Mississippi to the upstairs apartment where Susan and Romaine had lived before they went away to college. This started a happy relationship between Diane, her husband, Laurie, and Bill. When I came home from work, I often found him on the front porch with Laurie, singing to her, and being a good grandpa to her. Every noon, Diane fixed lunch for Bill, although he enjoyed cooking for himself when he was feeling well. He enjoyed being pampered by a young daughter once again.

During the day, Bill kept busy writing letters and reading. He was writing a book, *The Building of the Church*, which was all about construction of the Rock Spring Presbyterian Church and how they built only when they had the money and how he raised the funds to do it that way. Diane helped him put his writings together so that they could finally become part of the official records of the church.

I came home from the Mission during the late afternoon and was able to have dinner with Bill and spend the evening with him. This freed Diane up to have the evening with her family. During the evening hours, we had much to talk about. Bill wanted to hear about everything that was going on at the Women's Mission. I had someone I could brainstorm with. He shared his dreams for the Women's Mission with me, and I shared my burden and my dreams with him. God had been so good in giving me another husband who had a heart for God and for destitute women who were reaching out for help. I had been a widow for six years and now felt like I was a whole person again. I didn't compare him to Stauffer, but at the same time, both had some of the same qualities and certainly the same concerns for their fellow-man. I know that often, my children, including Susan who was single, went to him with their problems before they came to me. They enjoyed having a home again and having a mother and father, so their lives could get back to what should be normal for a family, to have parents and grandparents to visit.

Bill was a co-teacher in the men's Bible class at Central Presbyterian Church. I became co-teacher of the women's Bible class there. Although I became a member of North Avenue Presbyterian Church, we alternated going to his church and to mine after Sunday School. He never asked me to change my membership over to his church. He felt that my church was meeting Susan's needs. Because of his age, he wanted to see me established in the church that I had chosen when I came to Atlanta and which my children were used to visiting when they came home.

Bill was not very fond of vegetables. Before we were married, his doctor talked to him about his diet and the fact that his blood pressure was so low. He told him that he just had to eat more healthy foods. After we were married, he no longer seemed to have a blood pressure problem. Bill still didn't like vegetables but I always fixed them anyway. One evening, as I fixed dinner, he said, "I don't need any vegetables tonight. I had my vegetable at noon with Diane."

I said, "You did? What did you have?"

He said, "Carrots. I had a piece of carrot cake."

Our house was located on East Park Lane in the Ansley Park area and had beautiful, authentic, English gardens in the back yard. His gardens were on seven different levels because the lot was on a hill. Each level was faced with rocks that weren't bonded but fit precisely together as you see them in England. On each level was a different type of garden. He promised me a rose garden, and planted it for me on one level when we were married. Many hours were spent out in his garden pulling weeds by hand. As his health deteriorated and he became weaker, it must have been an unspoken frustration for him to see the weeds, and to see folks including Diane and Laurie and men from the Mission trying to weed the garden for him when they didn't know the difference between the weeds and the flowers!

Many years after Bill's death, I was sometimes asked why I spoke so often of my twenty-four years with Stauffer, and seldom talked about those five years with Bill. It seemed like I was a widow for a very long time and my marriage to Bill was like a five-year oasis. That sounds somewhat symbolic, but there were five years of relief, knowing that I had a provider and protector and someone who shared my joys and my sorrows with me.

Of course, when I lost Bill, I was alone again. I still had children with the problems that their own growing families brought. Because Stauffer was their father, my mind more often went naturally to him. I wished that he knew what was happening so he could share the joys and sorrows I experienced with our children.

Susan was married two months before Bill passed away. He wasn't well enough to perform the wedding ceremony, but he did agree to stand up and give her away. He was told he didn't even have to stand up but that he could just remain seated and say "Her mother and I." When it came to that part in the ceremony, he proudly stood up anyway and said "On behalf of her father, who is no longer with us, and her mother," he gestured to me, "I give this woman in marriage."

Then, he pronounced a special blessing on the marriage, which I don't imagine he'd planned beforehand. I believe it was something that God inspired him to do on the spur of the moment. Immediately after the benediction, Susan turned around. With heartfelt tears in her eyes, she just clung to him and thanked him for what he'd said. After we returned to the house, he was seated in his recliner beside the fireplace. Susan's husband, Steve, came up to him. He got down on one knee and said, "Dr. Huck, thank you for your role in the wedding ceremony. That was the most beautiful part of the whole service." I think that is something both Susan and Steve continue to cherish all these many years later.

Bill was always full of fun and always ready for a good, hearty laugh. He enjoyed all the children at all times. I remember when Susan and Romaine were at home and wanted permission to go somewhere. If they were afraid I'd deny their request, they went to him instead. We got a big kick out of that.

My memory of the predominant feeling of the five years with Bill was happiness. There was lots of laughter in the house. There was a great deal of sharing and good communication. After his death, both my children and his said that he lived much longer than he would have because of his devotion and love for me and not wanting to leave me alone. Every day he watched for me to come home from the Mission. Even during his hospitalizations, I stayed with him day and night. During these times, I was often torn between him and my job and I talked with him about resigning from the Mission so I could be with him all the time. He was a very wise man. He told me that he didn't believe that he'd be with me too long and that I'd need the Mission for my fulfillment after he was gone. When the Lord did take him home, I was so glad that I had the Mission to keep myself busy and to fulfill the vision that I had for reaching women for Christ.

In the five years that Bill was a part of my life, I have many happy memories. Bill loved unconditionally. He wasn't critical and was a very positive person. He was ageless. He looked into the future. He didn't look back and he didn't regret the past. He lived for the present but anticipated the future. He was not critical of my children but always welcomed them and was positive about their problems. He advised them wisely and loved them greatly. Those five years were very intense. We all wanted to seize every day. Carpe diem! We had felt deprived for the six long years I was a widow but we knew this couldn't last forever. When the Lord did take him home, our grief, again, was extremely intense.

He was in the hospital several times the last month of his life. During that time, we became acquainted with a nurse who did private duty nursing and she came to the house. I knew that whenever I needed her, she'd come and care for him during the day while I was at the Mission. When the private duty nurse was there, Diane took care of their meals. She was just being the daughter that she wanted to be. One of the last days that he was alive, he wanted to see Diane. He couldn't think of her name, and he said to the nurse, "I want the young servant girl." The nurse hesitated to tell Diane about it. When she found out, she wept and said, "The Lord gave me the opportunity to care for a man of God. Serving him was a privilege I didn't have with my own dad."

The day the Lord took him to be with Him, the nurse told me that I should stay home from the Mission. She knew his death was imminent and she told me that he could hear everything I had to say even though he appeared to be in coma. I asked him if he wanted me to read from Psalms. He didn't respond. I was reading Psalms 34:22 at the moment of his death. It says (NIV) "No one will be condemned who takes refuge in him."

Of course, I didn't recognize the moment of death, but the nurse did. He gave a sudden shout and that was it. It was all over.

The nurse said afterwards, "I have attended many people at the time of their death, but I never experienced anything like this. He was so quiet, and then it was like a shout of victory. If I didn't believe before, I would have to believe now when I saw this saint go home."

Life after Bill

It rained on the cold January day when Bill was buried. Coming home from the funeral, I felt empty knowing that I had to face the grief of losing another mate. The children weren't losing another father, but, for the younger children, and especially Diane who had been in the home and caring for him, it was a time of grief for them as well.

Because it had been a five-year marriage and he wasn't the father of my children, it didn't seem that my friends or other people could understand my loss. Yet, I felt very much alone. In going to the Lord for comfort and guidance, the verses given to me by Professor Hatch many years before came to mind: (NIV Philippians 1:12) "Now I want you to know, brothers, that what has happened to me has really served to advance the gospel." (NIV Philippians 1:19) "for I know that through your prayers and the help given by the Spirit of Jesus Christ, what has happened to me will turn out for my deliverance."

I realized, as God ministered to my heart, that the first husband God gave me shared a vision with me. I shared Stauffer's burden for the salvation of men and women who were in bondage to whatever their sin of bondage was, to set them free in Christ. I cared not only about the people that I ministered to, but I was concerned that many other places be started so that the Gospel could go forth. Stauffer had a vision for pioneering in new ministries and for preaching the "Good News." He had the gift of evangelism.

Being married to Bill, I had received a new dimension of ministry. That was not only caring about the people that I was working with to reach them for Christ, but also to take care of their social needs and to have avenues of access where those social needs could be squarely addressed and where they could enjoy a more fulfilling lifestyle as a result. The Lord comforted my heart to know that the Gospel was still going forth and people were still coming to know Christ in the places that Stauffer had started. The Men's Mission started by Bill many years before had provided me with an open door to start the Women's Mission. Now there were women in the Atlanta area who were hearing the Gospel and who were adopting a different lifestyle because of the discipleship they received.

The 14th chapter of John was a great comfort to me in my personal grief. In the quietness of my home, I sought strength and comfort through God's word and through the comforting of my children. I realized that I had to keep my grief within myself and within the confines of the home. When I was at the Mission, I had to be the professional. I had to act in a way that was helpful to the women as I reached out to comfort them and meet their needs in their time of grief. It was essential to keep the two very separate.

During the five years of my life with Bill, the Women's Mission made continuous progress. My entire staff consisted of residents who had gotten back on their feet because of the Mission ministry but didn't have a family to return to. I personally trained the cooks and my assistant and those who sorted clothes to take their place on the staff.

I knew that traditionally, in Men's Missions, older men, converts, became assistants and eventually became Mission directors. It is generally thought that the people who want to be on the staff of Men's Missions should be older men. Early in the history of the Women's Mission, Debbie Berkholtz, a very zealous young woman who was only in her early twenties, came to see me. She had been to a Campus Crusade rally on the West Coast. While there, someone from Atlanta told her about our Women's Mission work. She flew to Atlanta, came to see me, and begged me for a place on the staff. Because of her zeal and her passion for souls and her desire to serve Christ, I thought I would try her out, despite her relative youth.

At first, the older residents of the Mission resented Debbie telling them what to do. I had to gather them in the chapel and tell them that Debbie was there to stay, no matter what kinds of "road blocks" they put in her way. I specifically mention road blocks because one day some of the women put actual blocks in front of her car. They decided they were going to hassle her and force her out of the staff position. She couldn't move her car forward or backward. I told the residents that Debbie was not going to leave. If they were unable to accept her leadership and authority, they were the ones who would be going somewhere else. After that, they started accepting her.

This incident set the stage for my realization that if there was an age group that really cared about Mission work, it was the young people. If they were ever to be trained, I would have to be the one to do it. There were no other Women's Missions where they could be trained. God was clearly leading me in the direction of staff training and development.

During this time, there was an older woman who wanted to come and work with me. She was going through a personal time of grief. This didn't work out at all. She was so possessed by her own neediness that she couldn't separate herself from the desperate plight of the women we were serving. She wasn't able to minister effectively and wouldn't have been until she'd gotten a great deal of help for her own personal issues.

I saw the critical need for the staff to be non-condemning and non-judgmental. They needed to accept the Mission women as they were and love them unconditionally. These characteristics were present in the first young women who came to work with us.

Around this time, a young woman, Kathy Kelly, came from Baltimore, Maryland, and asked for a position. I saw the same youthful zeal in her. She fearlessly proclaimed the Gospel. I remember saying, "Kathy, if you didn't have someone to witness to, you would witness to a fire hydrant on the curb!" Her energy was boundless, but caring.

The Mission took on an altogether exciting new direction when we started seeing the Spirit of God using these young women in the ministry. Not only did they bring the new residents to a saving knowledge of Christ, they also discipled them in their new faith and loved them unconditionally. They took them places and included them in our fun times. Social functions were planned for them with outside groups. God was so good!

During the time that Bill was still living, a woman who was in social work with a city agency came to my office and asked for a job. Traditionally, the Missions themselves didn't have social workers. However, we had women with such diverse needs, the pregnancies, the battering, the numerous and complex social problems, that I appreciated the necessity for having a social worker on our staff. I had to take it to my Board of Directors and explain the need to them.

When a destitute man comes to a Mission, his obvious needs are for food, shelter, and employment. Some need rehabilitation of one sort or another. A woman comes to a Mission through agencies or churches and her needs are more complex. Because of her emotional nature, and frequently because of her dependent children, the referrals and networking needed in her rehabilitation require a great deal of social work.

The Board of Directors gave their consent for Pat Beaver, the social worker, to be on my staff. She was a very resourceful person who knew all the local agencies. An entirely new dimension to the rehabilitation of homeless women was added to the Mission. Two hurdles had been cleared. I now had administrative assistants as well as a social worker!

During the latter part of this five or six-year period, we started seeing an increase in women whose problems I did not understand. Henrietta was an example of this. She came to us from a downtown church after being evicted from several apartments. Yet, she held a responsible job in a very exclusive dress shop. She dressed meticulously and had beautiful clothes, obviously putting all her money into her wardrobe. On the occasion of our New Year's Eve reception, she somehow was convinced that she was our hostess. This was an annual event open to the public for anyone who wanted to stop by to say hello to the residents of the Mission. She greeted our guests as though she was the lady of the house. In reality, she was just a resident like all the others. Another time, I came in on a Sunday afternoon and she was sitting in the dining room smoking a cigarette during our chapel time. She'd violated two rules: smoking in the dining room and missing chapel.

I said, "Henrietta, you need to be in the chapel. Why aren't you there?"

She said, "I'm not in the chapel and I don't plan to go."

I told her that as long as she was a resident, she needed to attend chapel. She continued to push the limits and began to exhibit unusual behavior. I took her into my office and said, "Henrietta, I wish either that your eyes gave away that you were on drugs, or that I smelled alcohol on your breath. Then I'd know what to do with you. As it is, I don't have a clue."

Eventually, I had to evict her. After obtaining legal advice from an attorney on the Board, I put her things in the hall and locked her door. Much later, I learned that she had mental problems and suffered from delusions of grandeur. Then, I felt profoundly ashamed for being so unprepared and inadequate to handle this type of problem.

There were other times that we had women who were obviously mentally disturbed. One was catatonic and just sat in the hall and stared. Another was aggressive and paranoid. She reported us to the authorities for things that I knew we hadn't done, like giving the women only bread and water and then poisoning their food. I tried to call the hospital to ask them what to do. Both women had been hospitalized, but had been discharged and were not taking medication.

These were some of the frustrations I had. Sometime later I learned that Georgia had passed a law that these women had to be discharged from the state hospital if they were not presently dangerous either to themselves or others. This was a major change in the rules. Now, mental health patients had to be actively suicidal or a real and present danger to others—actually threatening someone else with imminent harm. The doors of the state mental hospitals across the country were thrown wide open. The original intent was for these patients to stay in the least restrictive level of care such as a half-way house while taking medication if or as needed to keep them in touch with reality. Things somehow didn't seem to work out according to plan. Instead, these women were showing up on our doorstep in increasing numbers, unable to cope and without medications or treatment plans.

I mentioned earlier that we always had some residents who were pregnant. Missy comes to mind, a strikingly beautiful young woman who had been an entertainer. She refused to go to chapel. I told her that she had to attend as long as she was our guest. This was one thing I was firm about.

Missy said, "Well, I'm a Catholic. If your daughter was pregnant and in a Catholic organization, would you want them to insist that she go to the Catholic services?"

I responded, "Yes, I think if she accepted the hospitality and the support of a Catholic organization, she should follow their rules even if it meant going to their worship services."

Missy ultimately agreed to cooperate. When she finally had her baby, she had to sign the adoption papers. She was in grief over giving up her child. One of the church volunteers who had met her at a chapel service visited her in the hospital and gave her a devotional book. She showed her concern and her love for Missy. Missy returned to the Mission after the baby was born. Of course, we allowed her to stay until she was strong and well enough to get back to work.

The next time she came to chapel, she stood up and said, "I must tell all of you ladies something. When I came to the Mission, Mrs. Moses said I had to attend chapel and I became very angry. However, as a result of attending, a Christian lady gave me a book. With the help of that book and with some psychological help that I'd had earlier, I succeeded in overcoming the grief of giving up my baby. I just wanted to be all right. Last night, I woke up and I realized I would never see my baby again. I thought my heart would break and I dropped to my knees and I took Christ as my Savior and asked Him to forgive me for my sins. This morning, while ironing my dress, I had a light heart. I knew I was forgiven and I knew my baby would be in good hands and I could pray for her always."

I could go on and on with numerous illustrations about the excitement of working with these women who were so needy. A woman named Eloise came into the Mission. She had been raised in a fine, moral family, and was brokenhearted when she discovered her husband was sexually abusing her niece. She divorced him and then turned to drinking. She just kept going down. She took a position on the staff of a large retirement home. There, she was hired by individual families to watch over the care of some of the older people. After several years of this, one day, she took a patient to the psychiatric ward at Grady Hospital. She saw that the young doctor was very compassionate with her patient and said to him, "I have an alcohol problem. What in the world can I do about it? I'm just desperate."

He said, "The best place that I can recommend is The Women's Mission. They really help people like you."

She was a woman in her early fifties. I could see she had been a professional person. I said, "Eloise, do you really want never to drink again?"

She said "Mrs. Huck, I would rather die than take another drink. And yet I can't quit."

I then asked her, "Do you want sobriety enough to leave Atlanta and spend two to three months in a Christian Rehabilitation center in North Carolina?"

She said, "I do."

I said, "Well, bring yourself and your clothes and come in. We can help you."

When Eloise returned several months later, she became one of our trusted employees. She took an important part on the staff in transporting some of our women to the industrial department of the Men's Mission where she was responsible for the conduct of the women. Often, I used her in the capacity of an assistant as well.

When we opened the doors of The Women's Mission, we just had some guidelines, knowing that the rules would follow according to the kind of women we had. After the first six years, we ended up with lots of rules, simply because of the problems that came up.

When Stauffer and I ministered at The Anchorage, we had our hands full with the eight alcoholic women there despite that they all had homes to return to. They were all self-centered and selfish (i.e. the sin nature was evident). We tried to cope with their personalities and tried to have programs to help them in their battle with their addiction.

Here I was now, in Atlanta, with women who had lost everything and who found themselves homeless, destitute and without friends. We had thirty-five women at one time. Perhaps nine were pregnant, and maybe ten or twelve had an addiction problem. Others were deserted, battered women perhaps. And now there was this new group of women that were mentally disturbed coming into our midst. Yet, it seemed that with thirty-five women, I was no busier and there were no more crises than there had been with the eight women at The Anchorage who had only the alcohol problem.

In the setting of the Mission, I observed that the alcoholic women interacted much better than the alcoholic women had at The Anchorage. I wondered why. Ultimately, I came to several conclusions. First, at the Mission, there were only two or three women with private rooms. We just didn't have very many single rooms. Most of the women were in rooms with two, three, or four others. When a woman came to the door requesting admission, we simply brought her in. Questions were asked later, because it was a Rescue Mission. The new arrival always went into whatever bed was empty. In the room with four beds, there might be a pregnant woman, an alcoholic woman, or a woman who was just out of a job and maybe abandoned by her husband or maybe was never married. Thus, there was always a diversity of women in each room.

I observed that it is the nature of many alcoholic women to feel like they have a monopoly on the world's problems and that life has dealt them the kind of hand that gives them the right to drink and to feel that everyone needs to cater to her problems. In the setting of a Rescue Mission, in the presence of a pregnant woman and women with other problems, the sensitivity of the alcoholic woman brought out her caring and nurturing nature. I saw her start fostering the other women and taking on the responsibilities in that room of meeting the needs of these women that she saw were much worse off than she was.

I was always thankful to the Lord for bringing me into mission work. Early in my ministry, I saw that people who had lost everything were fully capable of returning to a meaningful life. Women who were won to Christ and discipled in the Christian walk seemed naturally to want a better lifestyle. It was my impression that the success of returning them to living sober lives was higher in the setting of the Rescue Mission than it had been in a setting like The Anchorage. It appeared to me to be this way even though the women at The Anchorage all had the same problem and the advantage of being able to return to their families. At the Mission, they had the benefit of a kind of therapy that brought them out of themselves and started them reaching out to others.

Reverend Kelly was the executive director of the Men's Mission. Increasingly, more mentally disturbed men were coming into the Men's Mission as well. He told me that he thought he would make rules that he couldn't take them in "Because the men in the Mission say it's a place for drunks, not for crazy people."

While it was therapeutic for the alcoholic women to nurture and mother the disturbed women, we concluded that the men did not have the same nurturing nature in them. They were angry that there were those who were infringing on a territory that they felt was exclusively for "drunks."

While the influx of mentally disturbed people during that year helped The Women's Mission set its future focus, it really upset the routine of the Men's Mission. I am bringing this out to show that while ours was the first Women's Mission, we were still in the pioneering stage, experimenting and seeing what the best way to minister to these women was. I had believed all along that it was not harder to work with women than with men, as is commonly believed even today. It is just different. It takes women to understand the emotional needs of other women. When Atlanta finally had a Rescue Mission for women, the director (me) was given the liberty to develop it to meet the needs of women. It was just as successful as any Men's Mission. Truth be known, it was undoubtedly even more successful. For one thing, the men at the Mission were allowed to continue drinking.

We learned by doing and we made up the rules as we went along. There was one thing that I was extremely strict about and that was that I would positively not allow the women to drink if they wanted to stay with us. Even if a woman was not drunk but just brought alcohol in, even on her breath, it meant immediate dismissal. It did not matter if it was ten o'clock at night. We put her out on the street with no fear of her being abused or getting into trouble. We knew that within a block or two, she'd be picked up by the police and put in the safety of the jail. Drinking on the streets was a misdemeanor. There were very few women who dared to bring alcohol in or to even drink when they were out. They knew that in this area I was ruthless and that I was not an easy mark like I might be in some of their other problem areas.

The primary reason for our success in keeping the women abstinent from alcohol was the training of my staff. I said, "If you show mercy to one alcoholic woman by letting her stay, if we have ten alcoholics in the building, you are going to have ten other women coming in drinking, feeling you should show the same favor to them and it would be wrong if you would not. So, we have to judge it quickly."

The end result was that through the sixteen years that I was at The Women's Mission, we had very few incidents of drinking. I know of no incidents of drinking in the building, and we had very few incidents where we had to put women out. The women knew that drinking was absolutely forbidden in the building, and they shared this fact with all the new arrivals.

The daily schedule and the rules were fairly rigid. The women were awakened daily at the same time. They had to be at breakfast at 7:30, fully dressed and with their hair combed. They could never be out of their own hall area in dressing gowns. They had to be fully dressed when they were downstairs and coming into the dining room. Before they came to breakfast, their beds had to be made and their rooms ready for inspection by the staff.

We had chapel services every morning of the work week right after breakfast between 8:30 and 9:00. Chapel services in the evening were only held on special occasions. Perhaps a church group had a particular program, or young people wanted to have a service for the women on a Wednesday or Thursday night. We scheduled them and announced that there was a special service that they were expected to attend. Evening chapel was not a regularly scheduled event, as our morning chapel was. On Saturdays, we did not have chapel in the morning, but we did have an evening service and other organizations were invited to come in and lead the service. On Sundays, we had a morning Sunday School. After that, the women were encouraged to go to one of the local churches. Our Sunday School was held early enough that they could get to their local church in time for Sunday School there. We had other churches come in every Sunday afternoon for a service. Sunday evenings were free for them to fellowship or to be with each other.

We learned that the women liked to talk in little groups. They didn't like large rooms where they could lounge but not visit with each other. They seemed to enjoy being in small groups, three or four talking at a time.

Each woman had her own program from the very beginning, according to her needs. The women who were looking for employment were required to go out every day right after chapel. Otherwise, all women who were able-bodied were put on chores immediately. The list of chores was made out new every week. There were always two or three women in the clothing room. There was always the cook, who was also a resident, and she could have as large a staff in her kitchen for preparing meals and for dishwashing as she needed. We served three meals a day, strictly at the same time every day. There were also those responsible for keeping the building clean.

While we made and adjusted the rules as the needs of the residents changed, we were able to start building the kind of staff that we needed. The office secretarial work was done by volunteers. For years, I had the volunteers do any typing that I needed done. Occasionally, I had other staff members who could type do some of the secretarial work as well. Yet, the staff also had to be busy in the halls working with the women so I had to depend a good bit on church volunteers who came in to help me.

In the kitchen were large, used, freezer chests that were donated by various people. Our menu always consisted of good nutritious food. We saw to it that the women had balanced diets and that the food was well-prepared. I strongly believed that the time of fellowship around the tables was important. The staff on duty ate with the women in the same dining room at the same time. When my family visited, they also ate with the residents.

In the basement of our Mission there were several rooms that were filled with clothing contributed by church groups. The clothing room was part of the ministry that was much needed by the women, but it brought more frustration to me than anything else. What frustrated me the most was the distribution of these clothes. We got all these clothes in, from underwear to winter coats and shoes. God always provided a resident who enjoyed sorting clothes as well as supervising other women in sorting clothes. There were always plenty of clothes for everyone. However, a woman would come in with just what she had on her back and maybe a few things in a small bag. When she left, she'd have boxes full of clothes. We learned quickly that if a woman needed clothes, instead of going and begging clothes from the resident who was in charge of clothes, she had to come to me or one of the other staff members and make her request. We then gave her a piece of paper and told her what she could have. For instance, if a woman came in with nothing but the clothes she had on, we'd first determine with her what her actual needs were. Besides a week's supply of undergarments, we would list several changes of casual clothing and several dressier outfits. Then, with this list in hand, she could go shopping, as it were, in the clothing rooms, and have her list checked off by the woman in charge. Only in this way did the process become manageable. The security of most homeless persons seemed to be in their possessions. They often tried to get as many clothes as they could, even things that they didn't actually need at the time.

Billy Hightower was an older woman who came to us from the Georgia Regional Hospital as an unemployable alcoholic. After she'd been there a little while, I realized she had more serious problems than her alcoholism. She had been in and out of hospitals many times for her alcohol problem, but she also was very disturbed, though not psychotic.

Early in her stay with us, she turned her life over to Christ and made the commitment to serve Him the rest of her life. She was a hard worker and I soon learned that she could manage the clothing room with firmness. She was very much in tune with what we wanted to do. She worked tirelessly in the clothing room and I was always proud to take visitors into that area after she took over. She remained the director of the clothing room all the rest of the years that I was director of the Mission.

Billy loved her Bible. She loved Bible study. She especially liked when Dr. Huck came on Thursday mornings to have the morning chapel. The residents that had been with us through the years and had positions like Billy's really grieved Dr. Huck's passing.

If we allowed a woman who was already on welfare to stay for any length of time for rehabilitation, we charged a minimum fee for room and board. The primary reason for this was so that she would not lose her means of support upon leaving and starting a life where she would have to pay her own way again. Hopefully, her rehabilitation included training for good enough jobs that she could go off welfare. If a woman had no money at all, she was not charged. This was contrary to the way it worked in a Men's Mission where two or three dollars was required for a night's stay. A man had to be able to go and wash some windows, unload a truck, or do something to get enough money to return to the Men's Mission for another night. We couldn't do that. I couldn't tell a woman that she had to pay her way if she was there one or two nights because the only means she had to earn quick money was in a way which we were discouraging. One reason for The Women's Mission was so that a woman would have a place of refuge. We didn't charge women who had no money and we didn't expect her to go out and get that quick buck.

If a woman came in at the request of Traveler's Aid, she automatically received the services of their social worker and ours didn't get involved. She could stay with us as long as both social workers agreed that she should stay. Traveler's Aid paid for as many nights as she was at the Mission. This was good for us, because we received some income through that woman staying with us. It was also good for her because she heard the Gospel while she was with us. Many of our transients came in through referral from Traveler's Aid.

All the social service departments in the city actively used our services. They were grateful because they didn't have to put the single women up in a hotel while they worked on their problems. We charged much less than a hotel, so they sent transients to us. Many times, Vocational Rehabilitation was trying to work with a woman. If she was homeless, they sent her to us.

Every week, I had to make out the financial report for the Executive Office. I enclosed the checks that came in through different avenues of support such as contributions from individuals, churches, and social agencies. In addition, the room and board money was sent that was received from the women that could pay. This involved a good bit of bookkeeping on a weekly basis.

I had a salary, as did the rest of the paid staff. I submitted on a weekly basis the need for stipends to give to residents who were working in the building. Reverend Denkins and Reverend Kelly did the same thing. While none of the three of us had to worry about his or her own pay check every month, we were all charged with the responsibility of doing all the public relations work that we could. We were all used to PR and it was something we all enjoyed doing.

When I first went to the Mission, I was told that the Board of Directors would raise the funds a year ahead and that I would be in charge of spending it. I'd have a budget, but I didn't need to worry about finances. That was to be the responsibility of the Board. However, I soon learned that I played a large role in bringing contributions in through my speaking engagements. If I was to increase my staff to make the Mission more effective, I needed to increase our income to provide for salaries. I assumed more responsibility in this area.

I had many engagements in Sunday School classes and women's clubs to speak on behalf of The Women's Mission. Many of the contributions that came into the Mission were directed to the Women's Division. I sent personal letters thanking people for their contributions, and got more speaking engagements as a result.

Sometimes we got women in who were physically handicapped. They were destitute, and they were really unemployable at the time. They didn't know how to go about getting government assistance. Our social worker would send that woman to the Department of Family and Children's Services. The advantage of having a social worker was that she knew who would qualify and who wouldn't, and she only sent those to the office that she knew would qualify. When the woman received her first check, she had to begin paying room and board. However, then she could immediately start making plans to move out and become independent.

The pregnant women who came in were different from the ones I worked with at Faith Cottage in Asheville. There, all of them wanted to adopt their babies out. Some of them changed their minds, but very few. Those women knew that their babies would be better off with adoptive parents where they had both a mother and a father. Rather than return to their homes as single mothers trying to raise a child by themselves, they elected to have their child adopted. It was a new experience for me to have all these pregnant women who were throwaways. They had no security, and yet desperately wanted to keep their babies. We were really the only source of security they had. They saw us as a means to obtain security. We wouldn't try to talk them out of keeping their babies after the birth, but we would, in counseling, try to show them the reality of their situation. The social worker tried to show them the reality of single-parenting. However, this was a different group of women. They didn't have the stable background and the supportive family that the young women in Asheville had.

Many of our women came from out of state. They came to Atlanta hoping there would be jobs for them after their babies were born. Plans were made with the social worker beforehand to place them in the local housing projects with their new baby. Of course, their support and their checks started coming in while they were still at the Mission.

Some of our best workers in the Mission were the alcoholic women. We didn't charge them room and board because they didn't have an income. We also didn't encourage them to go on government aid because we knew they were employable. Because their rehabilitation was long term, these were the ones we put on the staff and gave them what we called a stipend. We gave them ten to fifteen dollars a week to take care of their personal needs as pay for the work they did. This also allowed them to feel that they were being compensated for their hours of work during the day.

All in all, our rules and life in the Mission were structured simply so things would run smoothly. Visitors often asked us if there was much fighting. There was very seldom a fight between the women. There were enough of the residents who took responsibility for themselves as well as for each other. Our staff of young committed Christians created a happy atmosphere that was comforting to a troubled population.

Occasionally, we had some well-meaning person who came in and spoke about the Samaritan woman, the woman who was a sinner. The women would come to me afterward and say, "We hear that same message all the time, like we are all whores and prostitutes."

I had to start talking to the groups and the visiting speakers to educate them to be effective witnesses in this environment. We are all sinners. We all need the salvation message. Most of these women were not prostitutes. We instructed the visitors to speak as they would to any group of women, while acknowledging that our women were there and were destitute for a variety of reasons. Some had been abandoned, and some were sick. They all needed words of encouragement and to know that we all have a loving and forgiving God. None of them needed a shaming message of condemnation.

The Mission was supported by Protestant and Catholic organizations throughout the community. No group was allowed to speak to the women unless they upheld the Gospel of the Lord Jesus Christ. False cults were not permitted. We had to be firm when false cults wanted to come in and proselytize.

Some of the women asked what church I belonged to. They wanted to be in the same denomination. I was careful to not tell them my denomination. I wanted them to know that Christ alone was the answer to whatever their need was. Simply joining a particular church did not guarantee their entry into heaven. I did tell them that belonging to a church was important as it provided a place to be with fellow believers for the worship of God.

I was often asked about my compassion for the person who was addicted. I told the women it took just as much of the grace of God to break the bondage of religion that I'd had as a child, as it did to break their bondage of addiction, which they had now.

I truly believe that God ordained that I should start The Women's Mission and that I was responsible that every woman who came in should hear the Good News of salvation. If a woman was just in overnight and didn't get to a chapel service, I had to just trust that the staff would somehow share their own faith with her. When a woman came to faith in Christ, I believed it was my responsibility and my staff's to disciple her in the Christian walk of faith.

We eventually used the same Bible studies that we had initiated at The Anchorage. It proved a bit more difficult to be consistent with this study at the Mission because the women tended to come and go more that they had at The Anchorage. It was constantly a struggle to disciple these women so they could grow in the faith. We did try to impress these two verses on the residents:

2 Corinthians 5:17 (NIV) "Therefore, if anyone is in Christ, he is a new creation; the old has gone, the new has come!"

Galatians 2:20 (KJV) "I am crucified with Christ: nevertheless I live; yet not I, but Christ liveth in me: and the life which I now live in the flesh I live by the faith of the Son of God, who loved me, and gave himself for me."

In our morning Bible reading and chapel service, we did a lot of scripture memory work. We also did a lot of singing. We tried to get the message to the women through song and through the singing of many choruses.

There were three divisions to the over-all ministry of The Atlanta Union Mission. In addition to the Men's and Women's Missions, there was a large rehabilitation farm, Potter's House, that was started in the North Georgia countryside many years before. While Dr. Huck was still director, he became burdened for the need for rehabilitation for the Mission men. After his retirement, and while he served on the Executive Board, his dream was realized. Potter's House was fashioned after The Anchorage in Albany. The name came from Jeremiah 18:2 (KJV) "Arise, and go down to the potter's house, and there I will cause thee to hear my words."

Reverend Strange became Executive Director of the three divisions of The Atlanta Union Mission after Bill retired. He was also director of The Men's Mission where he had his office. In the chain of command, I answered to him and he answered to the Board of Directors. Shortly after my arrival, Reverend Jim Soseby replaced him as Executive Director and Reverend Kelly became director of The Men's Mission.

Reverend Soseby immediately moved his office from The Men's Mission to a downtown office in the Healy Building. The three directors, Reverend Kelly from the Men's Mission, Pete Denkins from the farm, and I, had to go to his office every week with our reports and for a short staff meeting. When I saw the need for another staff member or for any changes in my budget, I presented it to Reverend Soseby. He could give me the okay unless he thought that my request needed to go to the Board. In that case, he'd give me the answer afterwards.

Since the Atlanta Women's Mission was a new type of ministry in America, it was quite a novelty. We received increasing news coverage, both in the newspaper and on television. There was really nothing going on in the city for homeless women except The Women's Mission and the Women's Lodge at the Salvation Army.

In reflecting over my life, I suppose it is normal to see things in different groupings. I see the first six years of ministry in Atlanta as one very specific and precious segment of pioneering in women's work. During this time I had Bill as a mentor and as a mate. We talked things over and prayed together. I knew his prayers were with me daily.

A new challenge loomed before me as increasingly more psychotic women came to us over the next years. The social workers from the psychiatric floor at Grady Hospital were sending them to us. We were not trained to cope with this new population. I sought ways to have them removed but found they couldn't be committed unless they were dangerous to themselves or others.

Georgia was the first southern state to deinstitutionalize the mental hospitals. It disturbed Bill to see my frustration in dealing with this problem. Our beds soon filled up with women who were mentally disturbed. Yet, how could I turn them away? This was a problem I had to cope with during Bill's final illness.

Shortly after Bill's death, I met Dr. Berry, a Christian psychiatrist and his wife, Edie, in a Sunday School class. He was a guest teacher, speaking on the subject of grief. I was early and when I entered the classroom, they were sitting there alone. We introduced ourselves. When he learned my name, he said he had known Dr. Huck. Because it had just been a matter of weeks since Bill's death, I was eager to hear more from Dr. Berry about his relationship with my husband.

After the Sunday School lesson, I talked again with them. He told me he was doing his Psychiatry residency at Grady Hospital and he'd like to offer his services to The Women's Mission. He asked me what I knew about the psychotic population. I shared with him my frustration over the fact that we were seeing so many more of these people. I explained that my policy had been to admit any woman and not to be selective about who I would allow in. The presence of psychotic women was increasingly a problem to me because I was concerned about their behavior. I didn't know how to dismiss the women I felt we couldn't handle. Only the week before, I had told the Chief of the Psychiatric unit at Grady that I would have to ban all of their referrals if he wouldn't honor my request to remove a woman that was a problem or that we were concerned about.

When Dr. Berry returned to Grady, he mentioned to his Chief that he had met the director of The Women's Mission. The Chief said, "As a matter of fact, we had an ultimatum given to us by Mrs. Huck. I wonder if you'd take it upon yourself to be our liaison person and work with her and us on their psychotic population as it increases." As a result, I made plans to go to Dr. Berry's office at Grady Hospital for a one-hour appointment the next week. The week after that, he came to the Mission and talked with my staff. Thereafter, I saw him every week for an hour. On even weeks, we met in his office where I described my current concerns about the Mission and asked for his wisdom. The odd weeks, he came to the Mission and listened to case histories and taught the staff how to work with these women. After our initial meeting, I asked him what kind of staff he thought I would need as our psychotic population increased.

None of us on the Mission staff had any education in social work or the current treatment of the kinds of patients recently released from the state hospitals. There was only one state mental hospital in all of Georgia and that was in Milledgeville. There had been between twenty and thirty thousand inmates there. Georgia passed the same law as the other states, that mentally-ill people who were not currently dangerous to themselves or others had to be discharged back to the care of their local counties. When that law was passed, regional hospitals were to be built throughout the state. The plan was for the social workers in Milledgeville to send these patients back to the new regional hospitals in their local counties. After stabilization there, they were to be released immediately into the "least restrictive environment" while continuing their medications. It was envisioned they'd move from halfway houses to independent living or group homes where they'd be stable and productive members of the community. In retrospect, this plan may have been overly idealistic. As soon as many of these patients were in a halfway house and stabilized on medication, they tended to drop out of the system. Some no longer felt the need to take medication. Some didn't remember to take it, and some simply neglected to take it altogether. Then, in a confused state of mind or in feeling closed in because they had been incarcerated in the mental hospital for so many years, they started wandering the streets, enjoying their newfound freedom. Many of these people had a halfway house somewhere in the state and just didn't return to it. Ultimately, they found their way to our door, many of them probably in the same state as when they'd first entered the system. They were homeless and destitute and now they were our problem.

One day, Dr. Berry said to me, "Have you heard on the radio that all fifty states are going to have to release their mental patients? They are going to deinstitutionalize all the mental hospitals in the country."

I said, "Well, that won't matter to us because Georgia did it several years ago."

He said, "But it will matter. Florida has never done it before and neither has Alabama or the Carolinas. A lot of them are going to start gravitating to Atlanta since it's the largest metropolitan area in the Southeast."

When I got home from meeting with him that day, I saw the news on the television. I was frightened because they said several hundred thousand inmates of mental hospitals across the United States would be released.

More and more disturbed women showed up at the Mission. Dr. Berry advised that we not accept these women unless they came through Grady Hospital or another psychiatric facility with specific medication orders. Of course, when we did accept them, we needed to start administering their medication to them. We couldn't let these women keep their medications in their own possession. First of all, they didn't take their medications reliably if they did keep them. Secondly, the drug addicts would steal them. The addicts didn't seem to care what the medicine was, as long as it was a pill and they could swallow it. We saw the wisdom of taking their medication from them and incorporating new rules in our Mission regarding these drugs. If a woman on medication was resident among us, she couldn't stay unless she came to the medicine line and took her medicine daily. This meant that a staff member had to stand at a locked cabinet door and give each woman her medication. The women would line up with a glass of water in hand. Not only did we have to hand out these medications, we had to watch each woman swallow her pills to be certain they actually got them down.

Dr. Berry was also a professor at the Psychological Studies Institute (PSI). He observed women in graduate school who wanted the experience of Christian social work. Many of them wanted to have the hands-on experience of working with behavioral problems of all kinds. He suggested we request help from this school if we needed additional staff. A notice was placed on the bulletin board and two young women immediately volunteered. They were eager workers and labored side by side with the women in cleaning and cooking and in any way they could just so they could learn Mission work. For months, they were a valuable addition to our volunteer staff. These devout Christian women were selfless in their nature and loving to the women.

I was really excited about this. Up till now, the main emphasis of our ministry had been spiritual and I wanted it to remain that way. However, I found that the staff became frustrated when there were social or behavior problems, or needs that these women had other than spiritual. I believed in using young staff members to teach the residents. They enthusiastically felt that if these women turned their lives over to Christ, they would be transformed. This is generally true, with long-term discipleship. However, we had a more transient population coming in that had mental, social, and moral problems that also had to be addressed in short order.

I saw in the first two PSI students a desire to figure out how we could win these women to Christ through helping them work out their physical and emotional problems as well. Once I was granted permission to employ new staff members to start working with the mental health population, I naturally put these two women on the payroll since they had volunteered their services without compensation up until now.

PSI is a Christian counseling program offered by Georgia State University. The counseling and the psychological education are obtained through the University system but are integrated with Christian principals. The program is done off-campus. These bright young PSI women were eager to learn how to integrate Christian principles into their psychological counseling skills while obtaining a Master's degree in Psychology. This meant that they had a double load compared with the other students at the University who just took the counseling courses. Many of the applications from the PSI students stated something along the lines of: "My parents saw me through my undergraduate curriculum. They will pay my tuition if I want to do graduate work, but I will have to work for my room and board."

Thus, a new phase started for the Mission. This was an exciting experience for me. Now I was seeing my dreams and my vision fulfilled of inspiring young women to care about reaching women for Christ and then teaching them how to accomplish that. I started hiring students for either two or three eight hour shifts a week.

Dr. Berry was one of their professors. He continued to come twice a month to our staff meeting where we presented the problems of the schizophrenics and other psychotic people to him. He made suggestions for working with them. I thanked him one day for teaching us how to counsel these psychotic women. He said, "Well, actually, I'm learning while I'm teaching you. In my residency, I am learning how they think and what goes on in their minds. Then, I suggest to you how to handle them and I learn from you how it worked."

For the next ten years, he was our constant mentor.

All across the country, increasing numbers of mentally disturbed people were wandering the streets and coming into the Missions. Dr. Berry was concerned about how other Missions were handling this problem. With the help of my national directory, we sent a detailed questionnaire to the several hundred Mission directors in the United States. We sent the questionnaire so that what we were learning by Dr. Berry's involvement might be of help to others.

They were asked if they had seen a change in the problems of their population and how they were handling it. Many of them returned the questionnaire, most of them responding with: "We are set up for alcoholics, addicts, and homeless people. We are not set up for crazy people and we don't accept them. We just bar them from admission to our Mission." Some said they just didn't know how to handle the problem. That year, when I went to the IUGM meeting, I asked one of the directors what he was doing about the problem of the mentally disturbed.

He said, "I don't let the crazy ones into my Mission."

I replied, "The motto of Rescue Missions is 'to serve the least, the last, and the lost.' The government is now setting up alcohol rehabilitation centers with federal money. You complain that the drunks are going into the government facilities. Yet, you deny the people that the same government is turning out on the street. We are no long serving the least, the last, and the lost."

I believed firmly in what I said. Upon my return to Atlanta, I shared my concerns with Dr. Berry. If we were really serving "the least, the last, and the lost," then we had to do something about the mentally ill people that were on the streets.

This was back in the relative "dark ages" of 1975. Everyone in the social service agencies or in social work of any sort was concerned about this stream of mentally disturbed people out on the streets. In our thirty-five-bed Mission, we were becoming overwhelmed by the sheer numbers of women who were on medication. We had to start turning away other women who were homeless. I knew we couldn't give preference to the mentally disturbed. It grieved me to have to turn anyone away.

In the meantime, Reverend Soseby made a request to a foundation for a several hundred thousand dollar grant to relocate the Men's Mission. There was increasing pressure from downtown businesses to get the Men's Mission out of their area. When this foundation investigated the stability and the credibility of the Mission corporation, they naturally had to look into how well all of the divisions were doing. After visiting The Women's Mission and seeing what we were doing for the psychotic and other women despite our crowded conditions, they gave the money with the request that it be used for the Women's Division. This was a major disappointment for Reverend Kelly and it was like a left-handed gift to me. I was overjoyed for us but sad for Reverend Kelly. I loved Reverend Kelly and the work he did at the Men's Mission. However, I believed it was providential that we could now expand our ministry and not have to turn women away.

In anticipation of moving the Men's Mission, the Board of Directors had previously purchased an abandoned school on two and a half acres of land in an industrial area of the city. It was in poor repair as a result of standing empty for many years. Reverend Soseby called me to his office and asked me what I would think about moving the Women's Division into the school instead of putting the men there.

I was horrified, and I said, "I just can't comprehend moving women into a place like that with all their needs, especially their need to feel comfortable and safe. Women are nesters. All the needs of my women are being put aside by your even suggesting that we consider moving into an old school building. It just isn't suitable. The rooms are huge, the ceilings are too high, and it's located in an industrial area."

He was at a loss to know what to do with this building when the grant came to us instead of to the men. The Board thought it would be easier for us to sell our existing building than it would be for the Men's Mission to sell theirs. They thought they had a buyer for the Men's Mission but it fell through. Reverend Soseby requested that I talk to some of the influential women of my acquaintance that had a heart for The Women's Mission and that also could speak for the church women of our city.

I called Ann Cousins, a prominent member of our church who I knew had a heart for our Mission. She agreed to accompany me to the school and give her opinion as to how the women of Atlanta would respond to moving The Women's Mission to the proposed site. We unlocked the door, went in, and took our first tour of the building. All was in a state of severe disrepair. We saw decrepit halls, rundown classrooms, huge windows, dilapidated blackboards, and wooden floors covered with debris, and we were in tears. Any copper such as in plumbing or electrical wiring had been stolen. There had been a lot of vandalism. We just couldn't believe that we might be forced into a situation like this. Nonetheless, we continued our explorations with an open mind. We stepped off the rooms to get a rough idea how many beds could go in each one and how the project could come together. We left totally frustrated and discouraged and I shared our reaction with Mr. Soseby.

A day or two later, I got a call from a man on the Board. He said, "I wish you could become enthusiastic about that building, Elsie. Unless you are enthusiastic, we can't sell the idea to the public."

I said, "It's hard for me to develop any sense of enthusiasm for this situation when I've been in the present building for over ten years and no improvements have been made here yet. The women are still sleeping on Army cots. They still have to force their clothes into the same metal lockers. The staff and I have tried to make it as homey as possible. The greatest need women have is to nest. They can't do that in bunk beds. I certainly can't picture them living in bunk beds or metal Army beds in those huge classrooms, and I can't comprehend how living in this situation would encourage them to feel like they want to strive for a better life."

He responded, "If we can make it cozy, if we can make it home-like, if we can do all the things to make the women feel like they are home with nice surroundings, would you consider it?"

I said, "Of course I would if we can make them feel cozy and help them develop a desire for a better life. I'd be willing to go anywhere so we can serve the needs of more women."

Soon, architects drew up plans and builders from Post Properties went to work. Barry Teague was high up in Post Properties and was on the executive board of the Atlanta Union Mission. Post Properties builds and manages a tremendous amount of apartment housing in the Atlanta area. Barry brought a high level of enthusiasm to the project, virtually guaranteeing its success.

Every classroom was divided into seven separate cubicles. Each cubicle became home for one woman. The partitions were six feet high. As you walked through a classroom, it was like going through a maze. Even though there were no doors to these cubicles, the opening to each woman's cubicle faced the wall of another cubicle. This way, each woman could feel like she had her own private space. Each cubicle had one twin bed, a chest of drawers, and a writing desk with a chair. Each cubicle was covered inside with attractive wallpaper. Each resident could hang pictures on the walls and personalize her space, making it truly her own.

There were eight classrooms with seven cubicles in each classroom and there was another large classroom that held nine cubicles. Altogether, this meant sixty-three cubicles, thus providing individual space for sixty-three women.

The library was very large. Seven different types of cubicles were placed in there. Each of these cubicles held several women. There was room for thirty women in the library. We wanted the library area for transients because we didn't want to turn down women who just came in for a night or two. We wanted to have space for women in need of refuge who were brought in by the police department, or for women brought by Traveler's Aid who needed a place during a short period of transition.

The entire project was coming together and I was thrilled to see the progress. All of the various bathrooms were large and were restored to mint condition. Carpeting was placed throughout the entire building, reducing the noise level considerably. Attractive colors of paint were applied to the walls of the wide hallways. Rocking chairs were placed up and down the wide hallway, providing comfortable seating for the women who stayed during the day, many of whom rocked themselves for a sense of comfort.

We moved into the new Mission shortly before Christmas. Everyone was excited. It was beautiful. The assistant and I each had a large private office. The staff that administered medication, the night staff, and the day staff that worked directly with the women all had separate offices. There was a big chapel in the auditorium. Not only was the inside lovely, but the outside was landscaped with beautiful flowers and elegant trees. There was a sprinkler system for the lawn. The move itself was a very delightful occasion. God had answered our prayers. He had transformed an old school house into a first-rate Women's Mission. I was truly overjoyed and humbled before Him for the great blessings He had bestowed on the destitute women of Atlanta. Once again, my God was faithful.

The transfer of our thirty-five women to the new location was a major task that had to be carefully planned and executed. We had to work particularly carefully with the women with emotional and mental problems to avoid arousing fear in them. They were afraid of change and were settled where they were. Before the actual move, I took a station wagon load of women over, just a few at a time, and showed them the beautifully decorated rooms with new furniture and allowed them to write down their first and second choices for the room they wanted. Remarkably, almost all of them got their first choice!

There was one whole area of the new Mission that we didn't open up at the time of the move because we wanted all thirty-five women to face the attractively landscaped spot that had been the playground. There was now a big gazebo and a picnic area with tables. They could even go outside during inclement weather and be protected by the roof and sit at the picnic tables and enjoy each other's company out there. There were new lawn chairs. It was just gorgeous.

Our opening made the news in Atlanta. The magazine section of the Sunday paper had a centerfold showing the silhouette of one of the women. The article was titled, *A Room of One's Own*. That was twice in a short time that we made the centerfold of the magazine section of the Atlanta Journal.

Instead of being downtown on Ponce de Leon Avenue with all its traffic, we were now on a quiet street in an industrial area. When we faced the back, we had a beautiful yard with real gardens. Our more secluded and protective environment was important because Atlanta was becoming an increasingly dangerous place, especially for the women who were vulnerable because of mental health issues. This area was much safer than the area around our old building.

The city even put a bus stop right at our front door. The women could easily step outside, walk down the steps to the sidewalk, and get on the bus. They could actually sit on the steps of the building, watch for the bus, and be down at the bus as it arrived.

The individual cubicles were essential, I believed, in the plans for the new Mission. Through our experience and our sessions with Dr. Berry, it seemed that the mentally disturbed women had confusion in finding their identity when they lived in a group situation in a room with other women. They became different when they had a room of their own. It was exciting for the whole staff to see that the women who seemed most disturbed and who had the greatest problems with reality started to act differently and exhibited appropriate behavior in our new setting. We believed this was directly related to the structure that we were able to provide.

The whole mission work took on an entirely new and exciting focus. I recognized once again that homeless and destitute men need to be where the action is. When they are lonely, they have to rub shoulders with other men. Homeless women feel vulnerable. They feel their shame. Because of their very nature, they need to be able to withdraw from society and from public view. They also need to be on a good bus route so they can get where they need to go.

It was December 1980 when we moved in. A young couple, excited about the Mission, brought us a Christmas tree and decorated it. On Christmas Day, we had a nice Christmas for the women who made the move with us. We didn't move all thirty-five women at once. Many of those who were with us at the old Mission found other places to go on a temporary basis and so we moved perhaps twenty or twenty-five women.

In January, we had the big ice storm of 1981. All means of transportation were shut down. The news media begged for places for homeless people; yet, we didn't fill up during that time. The homeless women couldn't get anywhere unless they could walk there. We were out in the industrial area of town. Some people came in from the local offices for refuge during those days. I couldn't get home. I was stranded when the ice storm started, as was the rest of the staff. The cook was stranded. Everybody was stranded. We had plenty of food, so we all settled in for the duration. I look back to those few days as a happy time of closeness to the women. We taught them exercises on the new carpets in the hall. During the storm, the Men's Mission and the Salvation Army filled to capacity. Churches were being asked to take homeless men in for refuge from the cold. We were still not full and the Board was getting restless.

At the next Board meeting, they said, "You said that you were crowded in your old facility and you still don't have many more than the thirty-five people you started with."

With confidence, I said, "You have to understand women. Men's' Missions fill up in the winter when men have to get out of the elements. Women stay in unsavory situations in the winter time, being afraid of the elements. In the summer, we will fill up."

The agencies kept sending women to us. By July we were not only full, we had a few cots outside under the gazebo in a fenced-in area in the back yard. We were full to overflowing in the summertime, another indicator that women's needs really are different from men's. People seem slow to understand that women's places are filled to overflowing in the summertime, while men's places can be closed down, at least the surplus places. Men tend to want to sleep in less restrictive areas when they don't have to fight the elements. When the weather is nice, men don't come to a crowded Mission. Men would rather sleep under a bridge than go and sleep in restricted places where they have to be under someone else's rules. Women tend to make an escape from a bad situation when they don't have to fight the elements. If there are children, they have to wait until the children are out of school and then make their break. Also, many times they take refuge in places where they are not quite as vulnerable as they would be out on the street. If women are going to make a change, they do it when school is out and when they don't have to fight the cold weather. Then, when they find themselves homeless, they need places like the Mission or any other shelter.

Before long, we maintained a full capacity of ninety-three women. Consequently, we needed a larger staff to provide around-the-clock supervision. Nine or ten graduate students worked two and three shifts a week. We needed to have two women on during the night and on the weekends when the rest of the staff was not there.

Our capacity was ninety-three women. We had room for thirty women in the intake room (the library) where we put the transients that needed a place for a few days to a week or two. That gave us sixty-three beds in the private cubicles that we realized were needed for rehabilitating women with other problems. We concluded that we had to keep our population by quotas and we couldn't have more than sixty per cent women with mental health problems. It was estimated that sixty per cent of homeless women had been in mental institutions for mental problems prior to deinstitutionalization.

Our revenue increased. A minimal charge for room and board was made to all the women on Social Security because they were unemployable or on medication. However, contrary to halfway houses, and with the recommendation of Dr. Berry, we just had the same minimum room and board charge as we did for any woman who was working. This system allowed the women to have extra money to save or to use when shopping for their necessities.

Our daily routine was well-established. Many of our women came for their prescribed medication four times a day. As long as they were on the medication, they were functional. We didn't allow them to go back to bed after breakfast. They had to follow the rules. They were allowed to rest during rest periods like all the others. We expected normal behavior from them. We learned that when we expected normal behavior, they did their best to comply and lived to their highest potential. It was an exciting time.

Occasionally, a church group came in and talked about healing. The women were then asked to come forward for healing. I was generally impressed with these groups, except when they urged the women to quit taking their medication. Groups like that were not allowed back. I reminded the staff that we weren't doctors and that we weren't God. If God were to touch a woman and heal her mind and emotions so that antipsychotic medication was no longer necessary, then the doctors would wean them off. I am happy to report that this happened many times. There were cases where women who were on psychotropic medications required less and less until some were finally off of it, for which we were very grateful.

This special group of women was very sensitive to spiritual things. They were good at writing poetry and at art and handcrafts. It was an exciting era in the life of Rescue Mission, because our work with the mentally disturbed population was so successful. Many of them, regardless of diagnosis, found apartments and subsequently did well living independently. One could only accept the fact that many of them would have to take medication the rest of their lives.

Prior to deinstitutionalization, destitute women were seldom seen on the street. It isn't that they weren't out there. They simply kept themselves better hidden because they realized their vulnerability. Their homelessness was less obvious. They didn't loiter. Women coming out of institutions seemed less aware of their vulnerability. It wasn't until then that homeless women were termed "bag ladies." Invariably, these bag ladies were women with a mental health problem who had spent some time in one of our mental institutions.

We first became aware of the deinstitutionalization of the mental hospitals back in about 1975. I had to let the folks at Grady Hospital know that unless they could help us out and cooperate with us, we wouldn't take any more referrals from them. Two things resulted from that. Dr. Berry became their liaison person to work with us and train us and help us understand how to work with them. At the same time, the social service department of the Grady Psychiatric unit assigned one of their social workers to work with us. She visited one day a week to see how her clients were doing. This meant that if we were having any problems, we could contact her. This communication allowed us to better help the women socially as well as spiritually. This was a very good working arrangement and we had the constant cooperation of the local agencies.

We worked with these women in the early days of their release from Milledgeville Mental Hospital and learned very quickly that they had many fears. Those first residents that came to us had memories of being forced into the mental hospital. Many times, they were actually handcuffed and put behind the locked doors of the mental hospitals as though they were felons. They had many fears and a lot of mistrust. While paranoia is frequently so much a part of the problem with schizophrenia, a lot of them had normal fears and normal paranoia. It was difficult for me to ask them to go to the hospital for anything.

One of our women broke her wrist. When I wanted her to go to the hospital, she thought I was railroading her and forcing her back into the mental hospital.

There were times when I had to write a letter to a facility on behalf of a woman. When I knew a woman needed to go to the hospital, even for evaluation on the Psychiatric unit or at any other clinic in the hospital, I had to write a letter saying, "Please see this patient. She needs care in your unit. When she has received her treatment, we want her back at the Mission and we will provide transportation," or something of that nature. I didn't seal the envelope. Instead of giving the letter to the person who drove her to the hospital, I let the woman carry it, knowing that she would read it and that she would be assured that I wasn't part of a scheme to have her committed once again.

We had a beautiful young lady come to us who had a nervous breakdown while she was studying with her husband in Europe. She had been hospitalized. While in Europe, she had studied under some of the finest calligraphers. She was an artist and she did calligraphy beautifully. She gave birth to a child when she was in Europe and her mental illness began afterwards. Finally, she returned home but never did return to normalcy. She was one of our residents. Her husband divorced her and later married again, taking the child. She couldn't cope with the feelings that came up when visiting her child. Even visits from her parents were a strain on her. My experience with this woman and others like her taught me that many of our people with mental problems weren't actually homeless and it wasn't that their families didn't want them. They simply couldn't cope with certain of the feelings that arose from contact with family members.

In our new Mission, our need for a cook was met in a great way. Our old cook, Jean Morris, was in failing health. She acquired an assistant named Chi Chi who came to us through the Georgia Regional Alcoholism Treatment Center. Chi Chi had been trained in a chef's school and had her chef's certificate. Shortly after her arrival, she made a commitment of faith. She soon took over as head cook when Jean retired. Chi Chi became a very devoted member of our staff and remained with us until after my retirement.

Events occurred shortly after Dr. Huck's death that reaffirmed God's call to me to reach out and speak for the women who were so overlooked in the other large cities of our country. Several hundred Men's Missions were in existence. Little if anything was being done for women by most of these Missions. Heavy on my heart was my desire for the Boards of Urban Missions and volunteers from these wonderful Rescue Missions across our country to take up the burden and do the same things for the women in their cities that we were doing in Atlanta. My concern was made greater by the desperate need of increasing numbers of vulnerable women on the street.

A Voice Crying in the Wilderness

Two needs weighed heavily on my heart. My concern for the women across the country almost consumed me. The Board of Directors and the people of Atlanta were listening, but Missions elsewhere seemed unconcerned about the great need of the women in their areas. Maybe they were just uneducated. Additionally, homeless women with children were not being served, even in Atlanta. I felt very much like I was crying alone in the wilderness, like I saw something that no one else saw.

After much prayer and preparation, I took a trip in 1977 to the IUGM national headquarters in Kansas City, Missouri. Seminars were planned for the directors and their wives. At this time, Larry was living in Omaha, Nebraska. Diane and her children and I drove to Omaha. On our way back through Kansas City, we visited the Wooleys. Diane knew and loved the Wooleys. We were welcomed into their home and Bill and Madeleine took Diane and me out to dinner that night.

Reverend Wooley took Stauffer's place as director of The Anchorage when we moved to Dothan and he served there for ten years. He resigned as director of The Anchorage when he became the executive secretary of the entire IUGM organization. Madeleine, his wife, became his private secretary. He not only organized the International Convention each year, but he gave a detailed report of his activities during the year as he visited missions across the country.

Before I set out on this trip, I carefully wrote out and prepared a five minute delivery on the plight of destitute women as experienced in Atlanta. During the conversation at dinner that evening, I approached Bill about my burden by saying, Bill, you know what I have been doing for the last years at The Women's Mission. You know I would much prefer being the wife of the director of a Rescue Mission, rather than being the director myself. God, in His providence, put me in my present position. I would like to know why there is not more done for women by the Missions of our nation. I wonder if there is anything you could do for me in this area.

He was a jolly fellow, and started laughing heartily. I didn't think I'd said anything humorous. When he composed himself, he said, "I'll see what I can do for you."

I replied, "That's great!"

He said, "I'll see what I can do to find a husband for you so that you can be a director's wife!"

This was a typical example of the attitude toward the women's role in the IUGM in those days. Women were supposed to be secretaries, or housemothers of any branch work that might have anything to do with the Mission. When I went to conventions, I was the only female director of a Rescue Mission. I felt like the convention was planned for men and their supportive wives and staff.

The president of the IUGM was always an executive director of a city Mission who was voted in by the delegates at the time of the convention. Morris Vanderburg, the director of the large Mission in Kansas City, was the current president. He had been the president for several years. I felt that I could speak to Wooley and Vanderburg to see whether they could influence the delegates at the next convention to start something for women.

I made an appointment to have breakfast with Morris Vanderburg the next morning. During our time together, I asked if I could have just five minutes on the floor when all the delegates were there, just five minutes of time to challenge the directors of the Missions to start Women's Divisions. I told him I had a five minute tape that I could give him so that he would know exactly what I was going to say.

With a great, compassionate heart like Morris has, he said, "Elsie, I hear everything you are saying and I agree with you that this is a tremendous need. I see it right here in Kansas City, but financially the funds are coming in so poorly we can hardly make ends meet just with the program we have going. As far as the Missions across the country, if you were to deliver a challenge like that, I doubt that there would be a dozen men that would really hear what you are saying. This is my last year as president and I am a 'lame duck.' It is time for another election. My time has run out. There is really nothing I can do at this point to incorporate you into the program."

That was in the summer of 1977. It was four years later, in 1981, when we moved into the ninety-three bed Women's Mission.

The other passion and burden of my heart was to have an area where I could take homeless mothers with children. I thought this might finally be realized when we moved into the ninety-three-bed Mission. However, the mentally disturbed women took up all our beds that next summer and there was simply no room. We never did start a program, nor did we even have an area for homeless mothers with children there.

There were two acres behind the Mission that would have been suitable for cottages. Every time I showed anyone our beautiful building and lovely grounds, I said, "My dream is that some day we'll see cottages in the back for homeless mothers with children."

From the very beginning of my work with the Mission, when a mother with children called, I tried to get as much information as I could over the telephone and I instructed the staff to do the same. If she was going to be in town for less than six months, we referred her to Traveler's Aid. Although Traveler's Aid sent us the unencumbered women that came to their office, they were obligated to put mothers with children in a hotel room where they would be safe while they worked on their social problems. Homeless mothers with children who were going to be in town longer than six months were directed to a local church that I felt would be compassionate toward their needs. I was always grieved when a mother called and I had to turn her down. I remember so clearly the occasions when women came in and said, "I called some time ago and you all couldn't take me because of my children. Now the Department of Family and Children's Services has taken them away from me. I need to get my life straightened out."

On those occasions when a woman really did make a change and get back on her feet, it was still very difficult for her to get her children back from foster care. At the very least, she had to have a good job and an apartment with the right number of bedrooms, according to the number of children she had. The Welfare Department generally does not step in just because a mother is living in crowded conditions. However, if she ever loses them, it is difficult to get them back unless they meet all the strict requirements of the Department of Family and Children's Services (DFACS). I saw the agony of these DFACS mothers as they visited their children while under the care of another woman. I truly hoped that some day we would have a place for homeless mothers with children on our grounds.

When we moved into our ninety-three-bed Mission, the story was written up in the magazine section of the Atlanta Journal with beautiful pictures in the centerfold of the magazine section. It was in the spring of 1981 during the national convention. The Atlanta Journal Constitution is picked up and read all over the country and we received national recognition. I took a copy of the paper with me to the convention. There, a gentleman from New York came up to me and said, "On my way home, I'd like to fly through Atlanta and see your Mission."

As he sat in my office later that month, he listened while I spoke about my burden for Women's Missions in other cities.

He said, "If I tell you that there is somebody who might make a contribution or otherwise be able to help you, would you write down the reasons why a woman who has money earmarked to give to Men's Missions should give to start a Women's Mission instead?"

I said, "Yes, I'd be glad to do that. The country knows about Men's Missions but it seems people have to be educated about the need for Women's Missions."

However, I got caught up in the details of running the Mission and didn't get around to writing down what he needed. He called me some time later and said, "I'd like you to put down on paper everything you told me that day."

I reminded him, "We talked for well over an hour."

He said, "Well, I'd like you to just play your heart out on paper and mail it to me. I know some people that belong to an anonymous foundation. If their hearts were turned in this direction, there might be an interest in what you are talking about."

I took a week of vacation and went down to visit Eileen in Florida. While sitting on her deck, I wrote voluminously. Upon my return, a volunteer typed forty-two pages of triple-spaced information!

I called the gentleman and said, "I'm going to have to do a lot of editing and condensing. There are forty-two pages."

He said, "I've written many speeches and I've done a lot of writing. Just mail it to me and I'll work on it for you."

As a result of that, a grant came through an anonymous foundation. It was not a cash grant. Instead, travel expenses were to be covered for any opportunities I had to go to a city and assess its needs and learn if there was any interest in mission work. I shared this information with the concerned men and women in my circle of friends.

After much prayer and deliberation, the six of us who comprised the original board decided to start a new Board of Directors so that we could work on seeing Women's Missions started in other cities. This included Boyd Lyons, Ann Cousins, Anne Campbell, Markham and Edie Berry, Fleet Rogers, and me. "Ministries to Women USA" (MWUSA) was the name of our new organization. We prayed that God would open doors for us to promote women's ministries in other cities and states and to provide a place for training people to do this work. By this time it was 1984. MWUSA was incorporated in 1984.

The Atlanta Journal featured the new Women's Mission the second time in the magazine section. As a result, I had calls from distant cities about the Mission. On occasion, concerned women or couples came and observed for several days or volunteered for a week so they could go back home and pioneer in their city.

By 1984, I considered that I might partially retire from the directorship of The Women's Mission in the following year. Our Women's Division was fast becoming a national training headquarters. With the excellent staff of graduate students, I believed that by 1985 many trainees from other cities on staff as volunteers would greatly reduce the budget and I would be free to retire partially and the Atlanta Union Mission Women's Division would become the spring-board for ministries across the country. A professional movie company even made a video tape pro bono showing all facets of The Women's Mission. It was beautifully done so that we could mail it to other organizations all over the country.

However, in 1985, things did not come together as we had believed they would. The Board of Directors of the Mission requested that I retire completely as of that July. The circumstances of my retirement cut off my relationship with the Mission entirely.

Three days later, in the providence of God, North Avenue Presbyterian Church offered me an office in an adjoining building. I was now into another phase of my life.

Personal Life Following Retirement

During the five years while Dr. Huck was alive and we had our family life, many good things were happening. Seven of my sixteen grandchildren were born during that time. We have albums full of pictures of the babies and the children who were already toddlers during those happy years when we lived by McClatchey Park. Eileen lived in Florida and visited us often.

Audrey had been living in Texas with her two children and during this time she moved back to Atlanta. A year after Dr. Huck died, she came into my office and told me she had a lump in her breast and she was going to have a biopsy. She told the surgeon to remove her breast completely if the frozen section biopsy showed malignancy while she was under anesthesia. She didn't want them to wake her up only to put her to sleep again. I went to the hospital with her that day. The surgeon sent word out that the frozen section did, indeed, show that it was malignant and he was going to proceed with a total mastectomy. Her children were about five and seven at the time. A year later she became pregnant and was in turmoil about what to do. One doctor told her to have an abortion or she would surely die. Another one told her not to. She went to several doctors and they differed in their opinions. She went to several preachers and they differed in what she should do as well.

She came to me and she said, "Mother, I have to decide. I know you wouldn't have an abortion."

I sat before my daughter as she asked me to decide. I had to be very honest with her. Though I hate abortions, I said, "Audrey, you have two children. I'm so neurotic about my own body and my own health that if I were facing what you are, I just might decide to have an abortion. You are going to have to take me off your scale. I can't weigh in on either side. This is something that you are going to have to decide yourself before the Lord."

She decided to have an abortion and went in for it on a Monday morning when the rates were a little cheaper. I didn't know she was actually going through with this. As she sat in the waiting room, she heard the women around her talking. They were healthy, married women for whom it just was not "convenient" to have a baby. Audrey got up, put down her admission papers, and walked out. She went home and wrote down her experience. Audrey loved to put her feelings down on paper when she was upset. She related her whole experience at that abortion clinic and explained why she decided to walk out. When she was all done, she entitled her paper *Murder Cheaper on a Monday Morning*. Subsequently, she submitted this paper to Guidepost Magazine. She was one of ten winners, but it was never published because they considered it too controversial. When her baby was born, she wrote another emotion-packed commentary called *I Wouldn't Send You Back*. That child was our little Jonathan.

Things went well for the next couple years. Then, one day, she came into my office with a hacking cough. I told her she'd better check it out.

She said, "You think the cancer is back, don't you?"

I said, "No, I didn't actually think of that." And I really hadn't. I just thought it might have been hay fever or an allergy and she needed to check it out.

As it turned out, however, the breast cancer had returned and had spread to her lungs. Her doctors said that her pregnancy with Jonathan had nothing to do with the return of her cancer. If that had been the case, the cancer should have shown up immediately.

She only lived another twelve months and then went home to be with the Lord. The last year of her life was really difficult as she struggled with her faith and her belief for a healing. She suffered a great deal as did those of us who were close to her. Her husband, Marion, was particularly supportive. In addition to Marion, she left behind the three children ages three, eight, and ten. While I had already experienced the grief of losing a second mate, I now faced the additional grief of her loss and the grief of seeing my three young motherless grandchildren. She passed away April 6, 1979, and was buried on Palm Sunday. The following Sunday was Easter. After church, we took the children to the grave. All the flowers and trees throughout the cemetery were coming to life. This gave us an opportunity to talk about the Resurrection.

God was with us in our grieving, but we still had to find our way through it. I felt such a longing to have her father with me for comfort. When I cried out to the Lord, He showed me that He was the God of all comfort. During my journey through that grief, I was busy at the Mission and quite preoccupied. Otherwise, I could have been overwhelmed by dealing with the feelings of losing both my mates and now losing a daughter. My nature was to postpone facing the reality of grief. It was many months before I could sing the song *Because He Lives, I Can*

Face Tomorrow. That brought great comfort to my heart, knowing that we serve a living Savior and that we can face our tomorrows with His help. Death is so final. God gives and God takes away. God heals a broken heart. I watched the children go through these phases and saw they had to go through the grief of losing as well as I did. This allowed us to comfort each other.

To me, the most tragic things I have observed through the years were watching several of my children go through very painful divorces. Divorce is never really final because the children are affected constantly. They are torn all the way into adulthood between two parents that they love. Divorce is absolutely not normal. My children hate divorce as much as I do. God hates divorce. However, even Christian marriages don't endure sometimes. We had to face the reality of divorce and work through that grief as well.

Through these years, when I left the house and entered the Mission, I entered a microcosm of women in pain. It was my job to minister to them. Perhaps my personal emotional pain made me more compassionate and better able to comfort the women. We never had the promise that life would be easy when we became Christians. For many, I have observed that life may have become harder. As Christians, however, we are given grace to deal with our grief. No one ever said that everything would be ideal and that we could dictate to God what we wanted. The Christian life is a life of adventure. God walks with us and holds our hands through the hard places. The unbeliever suffers and goes through death without God. The unbeliever loses loved ones to death and does not have the comfort of knowing that he will see them again or even that God can provide. The unbeliever goes through divorce, either their divorce or their children's, alone. When we have Christ, He is right there with us. That is the comfort. That is why the Christian life is such a wonderful and great adventure.

> John 14:16-18 (NIV) says 16 And I will ask the Father, and he will give you another Counselor to be with you forever—17 the Spirit of truth. The world cannot accept him, because it neither sees him nor knows him. But you know him, for he lives with you and will be in you. 18 I will not leave you as orphans; I will come to you.

Stauffer always said, "We don't really start living until we are ready to die."

That is so true. That is what we found out was the reality of living a life truly full of joy.

God gave me many friends who shared the vision that I had for taking the Gospel, not only to Atlanta to women in crisis, but throughout the nation. Among these friends were those that were on my Board of Directors of Ministries to Women USA. They had now been functioning in that capacity for almost a year. There were many volunteers that were ready to stand by us.

I am thinking of Kathy Parcham, a young, married woman with no children. She was a volunteer chaplain at The Women's Mission during my last months there. Kathy was a seminary student, just finishing her graduate work and preparing for ordination. It was her desire to be ordained in the chapel of The Women's Mission. Kathy had a heart for women who were in crisis and who needed to know that in Christ was the answer to their problems.

During the last days of my ministry at The Women's Mission, and the severance that the women had to witness in my leaving them, never to return, she was truly a God-send. She had a true pastor's heart as she ministered to those women. She was also gifted in fund raising and helped in raising money for Presbyterian Village, a senior's community for Presbyterians. When I set up the office in the ministry center provided by North Avenue Church, she worked shoulder-to-shoulder with me.

Village Atlanta and God's Math

The newly-organized Board of Directors and Kathy and I prayed for God's guidance. Now that we couldn't use the Women's Division of the Atlanta Union Mission as we had formerly planned, we knew that God had something even greater for us. Our concern was that there was nothing in Atlanta for homeless mothers with children. It was quickly decided that was the ministry God was calling us to.

We started looking for land for a large building, seeking God's will for the direction in which we should go. Our mailing list of friends was very small but God gave us the faith to believe that He was leading us.

A Christian man in a county government office started looking for property for us. One day, he called me to report that he had three places he wanted to show me. He thought they might be appropriate to start something for homeless mothers with children.

The one property that appealed to me was a seven acre tract of land on a main route going south from Atlanta. The route was now bypassed by Interstate 85 so traffic was light. A stately, old, five-bedroom home near the center of the property faced the old highway. There were columns at the front entrance. No one had lived in the house for many years. I could see that the old place had a lot of potential. I'll never forget the day the Board of Directors gathered on the front lawn of this home. The spirit of God just burdened all of our hearts and we knew that this was God's choice for the location of our new venture. The price of this property was $185,000. We didn't even have money for a down payment.

We had been holding a foundation grant of $25,000 in escrow to venture out and start Missions in other cities. Because our efforts in that direction seemed to be thwarted at every turn, and because the need of homeless women with children was so great, the Board decided to use this money to start this new ministry instead. Debbie Shearer was immediately hired to assess the need with the agencies and work on the program. She was a young woman who had been on the staff of the Atlanta Union Mission. We also hired Kathy Parcham part-time in the development office to get out the newsletters and to help in developing the program.

This was another big step of faith for me. Although I was now eligible to receive Social Security, I needed another source of income. In reality, I should have taken a part-time job upon retiring from the Mission. There was no way I could live on my limited retirement income and maintain my large home. However, I knew that God had other plans for me and that I had to trust Him once again to supply all my needs.

After Dr. Huck's death, I had taken out a sizeable mortgage on our house in order to restore it. Now, I had to meet the monthly payments. In addition, although the house was restored, the infrastructure started giving trouble. I knew that it would soon require major repairs. The house needed a young family that could afford it and take care of the property.

I began the process of getting the house ready to sell. About a year after I retired, I was able to sell it and I moved into an apartment. I didn't make my needs known to others, but simply trusted the Lord. The Board of MWUSA offered me a small salary. I believed that this was God's will. Again, God supplied my needs in a wonderful way. I was able to give my full attention to the ministry that God called me to.

I now found myself in a position before God where I had to look to the needs of a ministry and be responsible to a Board of Directors for the direction in which I would lead them. All along, during all the hard places in my life, God's hand was preparing me for the situation in which I now found myself.

By this time, funds were coming in through our small mailing list which took care of our monthly expenses. Our new property was purchased in 1986. The seller wanted $85,000 down and agreed to finance the remaining $100,000 over three years. We were to pay $10,000 in interest at the end of each year. We were able to make the down payment through three unsecured notes that two of the board members were willing to sign in addition to the original grant of $25,000 that we had.

God supplied our needs each step of the way. For a year, people contributed to a dream. They had no tangible evidence that anything we were doing would ever materialize. God gave us enough friends that shared our vision. It was a blessing to see the people of God reaching out by faith and looking forward with us to the time when we could take homeless mothers with children, give them the Gospel, and help them get their lives back. Finally, we'd be able to minister to these women and their children as we had ministered to single women in earlier years.

A banker joined our Board. After we purchased the property, the banker recommended to the Board that they move in a family from the housing project. It was the mother, father, three young children, and a grandmother. The parents were concerned about their children's safety in the housing project. The banker knew they were conscientious about paying their bills. Their presence there was also beneficial to us because our insurance rates were lower if the house was occupied. The Board concurred.

The next year was not without tests of our faith. Financially, and in the decisions that had to be made by the Board of Directors, our faith was definitely tested. I quickly learned that when you have a Board, there are those who are very "logical" and will want to see on paper how things are going to work out. It is more difficult for them to take a step of faith knowing that God will supply our needs because we are in His will. To them, God's math won't make any sense at all.

Within the year, our tenants brought more people in to live with them. A married daughter with children arrived and then another married daughter. Next to come was the other grandmother. I think there were fourteen people living in the house; all were related in some way or another. We required them to pay rent monthly, but expected to return their money to them when they left so they could make a down payment on a home. Their monthly rent was put in escrow by our treasurer.

At this time, the Board was getting restless. Some members just wanted to give up the whole idea. The banker created a crisis. He wanted no further part of this faith venture and refused to renew his note for $25,000. He insisted that the entire project be abandoned and was going to make sure that happened when he didn't renew his note. Without his $25,000, it looked as though the whole project would fall apart. Our whole venture appeared doomed. And then, suddenly, and at precisely the critical moment, the Lord laid it on the heart of an anonymous person to accept the risk and take up the slack with an interest-free loan for $40,000 that covered the banker's note and the unpaid interest expense. This was part of our donor learning to live by faith in his own life and this clearly was not a risk-free situation for him using the banker's logic. For us, we were again back on track. The banker left the Board, frustrated. Later on we were able to pay back the $40,000. The bottom line was that God's math worked and He had honored our steps of faith!

God in His providence now brought a man onto our Board by the name of Bob Lupton. Bob headed up a faith ministry in Atlanta. He knew the joy of seeking God's will, finding it, and then by faith going ahead and doing it. I was grateful to him when he challenged the Board on steps of faith.

The turning point came in a Board meeting when he said "Why do you have an intact family paying rent to stay in that house? We are telling the public that we're getting ready to take care of homeless women with children."

At that Board meeting, the decision was made to ask the family to leave. By faith, we believed that we should proceed with our plans and that God would supply our needs. We returned the money to the family. They used it as a down payment on a home and they didn't have to return to the housing projects.

Extensive restorations and repairs of the old house were needed. Many people pitched in. The pastor of a nearby Methodist church with members of his congregation helped some of our Board members and many other volunteers scrape and scrub and clean and paint.

Once habitable, we had to decide when to open. Some suggested that we wait until we had a certain amount of money in our treasury before we took the first residents. However, this was to be a ministry of faith. It was close to Christmas. I recommended to the Board that we take five homeless families, since there were five bedrooms. We had to believe that God would supply our needs.

The verse the Lord gave me was Joshua 1:3 (NIV) "I will give you every place where you set your foot, as I promised Moses."

I suggested to the Board that we'd already had the property for a long time. God had already given it to us. God would supply our needs when we put our feet into it by faith.

We admitted our first mother around the last part of November 1987 and two others quickly followed. A Christmas tree was put up early and pictures were taken. A newsletter followed, saying that we had started taking in mothers and children. The news was out: *Mothers admitted to Village Atlanta.* With year-end gifts, I think we took in about $30,000 before January 15. God had indeed honored our step of faith.

We now had two staff members at The Village, Debbie Shearer and Chi Chi. Debbie became our director of Village Atlanta and was also our counselor. Chi Chi came as her assistant. She had been our cook for many years at The Women's Mission. Eventually, she left there to work as the chef in a local restaurant. When she came on board, I told her we didn't need anybody in food service. Our need was for an assistant and somebody who could be a housemother and who could teach the women to cook. She was excited to accept the position and we were on our way.

Our development office remained downtown in the Ministry Center. We had monthly board meetings and sent out monthly newsletters. Every quarter, we were able to pay the interest on our notes as well as meet our growing expenses at

The Village. Village Atlanta was no longer just a dream. It had become a reality. Cash contributions increased and we began to receive contributions of goods and services as well.

Our long-range plan called for having buildings on the property where we could provide different levels of intake and rehabilitation for these mothers. We decided our first building should consist of twelve efficiency apartments to be used for purposes of long-term rehabilitation. The estimated cost of that structure was $200,000. Facing us was the need to pay off the notes amounting to about $75,000 owed to our Board members and the $100,000 that we still owed the seller by the end of the third year, plus his interest for the third year.

In our newsletters, we showed the plans for the proposed building and outlined the costs of construction. Foundations in Atlanta stated they would give us "sizeable" grants when the time was "right." To them, this meant when we owned enough assets. All we could offer the foundations was debt and a dream. We didn't actually own any assets. It seemed as though we just couldn't get a break. Our operating budget was being met by our newsletters. God blessed that problem area.

The debt that we owed was mind boggling. We owed the purchase price of the property. In addition, we had to raise funds for the new building. Finally, there was the cost of restoring the old house so it could be used for offices. All of this was an enormous undertaking. All the while, we had God's assurance that He would ultimately supply our needs. We had to rest in His faithfulness. This assurance made the adventure exciting instead of frightening.

After hard work by the Board, the notes were paid off to the Board members. We still had to pay $110,000 at the end of the third year.

I did some figuring. We had paid off $85,000 worth of notes. The property was worth much more than $100,000. I knew that we couldn't take a first mortgage out on the property and see to it that our seller was paid and cover the cost of the building and renovations. With the going interest rates at the time, it would cost us about $1,000 a month on a thirty-year note to finance $100,000. Although expensive, at least that was something we could incorporate into our budget. It was difficult to get hold of any of the funds from the grants we had already gotten. We were concerned about the $200,000 needed for the new building. We knew we had to position ourselves to get the foundations to start releasing the funds they were waiting to give us at the "right" time.

One day, we were visited by a middle-aged couple who represented the Holyoke Foundation. They said they had heard of our proposed Village and asked if they could talk with me. I eagerly showed them the grounds and then took them into the house and introduced them to several of the mothers. I told them about the proposed cost of a new building and about our operating expenses.

In conversation, the man asked, "In looking at the financial needs here, if someone were to provide you with $100,000, how would you spend it?"

I said, "If somebody gave me $100,000, I'd get rid of the debt on this house."

To this, he responded, "But I thought you were looking for money for the new building."

I said, "We are, but if we had the property free and clear we could give a financial statement of our assets and start writing grant requests to the different foundations."

A week later, he called and said "Mrs. Huck, my wife and I talked it over. We have a very small foundation but we can lend you the money. We can't give principal in the form of a free grant. We can lend you the $100,000 interest-free that you owe your seller. You did your homework well and you are right about what it would cost you for thirty years. If you accept our interest-free loan for $100,000 and take care of that debt, it will cost you $833 a month and you will have the entire loan paid back to us in just ten years."

With a great deal of rejoicing, we informed the Board of his offer. We incorporated the $833 into our operating expenses, which were very low. It was like paying rent of $833 a month and at the same time we were paying off $100,000 debt in just ten years.

In preparing to write foundations for grants to build our $200,000 building, I called Alicia Philipp. She was the executive director of a central office representing several smaller Atlanta foundations. The Holyoke Foundation was one of those she served.

I said, "We still really don't own the building. How will I write grant requests?"

She advised us to say "Due to the generosity of the Holyoke Foundation, we are able to incorporate the cost of the building into our operating fund. We want to start a building fund and this is how much we want to raise."

That was the method we used in writing our requests for foundation grants. However, God in His providence had another plan in store for us that was even better. Throughout all this time, we thought we'd have to put out the building in bids. John Wieland, a prominent builder and a member of my church, came to me one day and said, "If you will let me put up the building, I'll do it at cost and you won't have to put it out on bids."

Word of this quickly spread to the board and our next meeting was a time of rejoicing.

I didn't hear from him again for some time. One day he visited for a second time and asked, "Elsie, do you have any funds in yet toward the building."

I said, "No, we don't. We just need that first gift. We haven't yet had the break of a first foundation gift."

He said, "If your Board of Directors will raise $150,000 in three months, I'll write out a check for $50,000 toward the new building."

Within a few days, we sent out another newsletter announcing that we had a challenge grant of $50,000. Within three months, we had surpassed the challenge grant and now had $250,000. Several foundations released their grants after they learned of the challenge made by the well-known developer. With the Wieland check, we now had $300,000. Isn't God good? His ways are beyond our abilities to understand.

Ephesians 3:20-21 (NIV) "20 Now to him who is able to do immeasurably more than all we ask or imagine, according to his power that is at work within us, 21 to him be glory in the church and in Christ Jesus throughout all generations, for ever and ever! Amen."

We planned for the building to be two stories tall. There were to be twelve efficiency apartments. Each mother was to have her own apartment where she could close the door and have her family to herself in privacy. There was to be a lounge on the second floor. On the first floor were the main entrance and a lounge for the women. Adjacent to the lounge, a large playroom for the children was planned. There was to be a large laundry room.

We planned to have a large day care center on the grounds. On the property was a garage with an apartment over it and we had hoped to put the day care center there. However, the garage was condemned. It was subsequently leveled and became part of the landscaping project for the yard. Now, we didn't know where to put the day care. This made us aware of our frailty as human beings to provide for ourselves.

Anticipating all of our needs, God in his providence directed us and solved the problem. We got a call from the contractor who said that he couldn't place our building at the planned location because of the contour of the land. We either had to build somewhere else, or start our building with a ground floor and build the two stories above that. Because of the way the ground sloped, the ground floor would have many windows on one side and none on the other. In the end, that's what we did. Everything worked out perfectly and we put our day care center on the ground floor.

Ultimately, the building cost us $300,000. But hadn't the Lord provided $300,000 instead of $200,000? Again, He knows better than we do what our needs are even before we cry out to Him.

The first three years of our existence, we operated our ministry from the old house. We took the first woman about the first of December 1987 but didn't move into the new building until 1990. During those three years, about a hundred mothers with about two hundred children went through Village Atlanta. Many of them stayed two or three months. God was gracious and some of them were able to stay even longer.

During that time, the communal living situation provided a real learning experience for all of us. These mothers were all destitute and homeless. They were all grateful for a place to live. There was only the one large kitchen, and bathroom space was limited. For three years, the happiness and the contentment of those mothers was just unbelievable. There was great joy in sitting around the table and eating together. God taught us lessons that we never would have known had we not been experimenting while living together in the big house.

I realize now it would have been premature in 1985 for Ministries to Women to go into other cities as consultants to encourage them and help them get started. We'd have been ill-equipped had we left The Women's Mission in 1985 and ventured out. Day by day, we learned from our loving, heavenly Father how to live and work with homeless mothers with children.

In 1990, we left the old house for the new building. Instead of five mothers with children, we could now accommodate twelve families.

Naturally, we had a larger budget. More staff was needed. Again, we were in the position of having to say, "Lord, what kind of program do we need? The whole situation is different. We have no more communal eating. Each woman does her own cooking." Consequently, we had to start incorporating yet another new set of rules and guidelines. Fortunately, we had enough staff that we could just adjust them as the needs arose.

When the move was accomplished, we immediately started restoring the old house to serve as our administration building. A dedication celebration of the new building was planned for June 1990, just three and a half years after we took our first woman in the old house. At the open house, I challenged the audience that in the providence of God, we'd like to see the whole village completed by the time of the Olympics in 1996, just six years away.

I was president of the Board of Directors. Every several years, we elected a new Chairman of the Board. In our administrative office, there was a director of development. Volunteers functioned as receptionists. Over time, the salaried staff increased as we became increasingly busy. As the staff increased, our budget increased.

As we prepared our budget for 1992, we realized that it would be almost $400,000 for the new year. Although God supplied our needs, there were times when our finances were stretched pretty thin. Funds did not come in fast enough to build up the kind of operating reserves desired by the treasurer and the new chairman. I observed them faltering often in Board meetings and I tried to encourage them to continue to have faith that God would supply our needs.

At one Board meeting, the treasurer said, "If no more money comes in, we will have to close our doors in three or four months."

I had to remind them that there was a time when we didn't even have enough money for our small staff at the ministry center. This was before we even opened the doors. We had to believe God and we'd had to take it one month at a time.

There was great unrest among those that wanted to have trust funds set up and to be a couple hundred thousand dollars ahead at all times for our expenses. The newly-elected chairman and the treasurer were people who simply could not operate by faith. They believed there was a financial crisis. This was at the time of elections for the Board. Those with investments and those whose faith hadn't been tried on the Board were in the majority on our executive committee. Simultaneously, the Atlanta Union Mission now wanted my ideas and my advice on what they could do to have something downtown for homeless mothers with children on an emergency basis. Although they were unhappy with me for wanting to do something for homeless mothers with children in 1985, they were now under a new president of their Board and a new executive director. I was happy to work with them as a consultant. I saw the great need for a downtown ministry. They, in turn, could use Village Atlanta after the emergency if there was a need for extended rehabilitation.

Great unrest came on the Board. Some of us were not frightened by the economy and wanted to continue our venture by faith. Bob Lupton, a great man of faith, had resigned from the Board two years before because his own ministry required fund-raising and he had to give all his efforts to his own expanding ministry. We were in the minority.

The end to all this conflict came in March 1992, when my precious Village Atlanta was gifted to the Atlanta Union Mission, debt free. In addition, a $250,000 cashier's check was given to the Mission so they could operate the Village until it was incorporated into their budget. For me, this was like giving up a child for adoption and it brought great grief to my heart to see it happen. I really had to struggle with this turn of events. I felt betrayed. I had many other feelings and it was a real emotional and spiritual struggle. The ministry was sold out by the board members who were poisoned by faithlessness. It seemed that my dreams were going up in ashes.

This was already happening when I went to see my pastor. He was new and had only taken the pulpit in 1990. I had never really poured out my heart to him before. He didn't know that the Board was taking this direction. He didn't know what I was going through. After hearing me out, he concluded, "Well, Elsie, the Lord has something greater for you."

I walked out of his office that day comforted but not encouraged. Again, I was reminded of what Mr. Hatch said back in 1964 about things happening "rather to the furtherance of the Gospel." Now, however, we were twenty-eight years down the road. I thought this all probably happened because the Board considered that I was getting too old and felt that they had to take things into their own hands, betray me, and put another organization in control. Now, did the Lord have something even greater for me than all this? My grief was second only to the grief of losing loved ones to death.

The transfer of Village Atlanta to the Atlanta Union Mission was a matter negotiated between Boards. A retirement fund was set up for me. I had seen God provide my needs in times of great need. I could again retire, this time without major financial concerns. This time, I could truly be a volunteer. Whatever I did from now on, I didn't have to worry about my personal needs. I could zero in completely on the needs of any ministry that I consulted with and worked with in the future. Philippians 4:19 (NIV) "And my God will meet all your needs according to his glorious riches in Christ Jesus."

It was hard to box all my things and leave my attractive office at Village Atlanta. My home bedroom became the place where I had to start all over again. Fortunately, my children were there to comfort me.

Once again I reflected on the twists and turns of my life. When I committed myself to God's keeping and told him to direct my path, there were directions that I sometimes rebelled against. Nonetheless, I always had the confidence that God was walking with me.

When I retired from The Women's Mission in 1985, at the age of 65, I thought I was prepared to be a consultant in other cities regarding all aspects of ministering to women. In the providence of God, He knew that before Village Atlanta I had no direct knowledge of working with destitute mothers with children. God knew that I needed that training and experience. Village Atlanta provided me with what I needed to consult effectively in other cities. Working with homeless women and with homeless women with children added another dimension to my fund of knowledge and experience.

I have now traveled to several cities to recommend whether they begin their labor of love with women and children, or whether they start with just women. I could have thought then that I was totally ready, but until I had formed a Board of Directors and until I had been in that seat and until I knew how political Boards can become....

Looking back, I did have devout Christians on the Board. Our original founding Board was made up of people who had a vision for Missions, not only in Atlanta, but in cities around the country. The ones who strongly influenced the later events came on the Board after the Village was started. In looking back, and if I had it to do all over again, I would make sure on the front end that each Board member had a vision for the big picture. Each member needs to be able to see beyond what we are doing currently. Each needs to be able to reach out by faith to regions beyond. Each needs to be grounded in the Word of God. Each needs to seek to walk by faith in unity one with another and believing God.

There is now hardly an area of concern where I can't provide some ideas or know where to find help for questions that arise in other cities. The cities that I have been to through the years include Tifton, GA; Knoxville, TN; Hot Springs, Arkansas; New York City, N.Y.; Philadelphia, PA; Toledo, OH; Bristol, TN, and LaGrange, GA.

Before going to Atlanta, my ministry was mostly with women who were not homeless but who needed rehabilitation. They had families to return to. When I arrived in Atlanta, it was the homeless women I worked with, and then the homeless women with children. My burden is now increasing for another group of women. They are not necessarily homeless and may actually sit with us in church on Sunday. We may rub shoulders with them every day. Yet, they are often in crisis. They are abused or battered women who are suffering loss and who feel afraid and alone.

Winding It Up

By the age of 73, I found myself with a rather inactive board. The few of us remaining were struggling with what God really wanted us to do with the little time that was left. On the one hand, the reality was that I had retired and was living happily ever after in a retirement community. On the other hand, I didn't see myself as retired because I was still open to going to whatever cities wanted me. Yet, sometimes I can't help but feel like I'm on the shelf. I'm not actively motivating people in a local ministry or having staff surrounding me and sharing my burden and seeing them pick up the load with me. I find myself having gone really full circle around. I've retired twice now, once from the Atlanta Union Mission and now from Village Atlanta.

Some time ago, I found myself with more time available to spend in the local church I'd attended since I joined in 1969. I really didn't know the people there intimately because my only "involvement" was the Sunday morning worship, and I knew from previous worship experience that's not really involvement at all. The rest of the week, I was busy with mission work or speaking in other women's groups or churches about the mission work. I wasn't really involved in the local church for all those many years. Instead, I was continually trying to burden the people of many congregations to have a real compassion for the homeless women.

So I felt really at odds as I finally strove to get to *know* these folks. In 1994, in the midst of my transition from retirement to whatever was next, I got a telephone call from a woman asking me to attend a retreat in Montreat NC, with the women of the church. I told her I'd "think about it" meaning I really didn't intend to go. I felt like a stranger who had nothing in common with these women. And yet I knew them as friends; or at least as acquaintances. Sometimes, almost with a longing in my spirit, I wished I had the kind of fellowship with them that they seemed to have with one another. I really didn't know how to become part of them and I dragged my heels in signing up for the conference. Because she persisted, I finally agreed to go and I made the necessary arrangements.

It was in March of that year. Several of us rode with one of the women from the church. We got to the camp and unloaded our things. The conference was supposed to take place over a weekend from Friday to Sunday, but even before we left there were forecasts of serious snow in the mountains of North Carolina. Our group went anyway, thinking that those warnings would pass and no real weather would show up. However, when we got there, we found that a lot of people had already canceled. The entire South Carolina contingency took the forecast seriously and cancelled. The conference staff recommended we not stay in the cottages that were reserved for us saying, "You better take a block of rooms in the hotel near the dining room so you won't have to go outside to get there."

And so, here we were, our group of women, maybe about twenty of us. We had the luxury of each having a private room because of the cancellations. Our church was one of only two that hadn't cancelled by that time. The other church group had come from only a few hours driving distance away and they were already there. The conference staff had a lot of food in, expecting a large turnout. It's very beautiful in the mountains in March and they anticipated a large group. However, it started snowing the next day and continued on and on. We had no clue how serious the snow would become.

The woman who was the main speaker for the weekend was an author and contributor to Billy Graham's *Decision Magazine*. She said, "I want you all to write down what you expect to go away with from this conference."

And then I thought, "What on earth will I put down?" I just had no idea. All I could think of was.... I drew a complete blank. I was sure that the others would put something down that sounded really spiritual. In the end, I wrote down that I would like to know the women of my church on a first-name basis and that I would really like to get to *know* them.

Little did I know that the Lord was already answering my prayer. The three days of our Bible conference we were so snowed in that the cars looked like snow tents. They were totally buried under a foot or two of snow. There were warnings that nobody should be on the road because the state troopers needed it clear so it could be plowed and they could make rescues. The state troopers prohibited all travel in the area and absolutely didn't want us to venture out even as far as the highway. Consequently, when things looked like they were going to get just a little bit rough, the other church group pulled out entirely. The only people left on the conference grounds were the twenty women from our church and the entire hotel crew. And we had all that food and the big fireplace. We were stranded for six days. It was the worst snowstorm in history for that time of year. At night we'd all come out in our pajamas and sit in a circle around the fireplace and just talk. We were just like a bunch of young girls talking and getting acquainted with one another. When I went away from that conference, I knew that God had answered my prayer and I had gone full circle around now after retiring twice. At the age of 74, I had fellowship with my Church friends like I had when I was in my 20's. I was excited to feel like I was one of them and that no one any longer had me on a pedestal. It wasn't only I who felt estranged from them but I realized that they regarded me as being on a different level because I was a missionary. Now we saw each other as a group of women on the same plane but our level of friendship had become much deeper.

I came home rather excited, not knowing what the Lord had in store for me but convinced that the rest of my life I should never retire from working with street women. And yet, I saw all this falling away from me because more and more missions throughout the country were seeing the need. And it was no longer just the missions that I had helped start, but others that had started women's ministries were reaching out and starting even others. It was just like watching the concentric waves started by a pebble thrown in the water. There were now much younger people influencing ministries to women throughout the United States. Or maybe that happened while I wasn't looking—and was getting older.

Just a few months after that weekend in 1994, I was visited by representatives of the search committee for moderator of the women of the church. They wanted me to consider taking the position. My response was, "I've never had an office like that in a church."

Then, in 1995, I was asked again to be the moderator of the women of North Avenue Presbyterian Church. In praying about it, I recognized that though I had worshiped in the same church for twenty-six years since joining in 1969, I really didn't know the women there. As I fellowshipped with them and as I got to know them, I learned that many of them had deep hurts and grief. Yet, they seldom talked about their pain. They didn't want to make themselves vulnerable.

The current moderator who accompanied her said "Oh, I'll help you. It's you that we want regardless of whether you've done it before."

She happened to have been at that retreat months before. I felt in my heart this was something I couldn't cope with. I could cope with Mission Boards now. I could cope with staff meetings. I could cope with anything that had to do with missions. But of women of the church who had been part of the organization of the church, I had no knowledge. And so I did two things. First of all, I obtained an article about battered women on the street. Then I made an appointment with the young woman on the church staff who was responsible for the women's activities of the church. I respected her as a very godly young lady who had a real compassion for souls. I showed her the article and explained how this was my passion.

I said "Kathy, I don't know if you know that the women of the church want me to be their moderator and that I really don't want to do that and I would like you to understand why because I thought you would understand me in the context of ministry. First of all, I'd break the mold. I'm just me. I know nothing of the polity of the church. I'd conduct business meetings as we did in the missions. Whatever the proper form of things is, I'd definitely break it."

She looked straight into my eyes and said, "Elsie, perhaps the mold has to be broken. Maybe that's why they want you to be the moderator."

Then I said, "Also I have something to show you," and I gave her my article on the plight of the battered women with children.

And I said, "More and more missions are springing up for women; still, little is being done for women in danger on the street who left home because of battering and took their children with them."

She listened to me intently and then went to her filing cabinet, pulled out an article, and said "I want you to read this." She gave me a few minutes to peruse it. It was about the many, many, many battered women that are sitting in the church pews and she said "Elsie, there's women right here, members of this church, that are battered. The pastor knows about it. I know about it. You'll never know about it even though you sit with them in church."

The article she gave me also told the story of a missionary on the mission field married to a battering husband and nobody would believe her so he got away with it. One time he almost killed her. They finally returned home. She said, "You know, one thing I am really burdened about is that the women of our church need to face the reality that the homeless people you reached are sitting in their midst. They need to know that a lot of women in the church pews are hurting."

I went out of her office, still not convinced. I took one more step, and went to see a woman who had been moderator several times. I looked up to her as a highly educated, intelligent woman, and the historian of the church, who knew all the social graces of Atlanta. I said, "I recognize you've been moderator several times. I don't know if you are aware that I have been asked to be the moderator and that I don't feel qualified."

She looked at me in surprise and said, "Oh, but you are. We need you."

I realized that the discussion regarding the search for moderator had gone beyond the search committee and that even she had been in on it.

Moderator is the Presbyterian term for president of the women of the church. The moderator will preside over meetings, decide what direction the committees should go, come up with ideas, and come in with fresh ideas of what the women of the church should be doing, and then motivating the committees and the women of the church to follow the vision you have for your tenure in office. So having the past moderators encouraging me but also having a church staff member so burdened and convincing me that in our very own church (which was a middle and upper class inner city church) where the church took great pride in their history, this situation existed where women were hurting. So as I prayed about it, I felt that I had exhausted everything that I knew, that my accepting it wasn't something I had fought for or even felt equipped to do, that I had to believe that the Lord was enlarging that prayer in the snowstorm that I would get to know the women of the church on a first-name basis and so I consented to do it. I just asked the person in charge of the Roberts Rules of Order and all that to be on hand because I was going to be very informal in the way I conducted the business meetings.

And so I once again ventured out on something new in my life, with the shocking burden on my heart that not all people that are hurting and are destitute are on the streets, as they had been in the work that I had been doing. I didn't do this as a continuation of "missionary work" but as I look back now I see that it was.

There was one schism that I sensed in the church. There were a lot of older godly women and there were a lot of young professional women and it seemed like the older women didn't get to know the younger women as they might. For that burden, we started organizing things so that each older woman had a young woman to disciple and to really be a friend to. A lot of the young women were there, but their mothers, perhaps both parents, lived maybe in another state, and just to have an older women in the church be a substitute mother started bringing the age groups together.

There was another situation. There were the professional women who had started their families at the age of 35 or 40. These were doctors or lawyers or other professionals who now took a sabbatical because they were having children. So we also started special ministries not just for young mothers but for mothers of young children. Several of us, and I helped out here, took care of their babies and young children so that they could go out and have lunch together or go shopping or whatever. We did that once a month.

I never did find out, nor did I even seek to find out, who the battered women were in our church, but we diligently hoped that they were part of us and benefited by the times that we had together. More and more, as I continued, fewer and fewer opportunities came in from each of the other cities and I am sure that other younger women were asked to come to other cities in my place. I had to face the reality that there is a time for all of us to start withdrawing.

Yet, the Lord had put me in a new position in the church. I was now responsible for putting on an annual three-day retreat with a special speaker even like the one I'd attended at Montreat, a conference with wide appeal to the women of the church. I wondered if Colleen Townsend Evans might be available. She was the beauty star that accepted Christ and subsequently had a prominent role in one of Billy Graham's early films. She later married Dr. Evans. She had actually been at one of the retreats some years before and so I ventured to see if we could get her back. Although she was on the West Coast in California, and we were in Atlanta, in the Providence of God she agreed to do a three-day conference. Because it was Colleen Evans, we had a larger group than expected. I really have to think about what her subject was. I remember it was really geared to women but all I remember of the conference now was that toward the end she was telling about her own spiritual walk as the pastor of a prominent church in Washington D.C. and how she was so concerned about the women of the street. Here was the wife of the pastor of this prominent Presbyterian Church in Washington D.C. who would personally go into areas she knew to be frequented by women of the street and she'd talk to them and give them literature and try to influence them for Christ. She tried to get some of the women from her church to accompany her but didn't have much success. I sat there and thought, "Well, I'm glad to hear that she had that burden but it doesn't surprise me that church women didn't." I kept listening to what she had to say and kept thinking, "I hope these church women are listening. I hope they're getting something out of this because she certainly is speaking to all of them."

And then she said, "God started dealing in my heart, not that the women of my church could be influenced to care about the women of the street because I always thought they were self-righteous and above them and I was humble enough to go on the street and work with them and God convicted my heart. And then I saw myself as even more self-righteous than my Christian friends in the church because I was self-righteous in looking down on the self-righteous people. And I felt strangely that God was talking to my own heart and I realized that for years it would grieve me that so few people cared not only about the down and out in general but destitute women in particular. Not only did men look down on women of the street, but good church people did as well."

And so I became really interested in what this beautiful, godly woman, pastor of a congregation, and pastor's wife for years, had to say about her own spiritual journey. The next day she started closing up her series. There was a real stirring among the women of the church. After she closed, the program chairman said "We're going to ask our moderator to close in prayer." I wasn't prepared. I didn't know I was going to do that. I was sitting on the front row as the moderator of the women of the church just enjoying all the work that my program committee did after I had chosen the speaker and I stepped up to the platform and I...first of all, if I remember correctly, thanked God for Colleen and her messages and speaking to our hearts, and then I said something like "Lord, I think you spoke to my own heart as well" and I started with brokenness. I just said "God, forgive me for being self-righteous about the people that didn't care about the people that were on the street. I am a greater offender than any of them because I would, in my own heart, classify them as self-righteous and I was even more self-righteous than they, even as Colleen had been, and through my prayer I broke down and tried to close and then Colleen stood up and she...Everybody was still in prayer, but before I had finished she stood up and she said, "God is working in our midst and I wonder if anybody else has anything to say."

A girl who had not been in church for a while—she'd been on the church staff and her husband had abandoned her and in anger and bitterness against God she had stayed away from church for quite a while but she was there and she came up in tears, and she said "I have been..." and then she confessed that what had been always keeping her from the church was her own anger.

One by one came up, and I have never witnessed anything closer to revival than I did at the closing of that seminar. After a while, almost all the women were gathered around the front. Those that were the neediest, like the woman who was still grieving about her divorce, had special prayer as instructed by Colleen. One woman after another asked for prayer. We just reached out and put our hands on them as we prayed for them. I went home from the seminar with a real awareness of the presence of God and a real thankfulness in my heart. Here, I had gotten to know my Christian Church friends on a first name basis. God wasn't done with me yet, either, because I now saw myself as being one of them and wanting to be one of them. He had yet another work in my heart, that I would see the longing in women in the church and so God started doing that kind of work in my heart as well.

In 1992 when I retired from Village Atlanta, I was going through the grief and the loss of the Village and the staff and women who had become so dear to me. I went through a grief period second only to when I had lost a family member like my husband or my daughter. I felt like I had given away a child when I surrendered the Village to the Atlanta Union Mission. I had to strive to make sense out of it all and to find what the Lord wanted me to do. Remaining on my board were those few members that had the bigger picture of Ministries to Women USA. Village Atlanta was now in the hands of others and we had no tangible on-hands project and so there were only those with vision that stood with us, the Board of Directors. It was decided that since it was Ministries to Women USA I could spend a lot more time. When a mission or a social agency from another city would call me, I could go and spend as much time as they wanted in that city to help them.

There was also another burning issue that through this time there were small grass-roots ministries throughout metropolitan Atlanta that were calling and asking us to take a family. These were some good Christian organizations with compassionate people that were springing up in places within the metropolitan area but they only had room for an emergency family. They really looked to Village Atlanta to take their women on a long-term rehabilitation basis. Thus, they were all grieved when they knew that they wouldn't have my staff and Village Atlanta as they knew it to take the mothers and children they were trying to rescue. So together with going to other cities, the board with me decided that we would see what could be done locally to encourage these grass roots ministries. And while in many people's minds, because we'd had a lot of publicity throughout the city and were the first full-service rescue mission for women, and we were the first Christian organization to rehabilitate mothers with children on a long-term basis, yet, I had to recognize in the experience of those that sent women to us, that there were a lot of women struggling to reach out to help other women in distress. And so, Ministries to Women USA decided we had a local responsibility to be supportive of these grass-roots ministries and to encourage them because we did have a missionary vision. We were not just totally centered on scratching the surface like we were doing in Village Atlanta or even Atlanta Union Mission. The population of greater metropolitan Atlanta by this time was several million people. My staff had resources for knowing the grass-roots places. A lot of the staff members had gone out and were working in other ministries. One was the chaplain in a women's prison. We started compiling a mailing list of all the organizations that we knew that were reaching out to destitute women whether they had children or not. This was just to reach out to women who had lost their way.

I asked the pastor of my church about having a monthly luncheon and calling it "Networking Luncheon for Local Ministries to Women." I got immediate cooperation both from the church staff and from the kitchen staff. I knew that the women who would come were very busy so I determined it should be on a Friday around or shortly after noon. I knew from all those years of working with ministry staff and social agencies and people who were on the go all week that everybody tried to start wrapping up earlier on Friday. If they had a meeting to go to late on a Friday morning they would be able to go right home from there. It proved a good and a wise choice because we immediately had a lot of people respond by making reservations. We determined in the beginning that there was not going to be any actual program. We were going to get together to network and nothing else. We set up a microphone and had tags with the attendees' names and their organization. Some represented a church, a ministry, or a social service department, or were women's leaders of churches that were looking for volunteer work. Right from the beginning we asked the women at each table to stand up and tell us who they were and what they represented. We did that every month. When a new person came, I would call her to the microphone and say, "While the women keep eating, we want you to tell all about yourself and your ministry." And then they could ask questions. This was extremely effective because everyone was involved. It wasn't I who was standing up there, or a special speaker to give motivational talks. It was people that were already overworked in ministry and needed to know what was available out there for them. For instance, a chaplain from the prison wondered where she could send women where they would continue to be treated in a godly way and continued with their rehabilitation after they were released. The chaplain knew they would otherwise have no place to go to. There were women from the grass roots ministries for battered women or for girls who had run away from home who wondered who they could network with. We'd finish going through everything and then we'd close and that's when a lot of the real networking took place. It was interesting because at that point a woman might stand up and say, "I'm the president of the women of such and such a church. There are women in my church who want to volunteer. I had no idea there were so many opportunities in our city!

What was more interesting to me than anything was when young women wanted to get into Christian ministries of a social nature that reach out to help a woman in the name of Christ. They would come to the working meeting and listen to the different ministries and what they were doing. Several of them obtained employment. Even the directors found people interested in volunteering and in their programs. I found that there was a lot of networking not only during the half-hour after the formal networking was done but some lingered for quite a while getting acquainted and continuing the networking process. I also found folks exchanging cards and telephone numbers. In some cases, there was networking going on in between meetings during the month. I felt that this was certainly something that God had me do even though I was twice-retired from active hands-on ministries.

I also learned during that time that there were some who were even reaching out to other cities as well. I saw more and more that there were a lot of young people working in social service departments or elsewhere in county government who were believers and committed Christians who came for some information. I knew that the matron of one of the jails years before was a believer who liked to send her women to the Mission when they came out of jail. I knew that God had His people in secular work reaching out to know how they could help their clients meet Christ. Many times they weren't able to witness because of the restrictions of their own social work so they put them into the hands of a Christian organization.

Linwood Detweiler

In reading over what I've already talked about in the context of the timeline of my life, I can remember dates and years simply by when a ministry started or stopped or by my age at the time. And so I've tried to give a chronological record of my life and hopefully show how God dealt with me and document that life is constantly an adventure and that we are in God's school. We had to seek His will day after day and be open to anything that He wanted to put into our lives. In recounting the ministry that seemed to open up to me when I was trying to get over the grief of not having an active hands-on ministry in a mission or in Village Atlanta, I felt fulfilled in having the meetings with the ministries, the networking meetings, and also excited about what God was doing in the places where I was privileged to spend some time encouraging folks and helping them decide what direction they should go even with a project that was already underway.

I also told you about my coming to the point in my life with my church and how I came to peace about my relationship with church people, with the church at large, and how they played a role in my early life and now being filled with a sense of excitement, especially having that experience when I came to grips with my own self-righteousness about church people and their role in my life. I felt warmly a part of the church, and felt that there were just a lot of hurting people right in the church. I was now at a phase in my life, because I was into my 70's, where I at peace just being a part of the church and the things that were going on there.

Now, there's something else that was looming large in my life. I had been a widow at this time for maybe twenty years and many times one of my girls would say, "Mother, you need to go where you see eligible men. Now that you're not involved in mission work you need to look around and see about a husband."

And I'd always reply, "God knows where I am. I don't have to go seeking a husband. If that's in God's plan, He has one somewhere for me. Besides, my life is full and I've been free for a long time."

I also explained to them that I'd been independent and made my own decisions, with God's help, for a very long time. During those years there were sixteen grandchildren born. Now my older grandchildren were starting to have children so during this time I had become a great-grandmother. My oldest daughter, Eileen, was now answering when a child would call "Grandma!" So my life was changing. I certainly felt that I'd had a full life. Yet, there was that loneliness for companionship that was all the more noticeable after I didn't have to get up and go to an office every morning.

Two years after I retired from the Village, and before I'd had the experience as moderator of the women of the church, in the early spring of 1994, there was a message on my answering machine one day. I'd been away, and I don't know where, but when I returned home I was checking my messages and the voice on the other end said, "I don't know if you remember me but I remember you. It was back in our home church when we were in our late teens. I understand through your brother that you've been a widow for some time. I'm having a layover in Atlanta right now and I'm sorry that you're not in but maybe we can get together sometime." And so I listened to the message and he told me who he was. He was Linwood (same 1st name as my brother) Detweiler from Pennsylvania, and I immediately remembered him. I could still envision him in our young people's group. I felt a tinge of excitement that I should even get a call and I had some regrets that I wasn't home to receive it. Three weeks later, I returned his call one Monday morning. We got so busy reminiscing that we probably talked over an hour about the times more than fifty years before that we'd last seen one another. He asked me if there was any place where we could meet, maybe a Bible conference in my area, saying that he was anxious to see me again. We decided on meeting at The Cove in North Carolina where Billy Graham has his conference grounds. Lin made arrangements because he knew the speaker that he wanted to hear and it was decided that on the 24th of June I would fly to Asheville and he would drive down from Pennsylvania.

Now I must tell you a little bit about Linwood. I did remember him and it was before he ever went on to seminary and subsequently took his first church in Springfield, MA. He married when he was in seminary. While in the church in Springfield, three little girls were born to them. He was there about twelve years perhaps. After building up that church, he wanted a new challenge and he took a church in Souderton, (near Philadelphia) Pennsylvania where he remained for perhaps right around fifteen years. After he felt that that church was at its height and built up, he wanted another challenge and he took a church in Patchogue, Long Island, staying there until he retired. So, during his right on half a century of pastoring, he'd only had three churches. He remained in contact with many of his parishioners from all three churches. His life had been very interesting.

We met in North Carolina over a long weekend and, of course, we'd get together for breakfast and spend the day together. During the time between services, we'd chat, reminisce, and get acquainted. At the end of that long weekend, he drove to his home in Pennsylvania and I flew back to Atlanta.

That was in 1994, even before I became the moderator of the women of the church. God was doing some interesting things at that point. For one thing, I was asking God that I'd get to know the women of my church on a first name basis and he was preparing the answer to that prayer. For another, He was preparing an answer for my loneliness. I was having a telephone relationship with a man who had been a church pastor for many years. Linwood and I had a lot in common. We were both of Pennsylvania Dutch background and my oldest brother Linwood was married to Lin's first cousin. Strangely, our paths never crossed through all those years. However, when Lin visited his cousin and my brother, it was they who told him that I was widowed. This was after Lin's wife passed away. Consequently, Lin called me when he had a layover in Atlanta. I was very pleased that he called and that he would be interested in me. However, I was primarily interested in having a Godly male to have fellowship with even if it was just on the telephone or to occasionally meet at a Bible conference. And yet, I also found myself infatuated. I use that word advisedly, understanding that the dictionary definition is: "possessed by an unreasoning passion or attraction."

Because he didn't seem to have any knowledge…was very interested in what my life was like for those many years, but he didn't seem to have a real grasp of mission work, so we would talk on the telephone quite frequently and because of our ages we would enjoy reminiscing and saying "You know, here we are in our seventies…" and he would kid me about me being Sarah and he was Abram and he would tell me that he was one of three boys and that I was his sister that he never had, and so that was the kind of a relationship that we had. I was the sister he never had. He was comfortable on the telephone and while writing letters.

As time went on, I sensed that he was really wanting a mate, wanting to get married, and I still took the attitude I wasn't sure because though he didn't propose I felt that I couldn't encourage that kind of a relationship because I still had ministry on my mind. I was surrounded by several of my married children and so many grandchildren and so in that area I did have a full life. I was content for things to continue as they were, and, as a matter of fact, although we would call one another, there was one point that he made several calls to me and I didn't call him. It was kind of a mutual thing as friends that we would call one another. And it was during that time that I even tried to set up an office in my home so that I could get started on something else for Ministries to Women. It was my second year in office as moderator to women of the church that I had that experience that I described when our weekend conference ended up with a real time for me of searching my heart and I went home certain that God was not done with me yet, certain that I really had some more growing to do in my relationship back into the church as a church member, and certain that working for the body of Christ in that setting was something God wanted me to do. I can look back now and see that when Lin first contacted me in 1994, I thought it would be boring to be married to a man like that who just always had middle and upper class people in his congregation and spent his summer at Bible conferences and if truth be told hadn't understood real Christian work. Maybe not "Christian work," but who just didn't have a feel for the down and out; and, of course, God had to deal with me with that, to show me that it wasn't my new-found, long-lost friend, Lin, who was taking a self-righteous attitude toward the ministry I was in. I was actually not only taking a self-righteous attitude about church people in general but about him in particular. I didn't share these things with him. It was just that God was doing a work in my heart. I didn't know then that all this time what He was preparing me for was to again experience the joy of being a wife and entering a totally new ministry after my retirement.

It was after about three years of this sort of relating that he said, "If you're up this way, please spend a weekend."

I said, "If there's a bed and breakfast place, I'll come for a day or two on my way to Minnesota to see my daughter."

And so I visited him in the Lancaster area in the beautiful Mennonite or Amish countryside, and saw his friends. But I went there, and even as I flew from that area to my daughter in Minnesota, I still just thought of it as another nice experience of friendship.

It was in January of 1998 that he called and said "If it…you know, you spent a few days with me here. Do you mind if I'd visit you some weekend and you can get a place for me and I'll spend a weekend?"

In February he called again for my response, and I said, "Well, that'll be fine but my sister is coming to spend the whole month of March with me so that wouldn't be very timely."

And he said, "Oh, what about April?"

And I said "Well, April I'll be busy because I have a granddaughter getting married in May."

And he said "Well, how 'bought June?"

And I said "Well, it looks like that would be a good time."

I'm just saying all this to emphasize that I just thought our relationship would continue as it had in the past. As June approached, he called me and said, "I have a grandson getting married in Chattanooga, so how do I get to Atlanta by car from Chattanooga?"

To make a long story shorter, instead of him bringing the car, he drove with some of his family to Chattanooga and I offered to drive there and pick him up, drive him to Atlanta, and show him where his room was. We had a very nice visit for several days and I showed him the sights of Atlanta, the things everybody shows visitors: Stone Mountain and The Varsity and other points of interest. When it was all over, he had to get a one-way ticket to fly home since he had driven down. When I took him to the airport and he got on the plane, he was very warm, and said he hated to leave me and he'd call me as soon as he was home.

About a week later when we talked, he said, "Do you mind if I come back and visit you in September?"

Of course I was looking forward to his visit because there was just something about his visit in June that was so different…and probably not because Lin had changed but because I had. Now there was yet another milestone to go in my Christian walk to be ready for that man of God that God had prepared for me so we could really have the kind of fellowship that I had craved. I was concerned about what to tell my girls as reasons why I wouldn't want to get married again. I told them, "God has given me two godly men for husbands. I have lived alone a long time and I am happy. I certainly wouldn't want to make a mistake the third time and have a bad marriage to end my life."

He came back again in September. To try to make that long story short, he came somewhere around the 18th of September and started talking seriously about the relationship that we had and that he wanted us to get married and one way that we could do it since he really loved the North, we would spend the summer in the North and the winter in Atlanta. That sounded real good to me. Also, by this time, I wasn't receiving any more calls to come to the different cities. Also the networking with all these various organizations had kind of run its course. I viewed all that as God's hand and that God had something even greater for me even though by this time I was 78 and Lin was 79. So we decided…we felt, well, that we might as well get married before he went back. None of our children knew about it and, naturally, I wanted to wait a little while and invite the children and just have family attend. He said, "Our children are from California to Minnesota to Florida so we might as well just go and do it and tell them afterwards."

So we just went and did it, and my children said later "Mother, you eloped!" And I said "No, we didn't."

And they said "If we had done that at 18 or 19, you would have called it eloping."

But it really wasn't eloping. We had just gone to one of the assistants on the staff in my church. I called her and I told her what was going on and asked, "Could you arrange it with the pastor?"

On the 22nd of September we were in Atlanta and applied for the marriage license. The next two days we had blood tests and just hand-carried everything from the courthouse to the clinic to wherever they needed to go and had all the papers in hand and at four o'clock on the 24th of September we stood before the smiling pastor of my church and one of his assistants and just Lin and me and we were married. So since we hadn't really gone away anywhere, it wasn't really eloping.

This is a whole, now, new start for my life. I know many of my grandchildren look up to me and to their deceased grandfather as spiritual giants which is…. When I see them feel that way I feel so humble because I know my own personal struggles whereas perhaps they don't. I know my fears, my doubts, and also my—at times not willing to take that step of faith when I should, so I realize in talking about this that even at 78 years of age God had to really prepare my heart for what he wanted to do in my life and I'm convinced that here on earth we are just going through a school. We are going through God's school and He is preparing us to be with him forever and we really won't arrive spiritually until we stand before Him because it's just by His grace that we are what we are and He knows our weaknesses. He knows our fears and He knows the struggles we have and I just thank God for my children and my grandchildren and know that God is going to continue to work in all their lives.

After we were married…I knew Lin was a good pastor and that he loved the Lord but I think I had some wonderful blessings and maybe some surprises. I had not had anyone…No one had ever joined me as a prayer partner praying faithfully with me for my children. Lin was the father of three children and the grandfather of ten when we were married. I was the mother of five and the grandmother of sixteen grandchildren and by this time four or five great-grandchildren. Within a week, we were coming before the Lord daily to have our prayer time together and then our intercession time. We started from the very beginning to name all of our families' children one by one and it just…. I was just so grateful to God that he gave me a man of God who was entering this phase of my life with me because I realized that even though he had to give up preaching, for the most part I gave up my entire ministry as well. But yet we had a lot to pray about for friends, missionaries, the ministries that we had been into…But we felt that our greatest calling together was the ministry that we had for these wonderful children and grandchildren and now great-grandchildren that God had given us. It took us quite a while, especially in the beginning, by the time we took each one to the Lord personally in prayer, each person even down to the last great-grandchild.

We have been married now for seven years this September, 2005. During this time, more great-grandchildren have been added. Looking back, I see how rich my relationship is with my grandchildren because of the twenty-four years of being a single grandmother. Even though I had my ministry, my children came next and then my grandchildren. During that time, many of them, when they got to the adolescent years, spent some time even living with me so they knew me as the matriarch of the family. There were mixed emotions when I got married because they felt that they had lost me; however, it didn't take long before they realized that they had gained a grandfather. Only the very oldest of them remembered ever having a grandfather.

Because of the kind of relationship Lin has with his grandchildren and I have with mine, we get calls from not only our children but our grandchildren all the time with prayer requests. We are always pleased when we get a call from one of the grandchildren saying "I just found out that I'm pregnant" and we're the first ones after their own parents they want to tell. Immediately, Lin starts remembering that unborn baby, adds it to our list and starts praying for that baby until the day it's born. It's been a humbling and a precious experience to have this ministry at our age now so we don't feel like we're on the shelf anymore. We have a ministry although we don't live in Ephrata, Pennsylvania, or in Atlanta anymore.

In fact, we are now living at Penney Farms FL. J.C. Penney started this place 75 years ago in memory of his father who was a Baptist pastor. Eighty percent of the 500 people here have either been on the mission field or have been pastors of churches so we naturally have a sense of belonging. It is an affordable place for us, and we are just as close to any of our children and grandchildren by plane or telephone as we would be in Atlanta. They are literally scattered from coast to coast, and I even have a granddaughter who is a missionary in Sweden.

Here, the Lord has opened up opportunities for us to serve. Lin is chaplain one day a week in the nursing home on the grounds and I volunteer in the Alzheimer's building and also in feeding some of those no longer able to feed themselves. There are many of these volunteer opportunities that provide meaning to life and daily fellowship with other Christians. Lin and I are very happy and are blessed by having this new life together. I am grateful to God that He continues to add adventure to my life story.

What I have written has been "My story." It is my legacy to you. Now, you, my children, grandchildren, and great-grandchildren, are living out your life story. The choices and decisions you make will determine your destiny. If there is one truth I intended to share with you by remembering my life in writing, it is that religion could not save me. Religion (or non-religion) held me in bondage. Sin held me in bondage as well. Only Christ could set me free so that my life could be lived with a deep joy and peace that no difficult circumstances could take away. "The just shall live by faith" is the scripture that describes my experience of living my life by faith all these years—years saved at the cross and freed from the bondage that my life was filled with until I was 15 years old when Jesus Christ freed me into living by faith. What an adventure of faith these past greater than 70 years have been!

I reflect on the 11 years that have passed since 1994 when Diane and Doug initially urged me (with tape recorder in hand) to sit on their deck overlooking their large Minnesota lake to begin recording my life's journey and memoirs. After many long hours on their part of transcribing and editing, they have given me one final assignment: they want another "last chapter." I have reviewed everything I said to this point on several hundred pages, and I marvel that God has given me these 85 years to prove His faithfulness and precious promises.

The first thought that comes to my mind is that happiness comes with our circumstances. Joy comes from within and only the God who made us can give us joy in the midst of any sadness or grief.

After reviewing and reflecting, I am now aware that I spoke little about my children and their lives after their father died. My own grief was for me and the loss of my lifetime partner in life and ministry; yet, my primary grief was for my children's sudden loss of their father and spiritual leader. He was their counselor and they relied heavily on him for his wisdom. Then he was gone and all of our lives and dreams were shattered.

As a family, we grieved together and comforted one another during the early days of being "widowed and fatherless." I realized that each of my children had to walk his or her own journey towards resolution of this grief on their own. For each of them, it was part of their own personal walk of faith. Each needed to take a different path to this resolution.

At the time of her father's death, Eileen, the oldest, was married, had two children, and was seven months pregnant. She sorely missed him and it was difficult for her to share her grief as she gave birth to her third child just two months later. Her husband was devastated. He was the grown son of an abusive father and regarded Stauffer with deep respect, always coming to him for advice. Later on, he became an emotionally, physically, and spiritually abusive father himself. His oldest son, our first-born grandson, came to live with me when he turned 16 in order to escape this abuse. Eileen found it imperative to file for divorce, hoping her husband would get help. She is now happily remarried, a grandmother several times over, and active in her community church.

Audrey, our second daughter, was also devastated by her father's death. She and her husband returned to the college where he was a student and where she was working. She wrote to me often of her grief as she had the gift of penning her feelings. She found it difficult to accept comfort from her husband or from scripture, and saw her older sister busy with three children while she herself was childless. A year later, she became pregnant with her firstborn. She and her husband moved back to Albany so her husband could continue his studies at the Junior College there. Upon the birth of their baby girl she suffered severe post-partum depression. No one could reach her or fill the emptiness she felt. After a severe weight problem, the birth of a son two years later, and promiscuity, her marriage ended in divorce. She quickly remarried to a man much younger than she, and moved to Atlanta where I was now living. With her children now in school, and trying to get her life back in order, she developed a recurrence of the cancer which I mentioned earlier. Facing death, Audrey finally came to know the presence of the Lord in her life and the sense of God's peace that we had all longed for her. She left three beautiful young children behind. Her 13 year old daughter, Audra, went to live with Susan and her husband. Marion, her husband, took on the full-time responsibility of raising the boys. He has done a commendable job and they both look to him as their father.

Diane was a second year student the year following her dad's death. She remained in school that quarter, immersing herself in her studies to cope with her great loss and grief. Throughout her remaining college years, she returned home frequently in an effort to fill some of the void resulting from the loss of her dad. The young man Diane married after she obtained her college degree was in the Air Force. He was a friend of Larry's, who introduced them. Diane had been influential in his confession of faith. I spoke of Diane often in my writings because she was part of our household during the years of Bill Huck's life. After her husband was discharged from the Air Force, he enrolled at Georgia State University and took a job in their Computer Programming office. When their daughter Laurie was three, a precious little baby boy, Christopher, arrived. However, within a year after Bill's death, Diane was faced with her husband's unfaithfulness. After two years of struggle and humiliation, she knew she had to let go, and granted him a divorce. Now, I had a daughter and her two children living in the apartment upstairs, and I was downstairs alone in our large home. We were all happy in that big house. It provided security for Diane and her children as she sought spiritual comfort and guidance from scripture, family and friends. Divorce is not easy when it comes to a Christian family, and Diane had to struggle through to peace amidst the stigma that she felt from her church and 'others' in the Christian community. After five years of single-parenting her children, Diane regained her spiritual self-worth, and yearning for a complete family circle. God then blessed her with a loving husband and a Christian home. They have been very happily married for going on 25 years. Her husband has been a major contributor to this book, seeing it through from its inception to its publication.

Larry, our only son, was 15 when his father died. He wept frequently while grieving his father's death, as he and his dad were just beginning to have an adult relationship. At the time, I felt he was doing some "healthy" grieving as he talked much about his dad. However, on one occasion when he was overwhelmed with grief, in his despair, he said "Mother, if something happens to you, I will kill myself." His expressed fears caused me great concern. Did my son inherit the obsessive fear of death that I suffered through in my youth? I knew that he confessed Jesus as Savior of his life. Surely he would not go through that same suffering. Up to this time, Larry's goal had always been to become a veterinarian. After Stauffer's death, he never spoke of it again. Then, easing into his adult life, he scarcely mentioned his father or his faith.

It was Larry's decision, with some persuasion on Diane's part, to attend Columbia Bible College where Diane was a senior. By the end of his first year, he had no desire to return. Rather, he went to the community Technical College. At the end of that year he married a fine young lady he'd corresponded with from college. After their first child was born, he showed, at times, the same fear of losing his new son, becoming very controlling in the baby's care. This same pattern of control was evident with the children that followed. Moving out of state, I thought things would be better for him as he would be nearer his wife's family. I hoped that he would find peace there from his all-encompassing fears.

However, his great need to control his life and the lives of those in his growing family escalated out of his fear. Anger and bitterness resulted. Larry sought relief from marijuana. This drug was the "gateway" into a life of illicit drug use. He deceived himself in its use to begin with, regarding it as "okay" since it was not alcohol and thought not to be addicting. His escape through drugs continued for more then twenty years.

When my son came to the place where he had no where else to turn, he came to me and said, "Mother, drugs are not my greatest problem. Fear is. I am scared to death and can only cope with life when I can have relief." I witnessed a broken man, pouring out his love for his children, and afraid that he would lose them.

My thoughts then turned to a time many years before when my son lost his father and in his grief he said he was afraid God would take me too. He had come back to that point almost 30 years later, now adding his four children to that list. Here's this fear again. I knew I was on familiar ground.

My thoughts turned to Hebrews 2:9 "But we see Jesus, who was made a little lower than the angels, for the suffering of death crowned with glory and honor, that He, by the grace of God, might taste death for everyone." And then to Hebrews 2:15 "and release those who through fear of death were all their lifetime subject to bondage." (NKJV)

I remember quoting to my son, Ps 37:5 "Commit thy way unto the LORD; trust also in him; and he shall bring it to pass." (KJV)

I quietly asked, "Can you commit yourself first of all to God? Then name your children, one by one, and put them in God's hands for His keeping?" After some hesitation, I felt I was on sacred ground as I heard him praying between sobs for each of his children by name, telling God he was giving them back to Him.

I believe God delights in His children just as we delight in our children. He loves us with an everlasting love. Jeremiah 31:3 "The LORD hath appeared of old unto me, saying, Yea, I have loved thee with an everlasting love: therefore with lovingkindness have I drawn thee." (KJV)

I believe Larry to be clean now, and he has a heart for God not encumbered with fear. Although his marriage did not survive, he has four lovely adult children who dearly love him. He has many regrets and a lot of fences to mend and with God's help he is reaching out to help others. His two daughters are married and in full-time Christian work.

Susan, ten when her dad died, remembers life mostly with me as the head of the household. She cherished the times with Diane when she came home from college and turned to her as her confidante. Her dad's death caused her great pain that I believe she internalized. Yet, the next years she was a trooper and was right by my side as we moved from ministry to ministry. At the Children's Home she took responsibility for the young children, and at the maternity home in Asheville, she was friends with the young expectant mothers. By the time she was fourteen, she did the grocery shopping, preparing dinner for Diane, Larry and me each night. During her high school years she helped at the Women's Mission and worked on the mission staff during her college summer vacation time.

Susan was the youngest of my five children, and the youngest child of large families seems to me to be the 'special' child to the other siblings, with an independent and fun loving personality. When we arrived from the North to the "Deep South" to pioneer in our ministry with 50 alcoholic men, she was only eight weeks old. From those early years till the death of her father she was the cherished little girl and was special in the hearts of all the alcoholic men and women, and their families who visited for the evening services and stayed for the refreshments afterward. She was the 'mascot' of our ministries, everyone's joy, as she was named Susan Joy. Yet, to this time, I feel that Susan is still seeking her peace with a God who would 'take' her dad from us when he was so vital to so many lives.

She really didn't know her dad well through her young years, as Stauffer was a man who became more involved with his children when they started reaching their teen-age years. I still grieve for Susan that she missed her dad, and continue to pray that she will experience peace from that void in her childhood.

Susan married her teen-age sweetheart. Because she had made many moves though her school years, she had a longing to live in one place while raising her two young daughters. After her marriage, she and her husband eventually moved to Ohio where they lived in the same house for more than 25 years.

Although God in His grace has allowed me to live to see Him work in the lives of all my children, my heart has been heavy many times through the years for the pain my children suffered through the loss of not having their father present in their lives. I have cried out to God again and again to remind Him of his many promises in scripture where He will be the father to the fatherless.

Ps 68:5 "A father to the fatherless, a defender of widows, is God in his holy dwelling." (NIV)

I believe the travail that a mother suffers until she sees Christ formed in her children is far greater then the travail she suffers through giving physical birth to that child. Through the years, I ministered to desperate women and in short order witnessed the transforming power of God in them. Yet in my own family, my answers to prayer were not so fast. My floundering faith would claim the promises of God, knowing that God, as their father, loved my children with a perfect love. He would complete His work in their lives in His own time, a work that He had begun in them as children when their father was still alive.

Oswald Chambers wrote: "We are always in a hurry because we live in time. God has the luxury of eternity but He is always on time." I had heard their earthly father call their names at the Throne of Grace many times. He did not live to see them stumble and falter, yet I found comfort in believing Stauffer now spoke face to face with his Savior, while I had to talk to Him in prayer by faith about our children.

If there is one truth that I intended to share with you by remembering and telling my life story, it is that religion cannot save you. Religion (or non-religion) will hold you in bondage in one way or another. Sin also holds you in bondage. Only Christ can set you free so that your life can be lived with a deep joy and peace that no difficult circumstances can take away. I have witnessed this in my own life through the years and in the lives of others during my many years of ministry.

"The just shall live by faith," is scripture repeated in Romans 1:17, Galatians 3:11, and Hebrews 10:38. I can paraphrase it by saying, "Those who have been set free from the bondage of sin by way of the cross (salvation and justification), shall live their life, daily, by faith in God." This verse is the scripture that best epitomizes my life from the time of my salvation to the present. At age eight, I was in bondage to fear and subsequently to religion. I was saved at age fifteen into a daily experience of maturing peace and faith. What an adventure these many years have been!

All this has culminated in a prayer ministry with Lin. I believe this present mission is the most important calling I have ever had. We pray daily by name and by need for each of you children, 27 grandchildren, and 28 great-grandchildren, as well as for missions, missionaries, and friends in need. Many souls were changed through the power of the Gospel during the ministry that Granddaddy Moses and I had, and then during the many years of solo service that God gave to me. Yet, this will be of less consequence when compared to your *life of faith* and the lives you touch. Almost every day the phone will ring, and one of our family will ask us for prayer and share with us their need. At other times, the ringing of the telephone is to share with us an answer to prayer.

Unlike us, God does not have any grandchildren. Just children. You and each of your children will come to this place of faith, too, like I did at the age of 15. If you will confess Jesus as your Lord and Savior, then God has a "wonderworking" plan for your life—an intimate life of faith with an ever-faithful God. That is my testimony to you, my children, of my long and always exciting life of faith.

> Rom 1:17 (KJV) "For therein is the righteousness of God revealed from faith to faith: as it is written, The just shall live by faith."
>
> 2 Cor 5:7 (NIV) "We live by faith, not by sight."
>
> Gal 2:20 (NIV) "I have been crucified with Christ and I no longer live, but Christ lives in me. The life I live in the body, I live by faith in the Son of God, who loved me and gave himself for me."
>
> Gal 5:17 (NIV) "For the sinful nature desires what is contrary to the Spirit, and the Spirit what is contrary to the sinful nature. They are in conflict with each other, so that you do not do what you want."
>
> 2 Cor 5:17(KJV) "Therefore if any man be in Christ, he is a new creature: old things are passed away; behold, all things are become new."
>
> Gal 3:11-12 (NIV) "Clearly no one is justified before God by the law, because, 'The righteous will live by faith.'"

978-0-595-37582-0
0-595-37582-0

Printed in the United States
64759LVS00004B/196-225